Bemba Myth and Ritual

American University Studies

Series XI
Anthropology / Sociology

Vol. 2

PETER LANG
New York · Frankfort on the Main · Berne

Kevin B. Maxwell

Bemba Myth and Ritual
The Impact of Literacy on an Oral Culture

PETER LANG
New York · Frankfort on the Main · Berne

CIP-Kurztitelaufnahme der Deutschen Bibliothek

Maxwell, Kevin B.:
Bemba myth and ritual: the impact of literacy on
an oral culture / Kevin B. Maxwell. – Berne;
Frankfort on the Main; New York: Lang, 1983.
  (American University Studies: Ser. 11, Anthro-
  pology, sociology; Vol. 2)
  ISBN 0-8204-0051-3

NE: American University Studies / 11

Library of Congress Catalog Card Number:
83-48769
ISBN 0-8204-0051-3

Printed by Lang Druck Inc., Liebefeld/Berne (Switzerland)

In Honor of

My Father and Mother

Their Fathers and Mothers

The Maxwell and Burns Families

ACKNOWLEDGMENTS

Many relatives, friends and colleagues have contributed their support, encouragement and expertise to me and this project. It is impossible to name them all. But I intend to include them all in grateful acknowledgment by citing these groups of people and special individuals as representative of their cooperation and friendship:

All the informants listed in the Sources Consulted.

The Bemba themselves, especially the late Honorable Mr. S. Mwansa Kapwepwe, one of Zambia's Founding Fathers, who was my gracious host and entrusted teacher for a week at his home Chiyembwe in the hills of Chinsali. Also the 80 year old grandson of the great nineteenth century king Chitimukulu Chileshe Chepela, Mr. Musonda M. Chileshe, who was my companion and teacher on several visits to Mungwi area. Also Fr. Telesphor G. Mpundu, my friend for 15 years and an untiring research assistant for long periods.

The Jesuits of Zambia and Oregon, the White Fathers of Zambia, the Sacred Heart Brothers of Malole.

Rice University for honoring the original form of this work with the John W. Gardner Award for the Best Dissertation in the Fields of Humanities and Social Sciences for 1983.

The Department of Religious Studies at Rice, and its Chairperson, Niels C. Nielsen, Jr.. Especially Professor Werner H. Kelber for his remarkable generosity with his time, ideas, and assurance. Also Mrs. Sylvia Louie, departmental secretary for deciphering and typing a difficult manuscript.

The Department of Anthropology at Rice, notably Professors Stephen A. Tyler, Richard Cushman and Edward Norbeck.

Dr. Michael H. Agar, Professor of Anthropology at the University of Maryland for his encouragement and direction in the early stages.

The fieldwork for this study was conducted while I was a Research Affiliate at the Institute for African Studies in the University of Zambia. During that tenure, Vice-chancellor Jacob Mwanza, Professors Mubanga Kashoki, Robert Serpell, Mary Frost and John T. Milimo were especially helpful.

Ms. Anne Finkelstein artistically reproduced the Bemba designs in Chapter Three.

Ms. Donna Montez of the Office of Advanced Studies and Research at Rice University who expertly typed the final form.

Mr. Orin Cassill of Peter Lang Publishing, Inc. for patiently introducing me to the world of print and contract.

To all of these and to the many unnamed friends I say thank you.

TABLE OF CONTENTS

A Review of the Literature

The Bemba people of northeastern Zambia were first mentioned in 1798 by the Portuguese explorer, Lacerda (R. Burton 1873, 50-164). Thirty years later, another Portuguese explorer, Gamitto, encountered Bemba chiefs. In his journal he described these "nomadic" people as living "by pillage and the chase," without "any religion" or "superstitious practices." Fortunately, that first word on Bemba traditional religion was not the final word. As Gamitto himself admitted, he only "passed through" their lands and could not speak of them with any accuracy (Gamitto 1960, vol. 2, 195).

Since then, the Bemba have been described in the diaries, correspondences, monographs and official records of adventurers, missionaries, commercial and colonial administrators, journalists, historians and social scientists. This has resulted in a conspicuously large body of literature on the Bemba. Some of it is important only to antiquarians. Readers interested in a full account of Bemba history and culture can consult the more valuable sources cited in the bibliography. This opening review will consider only those sections in the major works, which have some religious import. In fact, very little of the published literature on the Bemba is concerned specifically with their religious beliefs and practices. At its best, it indirectly treats of Bemba religion by integrating it within an economic, social, political or historical context, and, at its worst, tends to reduce it to such intricacies.

The sketchy nineteenth century sources show the Bemba engaged in extensive wars and trade that necessarily entailed their internal cooperation in a unified polity and their external contact with foreign cultures. Neither of these could help but have far-reaching effects on Bemba religion. For example, the recorded visits of Arab ivory-merchants and slave-traders, like Tippu Tip, to senior Bemba chiefs in the last half of that century may indicate possible Islamic influences introduced into the Bemba religious world.[1] In fact, the French naval officer, Giraud noted in 1883 that the Bemba Paramount, Chitapankwa, affected Arab customs (Giraud 1890, 256 & 263). This same impression was taken by the famous missionary Dupont, who, in 1897, could be sure that, before the arrival of Christianity, Allah and his prophet already had a stake in the religious ideology (Dupont, 1898, 246-58). Indeed thirty years before Dupont, Livinstone wrote that, in his meetings with the Bemba paramount chief Chitapankwa and senior chief Mwamba, he talked of the Christian God and showed pictures from his Bible dictionary (Livingstone 1875, 157-58).

Thus, in the last two decades of the nineteenth century, a veritable army of European missionaries and empire builders rushed into Bembaland. But their copious writings on what constituted Bemba culture included certain extraneous features already incorporated into the tradition from Christianity and Islam.

The bulk of this documentary evidence has been kept in European and African archives, where it has been combed through and summarized by later historians and ethnographers. This present study entailed re-examination of those records in a search for materials dealing specifically with Bemba traditional religion. The bibliography contains a full list of the sources consulted. Here follows a brief review of a few of the more useful documents, published and unpublished.

Published

Gouldsbury and Sheane cooperated in some of the earliest serious essays in Bemba ethnography, resulting in the publication of several articles and a book, The Great Plateau of Northern Rhodesia (1911). These devoted considerable attention to traditional religion, but their efforts were descriptive and not analytic.

The first professional anthropologist to study the Bemba was Audrey I. Richards. She published two books Land, Labour and Diet (1939) and Chisungu (1956) and over sixty articles based on her marvelously complete study of the Bemba between 1930-34. With a brief return to the field in 1957, every aspect of Bemba life, including its religious dimensions, is described and analysed with comprehensive clarity. Her work is not just the vade mecum for all students of Bemba culture, but has become a classic model for anthropological literature. As a colleague and pupil of Malinowski, Dr. Richards analysed religious phenomena in a strictly functionalist manner, discerning the effective relationships between magico-religious beliefs and the economy.

W. Vernon Brelsford, founder of the prestigious center of Bantu studies, The Rhodes-Livingstone Institute (now the Institute for African Studies at the University of Zambia), wrote a dozen important articles. Some of the bear on the religious implications of chieftainship, and one is a particularly valuable study of the Bemba royal undertaker and high priest, "Shimwalule" (1942).

For twenty years, Richards and Brelsford were the last word on the Bemba, except for a few sporadic monographs. Then, in the 1960's and 1970's, a new generation of Bemba scholars emerged. John Taylor and Dorothea Lehman shed some light on the effects, which Christianity and urbanization had on traditional religion in their Christians on the Copperbelt in 1961. Henry S. Meebelo in Reaction to Colonialism (1971) assessed the dynamics of Bemba resistance to political and cultural aggression, even in its religious forms. Finding the seeds of rebellion present in Bemba traditions, he put an end to whatever remained of the myth of a static Bemba society, locked into a timeless ethnographic present and only looking on passively while the world rushed by them under a basically expatriate impetus. Another study of Bemba participation in and promotion of a long trajectory of cultural change was D. Werner's "Some Developments in Bemba Religious History" (1971). Using linguistic and ethnographic data on the geographic spread of Bemba religious terms, he documents discernible adaptations and innovations within the traditional religious system of the Bemba. Werner anticipated the trend-setting publication of the papers from the Dar Es Salaam conference, The Historical Study of African Religion (1972), which emphasized the possibility of reintegrating the study of African religion with African historiography as a whole.

In 1973, Roberts published his masterful A History of the Bemba, where he circumstantially confirmed the political implications of surviving religious structures in the nineteenth century.

In 1974 Snelson wrote his well researched Educational Development in Northern Rhodesia 1883-1945. Describing the achievements of early missionary societies, he suggests that their introduction of education and literacy were significant factors impacting on traditional cultures.

Some of the materials consulted for this study are published in the vernacular. Tanguy's valuable history of the Bemba Imilandu Ya Babemba (1949) is compiled from the oral testimony of Bemba elders. The White Fathers' Bemba reader for schools Ifyabukaya (ca. 1928) contains a history of Bemba chiefs, which soon became a sort of canonical version of the Bemba charter myth of origins; in effect, it supplants the plural versions previously performed orally by Bemba specialists. Mpashi's Pano Calo (1956) redacts the many folk tale traditions of the oral culture into a single literate story-line; it also establishes the author as a sort of poet laureate for the tribe. Mushindo's Amapinda Mu Lyashi (1958) and Kapwepwe's Utunyonga Ndimi (1962) are useful literate renditions of the proverbial and riddling oral traditions.

Unpublished

The following unpublished dissertations are worthy of special note. Garvey's "The development of the White Fathers' mission" (1974) examines the impact of Roman Catholicism in general and the White Fathers' society in particular; it documents the adaptive resilience of the traditional religious system, despite the systematic effort to transform Bembaland into a "Central African Christendom." Maier's (1976) "Aspects symbolique de la vie bemba" investigates traditional religion

using symbols which the author convincingly argues are Bemba
categories of understanding.   J.E. Lane's dissertation "Politics
and the image of man" (1977) makes some valid theoretical points
applicable to Bemba myths and symbols; unfortunately, his
investigation is seriously flawed by his error in accepting an
obviously non-Bemba narrative as the Bemba cosmogonic myth (See
below, Chap. 3, 110, footnote 6). Frost's "Inshimi and imilumbe"
(1977) formally analyzes the structure and content of the oral
imaginative genres of the Bemba, shedding considerable light on
the oral dynamics of the culture.   Milimo's "Bemba royal poetry"
(1978) and Mapoma's "Ing'omba" (1980) study the style and content
of the praise-songs for chiefs; together they demonstrate how the
oral performer, a religious specialist, exercises significant
political and social functions for the tribe.   Lutato's "Stephen
A. Mpashi" (1980) shows how deeply rooted in oral tradition are
the novels of one of Zambia's most popular writers;   it
illuminates further the structures and forces of Bemba oral
communication.

Archival

        In preparing this monograph, the following archives were
visited: Archives of the Council for World Mission at the School
of Oriental and African Studies SOAS (University of London),
Public Record Office in London PRO, Archives of the Diocese of
Westminster ADW, Archives of the Free Church of Scotland in the
National Library at Edinburgh NLE, Archives of the White Fathers
in Rome WFA, Zambia National Archives in Lusaka ZNA, Diocesan
Archives in Kasama KDA, and Mbala MDA, Archives of the Ilondola
Language Centre in Chinsali ILC, Archives of the University of
Zambia UNZA, Archives of the Moto Moto Museum in Mbala MMM, and
Archives of the University of Zimbabwe AUZ.

        Some of the archival material pertinent to this review may
be briefly described as follows: The ZNA contains these District
Notebooks: Abercorn (Mbala), in the entry for April 1944, gives
recorded notes on the witch-covens, and, for May 1950, an account
of spirit-possession phenomena; there is also a report in June
1959 on the witch-finding movement.   Chinsali has an early entry
by Robert "Bobo" Young describing some religious beliefs and
practices; in a later section, Brelsford kept his excellent notes
on the religious dimensions of Bemba chieftainship.   Kasama
contains a 1955 entry describing the spirit cave of Changa and
the related customs.

        Not surprisingly, mission records and materials published by
missionaries are preoccupied with data on traditional beliefs and
practices.   The missionaries are often criticized for their
attempts to interpret Bemba religion according to Christian
categories.   In fact missionary perspectives on the Bemba were
neither more nor less aggressive than the general cultural myopia
afflicting European attitudes toward Africa.

Both Catholic and Protestant sources contain endless haggling over the "spheres of influence" assigned to them by secular administrators, who tried to keep missionary competition to a minimum. An unexpected sensitivity to Bemba religious sensibilities was displayed by the officials; they assigned the area East of the Chambeshi river around the royal burial ground to the Protestants, lest the greater personnel and material resources of the Catholics prove too disruptive a Christian intrusion into Bemba sacrality (Garvey 1974). Both Christian groups' documents abound in recorded triumphs over "pagan practices," which, fortunately, they sometimes describe at length.

Because some of this missionary material is little known and is made use of for the first time in this treatise, it is described here in more detail.

In the Doke Collection at AUZ are the copious Macminn Papers dating from 1913, which contain, among other things, a large amount of manuscript material on Bemba customs and religion. There is also an invaluable 10,000 page Bemba/English dictionary with over 22,000 word studies. All of these were written in Bemba and English in cooperation with Bemba associates, most notably Mushindo.

In the WFA: one of the earliest monographs Les Babemba (1907) by Emile Foulon, has several passages, complete with wonderful ink drawings, describing traditional religious beliefs and practices. In a lengthy French essay, N. Garrec (1916) makes observations on Bemba religion within the first decade of its Christian contact. The most significant single collection represents the distilled knowledge and experience of White Fathers; they collaborated over sixty years to produce a 621 page answer to 745 questions, systematically laid out in the Table d'Enquete sur les Moeurs et Coutumes Indigenes. This work, enquiring into every aspect of Bemba life including all the religious rites and beliefs, was finally redacted by L. Etienne around 1958. The diaries of over twenty-six mission stations with seventy years of entries deal with Bemba religion, witch-cleansing movements, spirit-possession phenomena, and the interaction of the tradition with Christianity.

In the KDA: a mimeoed, undated work by Sambeek entitled "La Sorcellerie au Bangweolo" distinguishes between traditional healing practices and witchcraft. The minutes of the meetings of the Archdiocesan Commission for the Study of Customs features the 1970 meeting on the spirit world of the Bemba.

In the MMM: The national museum collection of J.J. Corbeil contains a wide assortment of items from Bemba material culture, including witch-craft appurtenances, initiation pottery, royal emblems, ancestral statues, and musical instruments. The private note-system of Corbeil reflects on virtually every aspect of

Bemba culture especially the initiation rites and witch-craft practices.

In the ILC: there is a large collection of notes by L. Oger, E. Hoch, J. Sambeek, and J. Calmettes, all teachers of the courses offered for many years on Bemba language and customs. In a most valuable French manuscript of 79 notebook pages about the religion of the Bemba, E. Labrecque (ca. 1935) meticulously describes the various ancestral and nature spirits, the times, places, and rituals for worship of divinities; he also points out the religious dimensions of the social, economic and family life of the tribe. In a mid 1930's article in Bemba, F. Tanguy comments on the witch-cleansing movement *Mcapi* . In four early 1920's articles, a Bemba catechist Ng'andu Mwanse writes on death, funerals and divination. A two-part collection of <u>Bemba Oral Traditions</u> assembled by the centre's staff is a veritable treasure trove of early twentieth century Bemba folklore. A 300 page edited typescript contains F. Tanguy's writings on the beliefs, manners and customs of the Bemba. J. Ragoen's French manuscripts and J. Sambeek's 1922 Bemba manuscripts describe the traditional religion. The copious notes of B. Kapompole preserve his discussions with Bemba elders about religious traditions. There is also his 105 page typescript on traditional healing practices.

In the ADW: the Hinsley Papers (ca. 1930) contain monographs by Labrecque and Etienne with some valuable comments on Bemba religion.

Besides those White Fathers already mentioned, several others offered the perusal of their personal papers in aid of this investigation. G. Stuer at Mpulungu lent his photos, tape-recordings and detailed notes on the visit of "a witch-cleanser" to his parish. J. Gamache arranged two group discussions by Bemba catechists on the subject of the encounter of Bemba tradition with Christianity and lent his own valuable notes representing over 30 years of careful observation. T. Smeldt arranged visits with traditional Bemba priests and chiefs and provided his notes.

Field Work

Such written material, representing the distilled and formalized experience and knowledge of generations of expatriate students, gives very important access to Bemba culture. But much significant material has been generated in the oral medium by the Bemba themselves. Preparation for the present work involved actual field research among the Bemba in 1978 through 1979, and again in 1981. Visits were made to more than 50 villages for interviews with over 150 people. Among those interviewed were 10 "chiefs" *Mfumu* , 6 "traditional priests" *Shimapepo* , 12 "royal councillors" *Kabilo* , 17 "village-heads" *Mwinemushi* , 4

"traditional healers" *Shing'anga* , 2 "possessed-women" *Ngulu* , 3
"women-initiators" *Nacimbusa* , 1 "wife of the sacred relics"
Mukabenye, 1 "royal poet" *Ng'omba* , and 2 "witch-cleansers"
Mucapi. Many of the interviews were conducted at places
considered sacred in the tradition, like *Shimwalule* "the royal
cemetery," or on the occasions of traditional rituals, like
Cisungu "women's initiation" and *Cililo* "royal funeral" for
Cimbuka.

More than 50 hours of these Bemba language interviews were
recorded on 36 cassette tapes and later transcribed onto 979
typed pages. The transcriptions are being catalogued and will be
available at the Special Collections in the archives of the
University of Zambia by the Fall of 1985.

A caution is in order here about the use of these interviews
as "first-hand" evidence in this work. Once the original words
of Bemba informants have been taped and transcribed, control over
them passes completely into the hands of the interviewer. Not
only has the ethnographer provided the occasion and devised the
context for discussion, he has further managed the consequent
transcription with commentary and footnotes. The original
informants cannot superintend their textualized words nor amend
or qualify them by editing and reflection. This "oral
testimony," then, as Stephen Tyler explains, is not a real
dialogue

> but a text masquerading as a dialogue, a mere
> monologue about a dialogue since the infor-
> mants' appearances in the dialogue are at
> best mediated through the ethnographer's
> dominant authorial role [Tyler 1981, 3].

It is hoped, however, that the author has been honest and
responsible in re-presenting the words of the Bemba and is
seriously committed to discovering their meaning, not imposing
his own. This, of course, is the theme and variation of this
treatise as we examine the differing hermeneutics of spoken and
written words.

Literature on Orality

It was in comparing and contrasting the content of the
literature with that of the oral interviews, that the
significance of the media themselves became the focus of this
essay. By making use of the methodology of media studies, the
essay intends to fill an hiatus in the study of a particular
African traditional religion. It consciously adverts to the
difference between a formally oral-aural culture (i.e. pertaining
to the "mouth and ear") and a predominately visualist one (i.e.
pertaining to the "eye"). Although such concentration will not
rewrite the cultural history of the Bemba, hopefully it will add

a distinctive chapter to the history of their religion by attending to the dynamics of its oral transmission. Vansina (1965) drew attention to the oral medium but only in order to exploit it for its historical content. If McLuhan's (1962) popular premise is true, that the medium is the message, then, one must study the oral dynamics for their own sake.

Several prominent scholars in various fields have amplified this theory: a thorough understanding of transmitted content must explicitly recognize the significance (oftentimes decisive!) of the medium itself. There is the pioneering work of Albert B. Lord (1960) and Eric Havelock (1963, 1978, 1982) the American classicists, who study the oral matrix of Western classical culture. Walter J. Ong (1967, 1977, 1982) extends their work to a phenomenology and history of oral consciousness. J.C. Carothers (1959, 1972) applies psychiatric methods to illuminate the distinctive oral mind set of African peoples. Werner Kelber (1979, 1983), the American New Testament scholar, reconstructs the oral world of early Christianity. Don Ihde (1976) formulates an epistemology of listening from his phenomenology of sound. The British anthropologist, Jack Goody (1968, 1977), studies the consequences of literacy on contemporary oral cultures. The American anthropologist, Stephen Tyler (1978, 1981), conducts a comprehensive exploration of the socio-linguistic dynamics of meaning and communication clearly differentiating the hermeneutics of speaking from that of texts. Together they may be said to represent an Anglo-American oralist school of cultural studies (Kelber's coinage), whose methods and conclusions provide the general context of this discussion.[2] In particular Ong has developed the oral heuristic, which guides this work in selecting pertinent data for understanding the orally conditioned religion of the Bemba.

The Relevance of Medium-Analysis

A medium-analysis begins with this foundational perspective as a theoretical framework:

Culture evidences a progressive appropriation of the world by personal consciousness, which stores knowledge in memory or elsewhere. Technologies develop to control the world, and, at the same time (as extensions of human sensory capacities), intensify consciousness by generating greater knowledge. The differentiation and evolution of cultures occur primarily through the dominant media available for appropriating, processing and storing that knowledge (Ong 1967; cf Havelock 1982).

It is very difficult for people from a culture with a long literate tradition to appreciate just how radically literacy has affected their individual psyches and social structures. Literates sometimes have difficulty conceiving of cultural differences in anything except pejorative terms, scorning the oral world as primitive.   Ong refers to this bias as a "cultural squint" (Ong 1967, 20).

There is no need to debate relative superiority. Levi-Strauss (1966) has amply demonstrated that literates do not think any better, only differently, from oral peoples. Eliade (1959a) marshals impressive evidence that the symbol-making of "archaic consciousness" is as highly sophisticated a mental activity as conceptualization. Furthermore, psychoanalysts judge that those symbols can deliver their message and fulfill their function even when the message escapes explicit awareness and their meanings cannot be articulated with literate clarity and logic (Freud 1963; Jung 1958). S. Biesheuvel (1943) concludes that in the auditory sphere, the African's ability to grasp, work out, remember and create intricate relationships is by no means inferior to that displayed by the European in the visual sphere. As the Africanist Fernandez conjectures, many of the differences detected between African and European cultures "are really those between literate and oral culture" (1979, 285).

The key to a comparative understanding of oral culture lies not in the contrast of supposed "primitive" with "civilized." The distinction is located, not in mental abilities, but in technologies the mind employs for appropriating and communicating reality--the oral subject to acoustic laws and dialogics, the literate determined by laws of vision and logic (Goody 1977, 12-13; Havelock 1978, 224-25). In a follow-up extensive study of Vai-literacy, for example, Goody, collaborating with Scribner and Cole, concludes that, while cognitive capacities remain the same, access to different communication technology can effectively transform cognitive processes (Goody 1977, 18).

Different stresses, biases, specializations and operational preferences in knowledge-management are set up by the various media-technologies. On the one hand, oral-aural cultures (henceforth abbreviated to "oral cultures") favor a convocation of knowledge around a paradigm of sound. On the other hand, literate (visualist) cultures prefer an analogy with sight for their knowledge. The structures of psyche and of society are affected by the preferred sensory analogues of each culture. The dynamism of sound orients oral peoples toward a subjective and existential economy of knowledge and community. Literates evidence an enhanced capacity to organize efficiently and to verbalize objectively with the clarity and distinction proper to vision.

For Ong, the sensory analogue is the central hermeneutical key to the culture: "Given sufficient knowledge of the sensorium exploited within a specific culture, one could probably define the culture as a whole in virtually all its aspects" (Ong 1960, 16).

Ong lists a set of features which generally characterize an oral culture (1982, chap. 3). Its people are intensely aware of the power and action which their sounded words connote. Memory is the central act of their knowing powers and their knowledge is mnemonically formulated; successful knowledge is precious and has to be preserved for all practical purposes. Their thoughts and expressions tend to be simply additive rather than complexly subordinative; the existential flow of narration cannot be encumbered with reasoned structures. Any aggregation of ideas is synthetic and unyielding to analytic contemplation; their cumbersome load of epithets and clusters of clichés cannot be dismantled without breaking up valuable trains of thought which have taken generations to accumulate. Thought is redundant and its expressions are copious in order to give speakers time to think of what to say next and listeners time to stay abreast of what has already been said. Thought has evolved into a tradition to be handed down by wise elders who discourage intellectual originality; they prize the conservative effort to maintain the tried and the true. Expression draws heavily on the familiar world of human activity as a memorable model used to describe even non-human reality. Oral conceptualization and verbalization reflect the adversities of the human life-world; oral people engage in constant social altercations, and they struggle to survive in a dangerous physical environment. As uninhibited participants in any verbal exchange, an oral audience empathetically identifies with traditional wisdom, making only homeostatic adjustments to inevitable change. The thought and expression of an oral culture can be only minimally abstract; they are more easily recallable if they are closely confined to concrete objects and actual situations. Hence real-life circumstances provide the reference frames for classifying knowledge. Its verification depends on what real people say; even knowledge of self is set in the context of how society evaluates a person.

As this treatise unfolds, it will become clear that the Bemba fulfill all of Ong's criteria for classification as an oral people. How this oral culture is being transformed is the other ingredient of this discussion. Transformation implies interface and interaction of independent systems. In our context, the encounter of the Bemba religious system with Christianity is the interface, and their communication through their respective oral and literate channels is the interaction. Each system is characterized by a relative degree of openness and closure (Cf Ong 1977, 305-41).

At the time of their meeting in the mid to late 1800's, the expectancies of the two religious systems were asymmetrical: Bemba structures functioned inclusively "homeostatically" (See below, Chap. 3, 106), accepting, discarding or exploiting, the unstable resources of the other, while Christianity demanded an exclusivity and total acceptance of its order. Christianity was dogmatic and uncompromising in dealing with the more compliant

Bemba tradition. Bemba traditional religion, however, had a rich history of adapting to, and precipitating change (Cf Ranger 1975, 3-13).

The Christian missionaries encountered Bemba religion, while it was reeling from the stresses and strains of nineteenth century upheavals. The Bemba offensive wars to expand and solidify their empire, East African incursions of the slave and ivory trade, the defensive wars against the Ngoni, the sporadic forays of European adventurers, traders and missionaries, all set the background for the Christian entrance and a large scale of conceptual confrontation (See below, chap. 3, 91-2). There was tremendous potential for mythic and ritual change in the Bemba efforts to understand inwardly the forces impinging from these outward sources (Cf Lane 1977).

The missionaries sought to graft a few "native" customs onto the Christian tree, more to disguise than to actually reduce its foreignness. Some regarded the culture as abyssmally wicked and demanded that their converts break with their village ties and live in the new religious environment of the mission (Roberts 1965, 171). The Bemba, on the other hand, wanted to accommodate Christianity to the traditional religious system that enveloped and motivated them. History shows that the Bemba were not immediately willing to drop their old beliefs and practices, but only to adapt the new as best befitted their religious imaginations (Cf Ranger 1975). This capacity for persistent renewal and change ensured, for awhile, a certain survival of the indigenous religion, if not as a wholly integrated system, then at least in its peripheral features (See below, chap. 4).

The changing Bemba religious pulse was often in sympathetic vibration with Christianity. Even some of the hostile critique levelled at the tradition by missionaries was consonant with what the Bemba themselves perceived as its failure to respond to their altered religious needs. Bemba tradition, too, had a built-in readiness to import the spiritual powers of foreign symbols and techniques; their very alienness was conceived both as a potential for cleansing the indigenous system and a faculty for coping with unaccustomed circumstances (Cf Colson 1964).

But, more importantly, Christianity only _seemed_ to be competing fairly on the same level of ideology and value-system with traditional religion. In fact, Christianity took unfair advantage by substituting its own literate currency as the medium in the exchange.

The Bemba had no form of writing prior to their contact with the European world at the end of the nineteenth century. They did have cultural controls for meaning with functions similar to writing, like the _Mbusa_ in the _Cisungu_ ceremony (See below, chap. 2). Hall (1965, 99) intriguingly tells of an old Bemba device called _Ng'enga_ , which was a calabash marked with symbols by travellers to record details of what they had seen on their journey. [3]

A phonetic alphabet, however, is a technology of the mind, which preserves each sound of the language by a different sign. The introduction of writing distinguishes cultures more radically even than any of their material technologies and development. Havelock (1963, 1978, 1982) demonstrates how the writing down of Homer was a cultural intrusion of the first magnitude, a dynamic and, in some ways, destructive thunderclap in European history.

With the advent of literacy, the Bemba oral way of life and its modes of thought began to be undermined. This erosion of orality had been extended over five thousand years of European chirographic and typographic experience. It has been effected in a single century among the Bemba, causing massive cultural dislocation without adequate time for assimilation and adjustment (Cf Havelock 1978, 228). The net result was terrific disruption of the tribal mores of a people caught between the seductive attractions of a modernity, for which they were not fully prepared, and the ostensibly comfortable security of a tradition no longer adequate for their aspirations.

Hall notes the sombre suspicions of the colonial government that missionaries were preaching radical political ideas in their schools and making the mission stations enclaves of political dissent (Hall 1965, 108). The reality was that the subversion of authority was actually the more subtle revolution of the new mental technology, which literacy itself effected. The oral authorities of traditional religion were simply overwhelmed by this unfamiliar and very potent instrument. Christianity itself was a very complex intellectual system, refined by its own literate history. The stable concepts of Christianity were seemingly tailor-made for the religious reaction of the Bemba to the colonial system. Christianity began almost immediately to wrest control of the Bemba religious tradition from its oral authorities by writing it down and making the written version "standard" (See below chap. 3, 77 for related discussion of "dictionary meanings"). For example, both Mumena and Shimwalule are aware that their oral renderings of the tradition are not in line with the books written by the White Fathers. Shimwalule says "that the writings are untrue and confused" *E batunfyana ifintu no kulemba kwabo. . . baputula fye* . But Mumena apologizes for the discrepancies of his statements with what is written (Shimwalule VII; Mumena III). [4]

The traditional religious forces in colonial times were fighting a losing battle with their oral weapons against Christian literate logistics. Not only was the religious tradition subverted by critical scrutiny and editorial manipulation, but Christianity was promoted by the same means that ensure success in the modern secular order. In addition, Christianity was the religion of the new political power. It was the chief dispenser of the literate means of coping with the larger social universe and of gaining some of the material benefits available in the new colonial economy. Bemba villagers "thought that the source of the European's power and authority must lie in his extraordinary capacity to read and write" (Snelson 1974, 21; also 282-85).

The Christian missionaries, then, turned over the new literate means of communication to the new breed of Bemba elite. The young Bemba converts, the spes gregis, learned the literate skills, and, in the process, found their traditions subverted and their loyalties undermined by the propaganda of the Christian faith (Cf Snelson 1974, passim). The written word, not the oral word, was true, viz the Bible. Truth was open only to those who read; these readers acquired the knowledge and extracted the power of the Europeans. Literacy short-circuited seniority as the way to wisdom; the youth could claim to know the rules of life and to control religion better than the elders who could not read (Cf Idem, 272). The Bemba situation was analogous to the period when the oral traditions of Homeric Greece were committed to writing; "the quality of oral art practised . . . suffered because the linguistic brains of the community were being drained off into the scribal centers" (Havelock 1982, 168).

The missionaries were convinced that education was the primary means of converting people from their old practices to belief in Christ. But their enterprise was motivated not by the narrow pietism of just saving souls; they sought to improve the physical and social well-being of the people. The Gospel and literacy were borne on the same vehicle (Snelson 1974, 248-49 & 69). By 1925 5% of the population was enrolled in schools (Idem, 22). It is probable that in 1945 15% of the men in the country and 5% of the women were literate. In that same year, out of 2097 schools of various kinds only 51 were managed by colonial government; the remainder, totaling 2046 schools, were run by missionaries (Idem, 245-48). By 1964 when the independent Black African government finally took over, 2/3 of the country's schools were still run by missionaries. With African interests now paramount, between 1965 and 1971 primary school enrollment increased 80% and secondary school enrollment trebled (UNESCO Statistical Yearbook). By 1982, 49% of the population was literate (World Almanac).

Literacy in Zambia has already promoted remarkable changes in personality and social structures. It is inevitable that there will continue to be a marked acceleration and complexification of human interaction, as commerce, law, philosophy, art, science, religion and politics are carried on the wings of the literate medium(Cf McLuhan 1962).

Roberts acknowledges that the literate medium was as powerful and significant a factor as the content of the new faith and education for transforming the culture (Roberts 1976, 172).

If social revolution could be effected through literacy, _e fortiori_ an ideational reform in Bemba traditional religion would evolve, too. History, in fact, shows how the understanding and practice of religion are tightly related to the state of its communication media. Much of primal religion flourishes under auditory conditions. Since it is related to the invisible, it necessarily languishes under the conditions of a visual culture-- a truth exemplified in the demise of Greek mythic religion under the impact of literate philosophy (Havelock 1963; cf Ong 1967, 29-31). The treatise will argue that the demise of Bemba traditional religion is partially a consequence of the change from orality to literacy transforming the culture at large.

Bemba religious traditions do not seem to be explicitly distinct from other historical, political or artistic traditions; they function dynamically from within the total body of oral lore. Even in its heyday, oral religion did not represent a coherent integral account and was never a recitative prerogative of a single authority (Cf Goody 1972). The oral tradition could swallow up discrepancies in the flow of speech and the flood of interesting instances. The oral modes of rhetorical persuasion and an engaging spate of words in face-to-face encounter made inconsistencies difficult to detect (Goody 1977, 49-50).

As soon as this living religious world is written down, it is rendered soundless and its living words become muted and immutable. The hegemony of sight dulls the polysemous world of sound carried in a chorus of omnifarious authorities. The missionary writers anaesthetized the flow of oral plurality into a single textcentric purpose (Cf Kelber 1983). Their technology of mind enabled them to set down in a fixed space for visual inspection, editorial manipulation and leisured reflection, the otherwise evanescent tradition. The act of transcription itself transformed, in complex ways, what was orally transmitted. Their writing skill had developed in them special forms of linguistic activity related to particular kinds of problems and solutions which were entirely foreign to Bemba interlocutors in their oral medium (Cf Goody 1977, 158-62).

Complex and flexible traditions, recorded at different times and places, were written up as one uniform version and collapsed into a single authoritative perspective. Artificial unities, unintended by the oral authorities, were textually enforced by writers, unaffected by Bemba social controls. They were the ones who individually made personal selection and accommodation among the conflicting ideas and attitudes, available in the orally transmitted religion (Cf Goody 1968, 340). The scope of the Bemba data has been narrowed to focus on Christian catechetical concerns.

The missionaries, administrators and anthropologists, then, can be understood to have excised the religious traditions. In their place, they constructed and imposed their own systematic and complexly interrelated unity for their own purposes and according to their own conceptual framework. This was erected upon essentially fragmentary pieces of oral tradition, whose individual forms functioned diversely, perhaps even conflictingly, within their original political or historical forum of recital. [5]

European redaction of the oral tradition constructed plausible and familiar structures to accommodate Bemba religious tradition, and then lopped off or stretched ideas to fit the Procrustean bed of their own ideological preconceptions. This redaction of the tradition is certainly satisfying to literate expectations, but it might very well have violated its oral virtues. It lies like a palimpsest on the tradition. Soon, the written accounts, with an authority acquired by their very immutability, almost incestuously spawn second and third generations of literate renditions. Each of these reenforces the prejudiced selections and interpretation of previous literate accounts. Witness, for example the interdependent chain of White Father writings by Foulon, Molinier, Garrec, Tanguy, Sambeek, Etienne, Labrecque, Ragoen and Hering. These written materials are finally assimilated into continuing oral traditions, a process Henige (1973) calls "feedback."

Orality and the Scope of this Discussion

The medium analysis which follows pay special attention to the sounds of the Bemba life-world as relevant data for understanding (a phonological rather than a phenomenological approach), and to its main organs of transmission, the mouth and the ear.

The purpose of this essay is neither to prove nor disprove the oral-aural theory of culture and consciousness. It seeks to illustrate how the oral dynamic is indeed operative in and illuminative of the Bemba case. The scope of the treatise is not naively reductionistic nor exclusivist. It does state the case of media analysis emphatically, but its intention is relationist, accepting many other factors, complexly and intimately interrelated, as significant. Orality does not cause or explain everything in Bemba culture and consciousness (Cf Ong 1977, 9-10, 306-07; 1982, 139 and 175). And, obviously, not every item of the Bemba case contained herein can be accounted for in terms of the oral-aural theory. Nor can attention be paid to every item of data. But it is hoped that there is enough detail in the discussion to make a cogent argument of the data, converging on at least the plausibility, if not the verification of the oralist theory.

Finally, if this work gives a broad idea of the extent and variety of media ramifications in the study of Bemba traditional religion and its decline, and serves at least the prior task of alerting specialists to the problems and solutions inherent in a media approach, then it has achieved its seminal aim and registered a significance beyond the merely religious.

FOOTNOTES TO PREFACE

[1]Andrew Roberts denies that Islam had any influence on Bemba religion "because the traders never sought to proselytise" (A History of the Bemba: Political Growth and Change in Northeastern Zambia before 1900. Madison: University Press, 1973, p. 209). But Roberts himself documents four decades of Arab influence prior to European contact with the Bemba (Idem, 164-214). By the mid 1880's there was a permanent Swahili village established just north of Mporokoso, whose influence on the Bemba is recorded in the Kawambwa and Mporokoso District Notebooks (ZNA). (It is no coincidence that the largest mosque in Zambia today is in Nsama village.) Even ordinary converse between Bemba and Moslem people would alter the popular consciousness since the syncretic tendencies of their respective histories demonstrate that both religious traditions are highly susceptible to change and tolerant of alien practices and beliefs.

Robin Horton thinks that Islam exercised a "catalytic" influence in prompting African thought toward the idea of a supreme spirit whose embryonal features were already present in traditional religion ("African conversion," Africa 41, 2, 1971).

[2]The findings of the Anglo-American Oralist school do not go unchallenged in the academic world. Every position generates counterpositions and the oral-aural theory is no exception. Y.H. Poortinga in "Cross-cultural comparisons of maximum performance texts: some methodological aspects and some experiments with simple auditory and visual stimuli," (Psychologia Africana, Monograph Supplement 6, 1971) finds that visual and auditory accuity of educated adult "white" and "black" South Africans have no reliable group differences in either modality. R. Serpell in "Estimates of intelligence in a rural community of Eastern Zambia" (Human Development Research Unit Reports to the University of Zambia, 25, 1974) by studying the performance of Zambian and English school children on a series of copying tasks in various media concluded that the sensotype hypothesis is greatly overblown. S. Scribner and M. Cole in "Literacy without Schooling: Testing for Intellectual Effects," (Vai Literacy Project of Rockefeller University Laboratory of Comparative Human Cognition, April 2, 1978) suggest that it is schooling itself, not literacy per se that accounts for differences in cognitive performance. C.F. Oliver in "Some Aspects of Literacy in Ancient India" (The Quarterly Newsletter of the Laboratory of Comparative Human Cognition at the University of California, San Diego, 1, 4, 57-62, October 1979) cites the case of India which produced a highly developed, specialized knowledge and yet sanctioned only the oral method of transmittng it. R. Scollon and S.B.K. Scollon in "Literacy as Focused Interaction" (Quarterly Newsletter of LCHC at the University of California, San Diego, 2, 2, 26-9, April 1980) in a study of the Northern Athabaskans in Canada and Alaska argue for a pluralistic understanding of literacy and orality, having found that some oral traditions of the

Athabaskans represent a very high regard for human individuality
and distinctiveness.   While none of these studies disprove the
oralist   thesis,   they do indicate particularistic limitations to
its generalizations.   But the oralist theory as a whole   remains
valid.

[3]I found no corroborative evidence of such a thing among the
Bemba.   But the Luba people had a handsized carved rectangular
board   called a Lukasa across whose concave surfaces ran rows   of
beads   and   shells in special configurations.   It served as   an
esoteric   memory device of a secret society called the Bambudye,
who were the transmitting authorities of the oral lore concerning
the   mythical   origins,   and the political   and   religious
organization of the tribe.   The fingers of the reciter ran over
the complex patterns of beads and shells which symbolized the
specialized information stored there (Thomas Q. Reefe, "Lukasa:
A Luba Memory Device," African Arts, 40-50, 1977). The idea for
the Bemba Ingenga may have had a Luban origin.

[4]The citations in the text, which have only a name and a
Roman numeral, refer to a list of principal interlocutors and the
month when they were interviewed by the author.   The complete
table of interviews appears at the end of the Sources Consulted.

[5]The model here is based on Kelber's conception of how the
authors of the Synoptic Gospels redacted their oral traditions by
writing   the   story of Jesus (Kelber, The Oral and the Written
Gospel, 1983).

CHAPTER ONE

ORAL CULTURE AND ORAL RELIGION

This chapter will first flesh out the skeletal outline of an oral culture, which was provided in the Preface by a summary of Ong's position. At the same time, it will show how prominent features of Bemba culture conform to that model. Then, we will proceed to a general discussion of religious experience and expression, before focusing on a profile of Bemba oral religiosity. Finally, the characteristics of Bemba traditional religion will be considered and exemplified.

Orality and Culture

An oral-aural culture organizes itself around sensory analogues of sound--storing, communicating and retrieving its knowledge in a medium characterized by its own special features.[1] The constitutive features of sound are its evident dynamism, its signal of the present use of power, and its assimilation to the human voice and personal presence (Ong 1967, chap. 3; 1982, chap. 3).

Sound and Orality

Carothers (1959) contends that the spoken word, which is the medium in the "ear culture," is of its nature more dynamic, emotional and personal than the written word. For, sound at its source and in its reception is an active event, setting things in vibrating motion. Sound is an all encompassing event. It is a living something, something going on now, an "energetic happening." Sound "moves" with "an animated liveliness" (Ihde 1976, 82). It is apprehended from the front, back, up, down, all around, overwhelming its hearer with interrelatedness. The hearer is assaulted on all sides, and everything within range is registered. Space is diffused and the hearer is situated in the center of an acoustic field (Ong 1967, 128-129). In the case of our study the Bemba are oriented and attuned to a world of sound engulfing and overwhelming them. There seem to be no frontiers, only entrances. Situated thus in the actual midst of reality, the person interacts with all else. The Bemba are not related to the world as apart from, so much as they are related within the world as a part of (Cf Ihde 1976, chap. 3).

Oral peoples are on the alert for sound, because sounds are usually of direct significance. In a forest environment, like that of the Bemba, things and events are heard before they are seen. The ear is a better predictor of danger than the eye. People develop a facility for the swift interpretation of sound (Carothers 1972, 122-23).[2]

Because the primary sound of the oral world is that of the human voice, all sound is interpreted according to the paradigm of personal speaking (See below, chap. 3, 73ff). Moreover, there is a certain intrinsic connection between sound and interiority (Ong 1982, 71-74). The level of reality, at which the "personal" lies, cannot be seen, touched, tasted, or smelled. Its best indicator is "hearing" (Ong 1962, 26-40). The spoken word reveals the interior of one person and establishes an intersubjectivity, when the listener reciprocates with a voiced reply. Similarly, every sounding object resonates in the interior of its hearers, insinuating an inwardness of its source. This accounts for the oral proclivity to accommodate a knowledge of everything else to what is best known--other persons--without differentiating between subjects and objects, persons and things (Ong 1967, 84-5; 200-22).

A space full of sounds is assimilated to a place of ringing personal communications (See below, chap. 3, 80ff). Thus, oral people populate their resounding environment with personal forces, entering into dialogue with them and situating themselves at the center of a living cosmos. They thus give it a vaguely animistic, even anthropomorphic character. The sonorous universe is charged with emotions and imbued with quasi-human relations, to which the Bemba respond as participants in a dialogue. The Bemba accommodate the otherwise alien universe to the more familiar human world. They people the universe of things with psychic presences, with which they are conversant, and, thus, more compentent to control with the power of the spoken word.

Because of its sound, the oral word is of the same order of reality as the object to which it refers. The physical property of sound partially accounts for what has become an anthropological cliché--how intensely the power of a spoken word can affect reality in the consciousness of oral peoples. A curse or a blessing, for example, effectively produces what it signifies in its hearer. The oral association of word and effect is expressed in two Bemba proverbs: a) *Uushilumbula mfwa ni mukamwenso* "The one who doesn't talk about death is motivated by fear," i.e. to speak about death brings death about. (The word *kulumbula* is associated with the invocation in divination. To call out the name of someone or something is to conjure them up, to give them reality by assigning them a name as a known quantity.) b) *Nkalamo tailumbulwa* --"one does not mention the lion"--for fear of calling one up. (The effective power of the oral word produces the presence of its referent.) (For a discussion of the power of the oral word in witchcraft, see below chap. 4, 134ff).

Special features of Bemba linguistic, musical and rhetorical traditions illustrate how the very nature of sound is exploited in their oral communications.

Language. In a short monograph on Bemba art, Oger (n.d.) calls the language of the Bemba "their cultural wealth," "the jewel of African languages." The Bemba themselves have a conscious pride and love for their language and delight in mastering its poetic craft and verbal play (Frost 1977, ch. 5). Highly tonal in character, it makes use of variations in pitch to signal different meanings (Cf Kashoki 1967; Sharman & Meussen 1955), such as *Impanga* "sheep" and *Impanga* "bush." Distance in time and space are indicated by noticeably rising tones in the repetition of the word *Kutali tali tali*.

The importance of sound is intensified by the use of concordial prefixes and euphonic initial vowels to establish grammatical unity between a subject and all the other words in a sentence, as well as to exploit their alliterative potential. For example, let the reader sound out these Bemba sentences: *Abana ba bantu bali abasuma*, or in another of nine classes of nouns, *Ku mushi kwa muntu kuli ukubi* . Linguistic harmony contributes to and is product of the Bemba conception of the universe as a polyphonic whole.

The fact that Bemba specialists can make use of certain drums, like *Mondo* and *Lunkumbi* (Corbeil 1972, 33-5), as acoustic speech surrogates, underscores the tonal quality of their language. These drummers do not use a signal code, but actually produce the sounds of the language in a stylized form. They imitate words by reproducing tones and distinguish them by varying the pitch of the drums on the male or female "lips" *Milomo*. The talking drum, resonating and echoing through the Bemba area is a model of their oral noetic and oral life-world, drawing everything and everyone into an acoustic forum for communication (Cf Ong 1977, 92-120).

The Bemba language, like other Bantu languages, makes pervasive use of the phoneme "-ntu." It carries the nuances of a panharmonic ontology, which Africanists, like Tempels (1945), Jahn (1961) and Booth (1978), detect at the base of Bantu thought. The Bemba punctuate virtually every notion with the sonorous syncopation of the vital element NTU. *Muntu* refers to persons and *cintu* to things; *kuntu* and *lintu* locate in space and time respectively; *pantu* reveals the reason why.

Music. A great deal of tribal communication is committed to the sung word. For, music, a constitutive factor of all Bemba religious celebration, is at once a particular instance of intensified sound and an almost irresistible invitation to communal involvement. Because of its power to inject the community into a physical harmony with the rest of reality, music has become the primary and almost infallible medium of truth. (For a discussion of the role of music in spirit possession, see below chap. 4, 133).

Ihde, in his phenomenology of sound, argues that music has an "immediacy" for the listener, who is "dramatically engaged, and "participates" bodily in its movement; he refers to its "demonic" quality and "enchantment," which "calls upon one to dance" (Ihde 1976, 158-59). Like language, music has its own "grammar" and "logic" and "shares intentionality with human voices," but delivers its meaning more forcefully (Idem, 160-62).

In the oral world of the Bemba, music in all of its vocal, instrumental and choreographic rhythms clearly meets the demands of acoustic memory and validation (Cf Havelock 1982, 202-3, 344-45). Dancing, singing and drumming are musically reverberating devices employed by the oral society to set knowledge to meter and enshrine wisdom in dramatic ritual representation. The Bemba use these devices as quasi-linguistic signifiers, which are capable of communication at the highest level, with nuances, subtleties and refinements of thought. Through music, Bemba moral codes are transmitted, history is remembered, tribal interaction is stimulated, women are rallied, personal grievances are publicized, social cohesion is promoted, laws are promulgated, political procedures are influenced, spiritual realities are conjured up, religious duties are discharged--in short, music, the sound par excellence, ensures the continuity of Bemba tradition(Mapoma 1980, 36 and 66ff).

Rhetoric. Thought structures must necessarily fit the available media of communication. There is not any way for persons with no experience of writing to put their minds through the continuous linear sequence of thought demanded by formal logic; "highly analytical thought structures are quite simply unthinkable" (Ong 1971, 290). Lengthy oral verbalization, too, is performed, not analytically, but with a formulaic flair and arabesque flamboyance. It follows the artful conventions of public speaking. Verbal formulation and communication organize and exploit knowledge through the use of oratorical commonplaces. They seek to move people to action and decision, and deal with dialectical probabilities, not the certainties of logic. Oral communication is more preoccupied with unifying examples than with distinguishing proofs. Rhetorical delivery addresses an audience in a dialogical struggle, interacting and reacting with it, and trying to teach already well known truths by casting them in more delightful turns of phrase (Ong 1967, 53-4, 215-16, 222ff; 1971, ch. 1). Oral speech itself is not speculative or abstract. It is personally committed and partisanly disputatious. It seeks not to present a case for cool consideration, but to persuade an audience to active participation with its virtuosity (Ong 1967, 83-5, 194-96).

1) The Bemba have dialogical conventions, which ensure the interchange between speaker and listener, leaving no chance for a monologue or a "lecture." Rhetorical questions really expect an answer, as, for instance, wherever a number features in the discussion. A speaker will not say directly "five people" *Abantu*

basano, but "how many people" *Abantu banga ,* indicating "five" with a closed fist. Listeners respond *basano* "five" without missing a beat in the vocal exchange.

Silent cerebration is unheard of in the highly socialized vocal exchange. The Bemba do not think voicelessly, but need to cast their voices out to catch ideas. Bemba elders, for example, pour forth a stream of sound to give their minds time to catch up with their words, throwing in a variety of fillers, which are really rigamarole-- *Nakabushe, Nakamuno mpindi, Nakamuli lelo, Mailo masoshi, Namuli muku umo.*

2) The language rebounds with ideophones, contributing to the dramatic rhythm which punctuates the relationship between the word and its referent. For example, using *Kwisula* "to fill" is commonly followed by *Paa ,* an ideophonic intensifier "to the brim"; the speaker usually gestures with a flat palm covering a fist to complete the communication. Even blatantly visualist words referring to color, like *Kutuba* "to be white" and *Kukashika* "to be red," are relatively incomplete without their respective euphonic accompaniments *Che* or *Tutu .* An abstraction such as strength is ably rendered by the ideophone *Ndi Ndi Ndi ,* and the sound of tip-toeing is dramatized as *Nwa Nwa Nwa* (Nkandu 1981, 18).

Ideophones employ both the medium and the message, supplying an affective attitude to the listener attending to the performance. By varying inflection, for example, the oral narrator can use the diminutive *Aka-muntu* to express "a clever little person" or "a despicable little twirp." The direct medium of ideophones allows the listener to aesthetically experience the immediacy, freshness and vitality of an event and reinforces the effect of the oral word itself (Fortune 1962, 42-3). The onomatopoeic ideophone renders both the sound of the original experience and phonically represents the motion of the character: *Awa mu mukonko fubu . Mwatalala na tondolo* "He fell into the gorge *Fubu* (suddenly and heavily); all was quiet" (Mpashi 1978, p. 52). Ideophones draw attention to themselves by being phonologically different from the rest of Bemba vocabulary syntactically unusual behavior in grammatical construction (Lutato 1980, 192). In doing so, they also serve as the performers' signal to their audience of what is of major significance (Frost 1977, ch. V).

3) The Bemba are oral masters of "indirection and innuendo" *Nshintu.* The good speaker and listener are attuned to ingenious combinations of language, which subtly but never perfectly clarify the subject under discussion (Cf Simukoko 1978, 13; 1977 passim). In certain circumstances, speech is richer in hidden meanings and serves as a sonorous mask, a camouflage behind which thought hides; the interlocutor must be adept enough to detect its true face beneath the expressions. As the proverb says: *Icishumfwa nshintu taciikala ku muuba* "The person who is not

clever enough to understand allusive speech should not sit at a meeting of elders." From their earliest years, the Bemba are schooled in the skills of orality. Children, for example, play their favorite games with proverbs and riddles, acquainting themselves with the hermetic and obscurant powers of speech. The first part of a riddle *Co*?! is oblique and mystifying (Cf Kashoki n.d.) *Akape kashisula* ?! "a little basket which is never filled?!" the second part *Ciise*! is pithy and clear: *Kutwi* "the ear." The meaning is that a person's whole life is contained in the ear, the organ of truth and memory (Labrecque, 1931). "Proverbs" *Mapinda* are also called *Manshoko* from the verb *Kushoka* meaning "to take a circuitous route to one's destination when a shorter one is available" (Milimo 1978, 58). The similarities and contrasts in the rhetoric of proverbs and riddles, as analyzed by the folklorist Abraham (1968), can be applied to the Bemba usage. Both, he writes, use the stylistic features of poetry--rhythm, rhyme, metaphor and assonance--to deliver the meanings and values of a culture. Both riddles and proverbs enlist a dialogue by their balanced phrasing. The speaker gives the first part and the listeners supply the second.

On the one hand, the rhetorical purpose of a proverb (which will be treated more fully and specifically in a section of Chapter Three) is generally to supply comfortably traditional answers to recurrent ethical problems. It prescribes in clear and simple terms a course of action, which conforms to the community's values. Although it does not directly supply its referent, an alert listener can feel its moral sting in the conversational context. The proverb, then, proposes its bit of traditional wisdom, which is geared to persuade the group toward some edifying solution in their moral conflict. The rhetorical wit of its felicitous and artful expression makes the bitter pill of implied censure more palatable. For example, someone during communal work may remark to a lounging teenager: *Iyakula* "It is grown up." Another laborer will quickly add the remainder: *Tainukwilwa cani* "One does not pull out grass (for a roof or a broom) for it." The rebuke is well understood: the teenager, who likes to think he is mature, cannot expect the community to supply all his needs unless he cooperates in public projects.

On the other hand, the riddle, in order to be a rhetorical success, necessarily confuses its elements and hides its referent. Its wit is formulaic creation of perplexity--setting up apparent contradictions, withholding essential information or providing inconsequential evidence that misleads the listeners toward a false solution of the enigma it poses. Because the riddle is understood as a trick and is conventionally performed only in a game-setting, it is given license to broach all sorts of forbidden subjects and to explore the antisocial motives of a supposedly social traditional process. For example, out of spite or personal enmity, someone might falsely accuse another of witchcraft (i.e., possessing horns of malignant medicine). The ulterior motive may be to get the community to settle a personal score by appealing to traditional witchcleansers. During a riddling session a good neighbor may expose the perjurer with the riddle: *Co ? Akape kaisule nsengo ?* "What's a witch's basket full of horns?" The response could demystify the instance from its traditional witchcraft suspicion. It lays the blame squarely on the malicious chatter of the accuser: *Ciise! Kanwa kaisula na meno* "It is the mouth full of rattling teeth!" (Yamba 1947, 7).

A riddle thus participates in the liminal period of ritual. The community can temporarily court chaos by contesting, in order to modify, what the tradition teaches (See below, chap. 2, 48). In the game-setting, the community can safely permit the suspension of its sanctioned truths and values in order to channel the potentially destructive energies of riddling rhetoric (and ritual chaos) into a creative reformulation and reevaluation of its unifying bonds. So, although the content of a riddle varies with the times (except for those riddles supplied as rote drills for children), its **form, game-setting** and cryptic **function** in criticizing and up-dating the cultural lore, are traditional.

Thus, the aggressive and licentious character of a riddle's rhetoric is clear over against the more normative nature of the proverb's. However, even these lines may be blurred. For example, a well known riddle may pleasurably demonstrate societal knowledge and communal solidarity, and an original idea may be cast in proverbial terms or a proverb may be used to settle a dispute (Cf Abrahams 1968, 149-52).

In a culture, which otherwise prizes publicity and sociality, the rhetorical art of concealing speech in proverbs and riddles has several virtuous purposes.

a) It deliberately aims at engaging interlocutors in active dialogue. If they do not succeed in penetrating the partially shrouded meaning or inquire about uncertainties, the informant is content to leave them in error.

b) It also serves as a safeguard against publicizing information, whose significance or usefulness is privileged for a specialist elite. "Royal councillors" *Bakabilo* are especially versed in allusive language, called *Cibemba ca panshi* "deep or underground Bemba." They sometimes use a remnant dialect of Luba, because passers-by may overhear the affairs of state under discussion. Thus, insiders' jargon prevents divulgence of their knowledge and protects their powers (Richards 1971, 105).

c) Circuitous speech may also underscore the grave importance of a message. It must be ruminated over before it will be assimilated. This ensures that the deep revelation will be plumbed. Because of the effort expended, it will also be retained more readily (Milimo 1978, 67).

d) Most importantly, in religious matters, dissimulation is even more pronounced. Modesty shrouds the sacred as it surrounds sex. The exposure of religious things somehow profanes and violates their sanctity. Religion is supposed to be something which cannot and should not be fully explained. To understand it is to secularize it. For this reason, the Bemba in some ways prefer their religion uncontaminated by public explanation and kept a mystery, even to themselves. Religiously speaking, what is unsaid, what is ineffable is what really matters. Symbols and rituals obviate literal meanings. At the same time they encourage and suggest meanings for the initiated, they withhold and forfeit interpretation from an outsider. Thus a certain rhetorical reticence is built right into the oral culture, inhibiting open speech on religious matters.

Oral Knowledge

Besides being powerfully and personally dynamic, sound is also by nature evanescent. The tribal store of knowledge embodied in sound needs constant repetition for its survival (Ong 1967, 22). Information tends to be limited and scarce, sharing in the precarious quality of its medium. Oral society becomes conservative as it jealously guards its traditions. It preserves them in formulaic patterns and suspiciously resists any originality which might interrupt continuous themes and burden the social memory (Ong 1967, 24ff and 1982, 34-5, 41-2).

Forgetfulness is the enemy of oral culture, and its technology of mind is geared to facilitate memory in the storage and recall of information(Havelock 1982, 89-121). Oral peoples, then, devise and constantly repeat fixed, often rhythmic sayings--proverbs, songs, riddles, fabulous narratives of concrete actions and persons, as well as other aides-memoire, which manage their knowledge. They do not choose to be imaginative in their conception and expression. Striking imagery,besides being aesthetically pleasurable, is pedagogically essential for storage and recall (Ong 1967, 25; Havelock 1982, 134-36). Hence, knowledge is not abstracted from the speaking forum. Ethical norms and cognitional principles are taught indirectly through the memorable examples of specific agents, acting in concrete times and places (Havelock 1978, 43, 113 & 122; Ong 1969, 203-04). Cultural ideals have to be expressed "in symbols grown smooth and warm to the tongue through long and familiar use" (Tyler 1975, 111).

Given the idiosyncratic nature of spontaneous conversation, it must be channeled into such formulas. Otherwise, oral dialogue about important topics would emerge, as a linguistic anthropologist notes, "almost incomprehensible, a thing of irruptions and interruptions, of fits and starts, thoughts strangled halfway to expression, dead ends, wild shifts, and sudden inexplicable returns to dead and discarded topics" (Tyler 1981, 3).

Oral knowledge then is relatively rigid, typical and concrete, both in its expression and in its conceptualization (Ong 1977, 24-30). Bemba knowledge, with its oral matrix, tends to be thematic and formulaic, and is little given to speculation. Answers to questions seem almost prefabricated (Ong 1982, 33-6). When the Bemba respond to cultural questions, they tend to speak for everyone to everyone about perspectives which every adult already knows and scarcely dares to question. And so, the Bemba repeat what others say, or correct it only according to what they know the ancestral tradition(others!) says. They are not concerned to say something original, but to confirm and recall what has already been said. They are masters of the cliché, little given to analytic thinking, since the need to conserve what has already been thought requires endless mimicking of what has already been said on any familiar subject-matter (Ong 1977, chap. X; 1982, 38-9).

It has already been noted that a good deal of psychic energy is expended in an oral culture just remembering socially relevant information; otherwise it is simply lost. Unfortunately, this seems to have already happened, to a certain extent, in the Bemba case. The field research for this study was undertaken in the hope of acquiring lengthy and vivid oral accounts of the Bemba religious traditions. These did not materialize. It was disappointing not to find a coherent and categorized body of symbols and beliefs, which would stack up against what other investigations had accumulated. The oral recitals obtained were, for the most part, poorly developed and sketchily articulated. Possibly in its heyday the tradition was a more elaborate and sustained body of oral performances than survives today. Probably the detailed documents written up by earlier investigations were composites, assembled from disparate sources and edited into a coherent whole. They certainly betray more of a literate structure than what a mere transcription of oral performances would yield. While commenting on "a true written text" of a Hindu performance, Tyler notes:

> Compared to oral discourse it is far less rambling, less repetitious, and less redundant. It has few fillers, no false starts, no backtracking and spontaneous reformulation, and no sentence fragments. Its syntax is more complex and its sentences are longer. It is also marked by the absence of such specifically oral devices as echo words, interjections, vocatives, and other speaker interventions . . . . Finally, it is highly focused, containing almost no extraneous topical departures. It reflects, in short,

interesting <u>cognitive</u> <u>adjustments</u> <u>that</u> <u>are</u>
<u>partly</u> <u>induced</u> <u>by</u> <u>written</u> <u>form</u> (Tyler 1981,
13-14, emphasis added).

The early accounts of Bemba tradition written by missionaries and
others share many of those obvious literate dispositions.

<u>Unquestionably</u>, there is a third factor to account for the
meagreness of today's recitals. The guardians of the tradition,
being out of practice have forgotten a great deal. As certain
features lose their relevance to the society's life, they also
lose remembrance. An oral culture does not enjoy the luxury of
continuing to store items of knowledge, whose affects and values
are no longer attached. As soon as an item loses its emotional
or practical grip on a people, the item is dropped (Goody 1968,
307). Meaning alone is not sufficient to ensure survival.
Significance is required for sustenance.

Beliefs and practices that succumbed to missionary attack,
government prohibition, or the enlightened derision of younger
generations, are now tenuously preserved only in second-hand
accounts and the fast fading memories of elders. These are the
days of infrequent rehearsal of tradition. When someone enquires
about the reason behind this or that action, the Bemba employ a
short-hand response: "It is our custom" *Ulutambi* (White Fathers
1958, 500). Apparently, this is in part an evasive excuse for
lack of extensive knowledge about the tradition. But this
response also signals how deeply rooted in the tradition and how
authoritatively sanctioned an area is. It is an action that is
commanded by the word of the ancestors. Rather, it is an action
that discloses the ancestral will as definitively as *Lubuko* "divination": "I do this because our ancestors did it." The reply
communicates the profound and necessary connection between the
present and the past which justifies and gives meaning to the
present. It is an appeal to the sum of wisdon and experience
accumulated by successive generations in community (Cf Zahan
1970, 212). The Bemba validate their present action by invoking
similar comportment by their ancestors in a ritual "return to
origins" (Cf Eliade 1954, passim).[3]

Bemba knowledge reverberates in its oral communications as a
sort of "echo system" (Havelock 1978). Words of knowledge once
spoken have passed on and can only be revisited if they are
repeated. Reiteration, then, is also the device orality uses to
give an audience time to think over (audit!) what has been said.
Verbal echo ensures that no one misses anything and gives the
speakers time to think of what they want to say next. It also
serves to corroborate what was imparted the first time (Ong 1977,
chap. IV; 39-41).

In an oral economy of knowing, the purpose of the
communication is not to transpose knowledge where there was only
ignorance, but primarily to invite participation of the listener.

It allows the listener to get involved with what is well-known (Ong 1977, 118-19). The operational and participational nature of the sounding medium itself actively employs a kinesthetic, tangible power which surrounds and engages people corporally: "sound always tends to socialize" (Ong 1971, 284). By the power of oral communication, authoritative speakers, the community of listeners and the traditional subject matter are all united in the event of sound. They become a forum where there is agreement. The knower and the known are identified. The performer engages the audience (Ong 1982, 45-46). Such feelings of total immersion are characteristic of the oral life style and cognitive process (Ong 1977, 272-304).

Both knowledge itself and knowing persons become highly socialized, through the engaging medium of sound in the knowing process and because of the constantly repeated formulae (Idem, 122-28). Knowledge becomes a social possession in an oral culture and the knower holds it in communal trust. Anyone with special knowledge in the community wields special power (See below chap. 4, 113ff).

Bemba villagers sometimes feel inadequate when interviewed alone. They deem themselves capable of furnishing testimony only when they are supported by others. Whatever knowledge one has, one is always acutely aware that one has received it. Or one is painfully reminded of that by resounding, apodictic corrections of "mistakes" *Filubo* by the social group. Everything has been learned in the village "speak-easy" *Nsaka* , where everyone speaks with the active participation of all others present, rejecting or corroborating what is said. The Bemba derive a genuine pleasure and reassurance in finding mutual funds of knowledge which resonate and reverberate in the exchange at the *Nsaka*.

Oral Truth

This is the authentic dynamic of communication and verification operative within an oral society: society conditions and verifies what the others are reporting. It confirms only what is already consonant with its own ideas and expectations, for it rings true. In this setting, truth is indeed a socially constructed reality (Berger 1967). The organ of truth is the ear. The criteria of truth are the words of others. The evidence proffered by what society deems true is largely "hearsay," as oral aural implies. The act of grasping truth is not only "hearing" *Kuumfwa* what is said. The verb also has connotations of "obeying" the statement, of "submitting" to what others say, especially those sayings sanctioned by the tradition (See below, chap. 3, 75ff).

Robert Serpell's (1974) study of emic categories for evaluating intelligence among the oral Nyanja peoples revealed that indigenous elders rated children's intelligence on the basis of social behavior, rather than according to creative mental ability and personal initiative. The patterns of social propriety, which were highly valued, were characterized by the cooperation and obedience of children to traditional mores and tribal seniors. Although the evidence gathered for that study was from a Nyanja-speaking group, the Bemba manifest complementary criteria for intelligence. The "clever child" *Wacenjela* and "intelligence" *Mano* are functions of compliance and obedience registered in the Bemba word *Kuumfwa* "to hear, to listen to directions, or to obey." A proverb expresses the idea: *Mano mambulwa* "wisdom consists in being told."

"True" in the oral world, thus, has the ring of "trustworthy, loyal, faithful" (relative to subjective interaction). In contrast literate "truth" connotes "accuracy, objectivity, facticity" (relative to proposition). A primary consequence of the transition from oral to written discourse, as Tyler observes, is

> to replace honesty with truth, for the former
> is an evaluation of the speaker's character
> derived from the harmony of his words and
> deeds, while the latter is only a relation of
> words to words (Tyler 1981, 1).

Discourse among oral people has a preference, then, to quote reputable authorities (Ong 1967, 231). This trustworthy body of authorized knowledge is remembered and repeated in dialectically and rhetorically persuasive ways.

There is a certain reluctance of the ordinary Bemba to give away any information, which experience has taught them might be used against them. This can be attributed to their respect for that truth which belongs to the community. Everyone has a duty to preserve communal secrets and the deposits of tribal knowledge. These are not readily broadcast at large to foreign ears. Knowledge is the community's possession, socially cnditioned and communally constructed and transmitted. Truth is conceived in terms that serve the community's interests and needs.

This is evident even in very simple matters, as, for example, when one villager, Mpundu, enquired of a near-sighted old woman in his village whether Mwango were present. Without any hesitation she answered "No!" But, when Mpundu identified himself as belonging to the village, she acknowledged his right to know about its inhabitants with *Kanshi, mukwai, epo bali ba Mwango* "In that case, Sir, Mwango is present."

Truth is knowledge that serves to strength the community's bonds and to protect it from outside harm. If what a person says upsets community relations, then that person is called *Wa mulomo* "a liar," literally "one with a long lip." It would be a "lie"

Bufi, then, to report to a stranger on a person in the community, until it is clear that no difficulties will ensue from that information.

Another instance of social prevarication illustrates both the communal dimension of truth and the power of the oral word to effect its referent. Bemba persons may deny that they have acted against tribal ethics, when, in fact, everyone knows they have transgressed. They are really confessing. With their denial, they acknowledge that their behavior should have been in conformity with ancestral wisdom, and, by pledging amendment, they orally recreate their behavior according to communal ideals (Cf Ray 1976, 87).

The Oral Self

Because of this social consciousness and communal conscience, oral peoples do not develop a deep sense of individual self. Tribal patterns of thought and activity simply overpower the individuals, depriving them of privacy and delivering them over to such total exposure that they have no opportunity to withdraw into self (Ong 1968, 16-7). The Bemba think of one's interior as being a social personality of self + ancestral spirits, who control one's actions and are responsible for their good and evil consequences. Where formulated knowledge is assimilated by being constantly repeated in communal situations, it is far more socialized--and so is the person, who is conditioned by this knowledge of what everyone else is saying. The clever person is not the one who comes up with original ideas, but who recirculates the traditional ones in familiar formulations. These show how what one says and thinks is socially acceptable and sanctioned by the authoritative wills of the ancestors.

While copying and imitation are the general rule of oral noetics, there is room for a limited amount of common sense initiative. But such originality is unobtrusively inserted into the tradition by the gradual process of assimilation called "homeostasis" (See below chap. 3, 106ff). Or it may be couched in such traditional terms or delivered by so time-honored a form that the community scarcely registers its novelty. There is even a proverb to warrant this exception of singularity to the role of authorized socialization: *Mupashi wa mbiyo tawenendelwa* "another's spirit will not cover for you!" (White Fathers 1954, 481).

Where knowledge is a tribal possession, a person avoids solitary and original speculation, and never stands alone, as an individual against the world (Ong 1967, 231-35). Where community matters so much, there is less emphasis on individual values, like personal freedom, rights, responsibility and initiative. A highly socialized world of agreement and solidarity is the end result. Indeed, it is virtually impossible to escape the social formation which the oral tradition imposes. Every social occasion in an oral culture engages the person in the group's ways of thinking, feeling and acting, and molds the individual in the image of the community (Goody 1968). In the end, it would be safe to say that no Bemba tribesperson in the tradition would regard one's life as a separate thing. Oral consciousness is tied to community.[4] Even precision has an anti-social charge, as does privacy in any form--private or peculiar thoughts, eccentric actions, secret stores, anything which excludes communal interests and controls (See below, chap. 4, 123ff).

Oral persons, writes Carothers, are so completely integrated into society that they become intellectually conventional and do not see themselves as self-reliant units. The oral economy of knowledge so effectively socializes the people that they are afraid to speculate on unique personal lives, are highly extrovert, and regard unorthodox thoughts as alien, even evil (Carothers 1972, 121-22).

Orally conditioned minds are more exteriorized. Psychologically faced outward, they are little given to depressive syndromes, overwhelming guilt trips or feelings of unworthiness or remorse. Deep feelings are given release and overtly expressed in oral society (Ong 1967, 192-222; 1982, 43-5). Oral peoples experience "self" as physically beset by a human and natural environment charged with personal violence and incarnated in the high levels of surrounding sound. Thus, personality structures in an oral society are polemically posed, as if for combat with a world swarming with active and canny foes. Oral people, then, are rather inclined to publicly exhibit and exercise their hostilities in the verbal pyrotechnics called "fliting" (Ong 1967, 207-22). Such aggression is often ritually expressed, because conflict is mnemonically advantageous; something is best grasped by contrast with its opposite (Havelock 1978, 84). Their polemically textured culture tends to conceive of even non-moral areas, like the incidence of disease and disaster, in polarities of virtue and vice, and praise and blame. These are attached to heroic or heinous agents (even animals) in conflict situations (Ong 1969, 203-04).

Carothers further characterizes the oral African psychology as "monoideic." He refers to their tendency to conceive of the world in terms of its unity and coherence, where wish and reality, possible and impossible, knowledge and belief, thought and imagination, secular and religious, dreams and reality, body and mind, animal and human, animate and inanimate, are all interwoven and fundamentally one (1972, 120).

Ong contends that the oral proclivity to personalize everything (1967, 84-5) encourages these synthetic, synchronic and interpenetrating habits of mind (Idem 178, 316). Lord (1960), Havelock (1967) and Ong (1982) agree that such "situational thinking" finds its most connatural expression in poetic and metaphoric discourse (See below, 25ff).

Accordingly, in the Bemba mind, the cosmological, zoological, botanical, anthropological, geological and spiritual words are not artificially separate zones, but a symbolic whole (Cf Labrecque n.d., 18-20). They all converge on and interrelate one with another. There is a unity of life and time. Phenomena, which are regarded as opposites in the West, exist on a single continuum for the Bemba. All things exist in dynamic correspondence. Past, present and future blend in harmony. Dreams and daylight mesh. The dead and the living are in contemporaneous communion. Causalities overlap. Everything exhibits a complementarity, commensurability and compatibility, which the Bemba exploit in symbols and metaphors. These poetic devices are characteristic of the cognitional apparatus an oral culture employs to express its contact with truth and value.

Orality and Religion

Oral people perceive the religious dimensions of their existence with the same mental technology with which they respond to the whole of reality. Their religion will participate in the same oral features as does its general culture.

This investigation first needs to proffer a framework on which the religious discussion can hang. David Tracy has developed a suitable scheme, the context of which must be examined before it can be usefully applied to the oral religion of the Bemba.

Religious Experience and Expression

According to Tracy, religion functions diversely as just one more variable in a complex of perspectives for understanding culture (Viz., Freud, Jung, Marx, Weber, Durkheim, Malinowski, et al., also Tracy 1981, 167ff). Nonetheless, it also has its own substantive reality. On its own terms, the religious perspective addresses itself not to any part, but to the whole of culture, which it claims to form, inform and transform. Religion's dominating interest is in

> . . . the fundamental, existential questions
> of the meaning and truth of individual,
> communal and historical existence as related
> to, indeed as both participating in and
> distanced from, what is sensed as the whole of
> reality (Tracy 1981, 158-59).

Such a perspective then recognizes the presence of implicit religious horizons in ordinary experience and language. These are what religion explicitly manages in its own proper performances and peculiar language forms. The religious horizons of everyday experience are identified, on the positive side, as "peak experiences" of joy, loyalty, creativity, love, ecstasy, etc., and characterized, on the negative side, as existential situations of "angst," like death, evil, sickness, guilt, fear, tragedy, etc. (Tracy 1975, 91-109). Religion, then, is profoundly ambiguous both in its substance and in its function. While its power can promote the good and the holy, it can as well seem demonic. As with its experience, so is the language of religion ambiguously and tenuously poised at a limit (Tracy 1981, 158). Both seem to be in intrinsic interaction with what is disconcerting to all, frightening at times to each--_mysterium fascinans et tremendum_. At these limits of human experience and expression, a reality is disclosed which functions as the ultimate ground of all experience. Appropriate language about those experiences is both expressive of their limit character and disclosive of that final dimension, which Tracy terms "the whole." On this view, a sense of reality of the whole, delivered by limit-situations and limit-language, constitutes the self understanding of religion (Tracy 1981, 159).

We then accept and will make extensive use of Tracy's concepts of "limit" and "the whole" as key categories for understanding any experience and expression termed "religious." Our Conclusion will distinguish _between_ this _religious enterprise_ of phenomenologically describing the peculiar character of these existentially meaningful experiences and expressions _and_ the more transcendental task of _fundamental theology_. The latter seeks to reflect deliberately and explicitly on their cognitive claims. For the present purpose, it is enough that the next section will describe the phenomena of religious experience and language.

Characteristics of Religious Phenomena

The classic religious experience is understood, first of all, as an event, a happening, which is not produced by human subjectivity and cannot be accounted for as an ordinary turn of expected events. Its reality

> . . . however named and in whatever manner experienced . . . functions as a final, now gracious, now frightening, now trustworthy, now absurd, always uncontrollable limit of the very meaning of existence itself (Tracy 1975, 108).

Secondly, this uncanny experience is a powerful disclosure of the whole, erupting as a crisis within experience itself that promises to transform all previous experience and understanding. Since the "given" character of its reality is cognate to the fundamental "instinct of the human spirit for some relationship to the whole" (Idem, 193-94), this revelation of the whole becomes paradigmatic of the real and bears a claim to truth. Tracy writes that the unique subject matter of religion is an

> . . . expression of the whole believed to be, because experienced as, a manifestation of the whole by the power of that whole . . . [It is] a realized experience bearing some sense of recognition of what can be named reality and truth (Idem, 197).

Thirdly, there is a limit character to that experience and to the language used to express it. Tracy discusses strange human experiences evidencing a "limit to" dimension. In them fundamental questions are raised about the final dimensions of existence and a "limit of" disclosure--the realm of transcendence consciously intended by proposed answers. Some are liminal occasions of gracious opening, where fullness seems to be realized, and others are closures, where diminution seems to threaten. All are uncanny situations, where the whole of the human and natural universe comes alive and takes on a depth. These are the "hierophanies" (to borrow a useful term from Eliade), in which the whole confronts the community with final meanings and values. Most linguistic communities have developed a kind of "limit-language" appropriate to these empirical situations so qualitatively different from ordinary experience as to elude ordinary expression. The notion of limit implies at least a heuristic awareness of what limits. The limit-language of symbols, metaphors, myths, parables, proverbs, songs, etc., therefore, has a double intentionality. It literally refers to the dimension which is the immanent "limit to" a particular experience, and non-literally intimates the transcendent beyond, which is the "limit of" all experience. "Reference at best," writes Tyler, "is only part of the story, for as important as the relation of words and things is . . ., above all, the relation between the said and the unsaid" (1978, 181). Persons seem compelled to attempt an expression of the unspoken and unspeakable final horizon of meaning and existence. Thus, at the very limits of experience and expression, there is a claim that the ultimate dimension to life, one which renders it whole, is not totally subject to language. Something is left unsaid, something is unheard of. This ineffable reality is what is most sacred to most communities. This religious axiom has a refreshingly sympathetic response in linguistic anthropology where, after a comprehensive study of hermeneutics, Tyler concludes that "meaning . . . abounds . . . in the resonating silence of the unsaid--in that possibility of all meaning" (1978, 465).

Finally, the uncanny experience of the whole emanating from the very "grounds of reality" (Cf Tillich 1951 passim), elicits and empowers in attending persons a dialectic response, which includes: a)   a sense of fundamental trust and absolute

dependence on the whole; b) a sense of estrangement from the
transformative powers of the whole; c) a sense of release into
the gracious mystery at the heart of human experience (Tracy
1981, 201).

Any expression of that finitude, estrangement and remedy,
which the experience of the whole enables, will be inadequate;
for the experience of the whole is a radical mystery, which both
reveals and conceals its nature. As such, symbolic expression
seems again to be of special usefulness (Cf Ricoeur 1967).

Tracy provides a useful typology of religions. A religion,
as manifestation-oriented, may focus on the event itself, which
immediately discloses and intimates the powerful realm of the
transcendent whole. Or, as proclamation-oriented, it
concentrates on the language, which mediates and responds to that
event. When the sense of immediate participation of the whole
predominates through mystical, priestly, communal and aesthetic
means, the religious expression is "manifestation." When
mediated non-participation dominates in prophetic, ethical,
individual and historical means, the expression is
"proclamation." These are ideal types, the one not excluding the
other, implying only an emphatic strain of expression. Actually
all religious expression incorporates elements of both. A well
integrated religion maintains a balanced dialectic between the
originating manifestation and its interpretive proclamation
(Tracy 1981, 207-19).

While adopting these types to the discussion of Bemba
traditional religion, this treatise will add its own corollary.[5]
Religion under the dynamic of the oral word is of the type named
"manifestation." It is the word as powerful sound, and not the
word as verbal content, which is particularly operative: the
sound empowers the participation of its audience and saturates
them with a sense of belonging to the whole. Since literacy
facilitates the disentanglement of the self from the community, a
literate religion will be of the type named "proclamation."
Writing enforces a general sense of discretion that disengages
the sacred from the profane, the divine from the human, the
personal from the objective. Any sense of identity with the
whole is destroyed. The whole is understood to be radically
distinct from all else. The word which this religious expression
"proclaims" is detached from the sounding reality wherein it
originated. Religion as proclamation defamiliarizes the
transcendent as a totally other self. The transcendent addresses
another, finite individual self, uncomfortably decentered from a
complacent participation in the whole and alert to an ethical
response to the world.

Bemba Religious Experience and Expression

The Bemba, of course, do not speak of "the whole" nor do they have any terms in their language which corresponds to "the whole." Nevertheless it is legitimate to predicate "a fundamental orientation towards `the whole'" as belonging to the Bemba religion. First, a distinction has to be drawn between the spontaneously operative notion of "the whole" and the theoretical accounts of its genesis and content, which differ from religion to religion. The notion of "the whole," which Tillich calls the "element of ultimacy" (Tillich 1951), functions as an invariant common to all religions. This is the case no matter how they account for it theoretically. The notion is prior to any concrete or symbolic conception of the whole. It is immanent and dynamically operative in religious practices and beliefs. As an intention of the whole, it is all pervasive and it underpins all religious contents. In short, it penetrates them all, constituting them all as religious and transcending them all. The whole is, in principle, inconceivable and ineffable. In fact, all conceptions and expressions of the whole are inadequate, though the attempts to do so admit of more and less.[6]

It has already been noted that the oral Bemba have learned to comprehend their world with a sensorium specifically organized around hearing. Hearing is the primary sense which gives the Bemba satisfactory access to the real. That world, through the physical properties of sound itself, surrounds them and situates them at the center of a powerfully reverberating environment. The Bemba liken their sounding world to a dialogical partner with whom they are personally conversant in a mutually revealing encounter.

In the Bemba experience, those active, powerful, personal presences, manifest in sound, constitute what Tracy describes as its properly religious dimension. Agreeable to Tracy's other terms (1981, passim), unusual sounds, originating in nature, are events outside human control and thus have the tone of the uncanny. The sounding event is revelatory, insofar as it is assimilated to the personal. It is also holistic, insofar as it is experienced as all-encompassing. It is transformative insofar as it physically sets hearers in sympathetic vibration at their interiors. Experience has a limit-character, as meaning and value beyond the time, place and fact of its occurrence are assigned to it. The language used to express it transcends ordinary usage. Finally, responding ambiguously, hearers exult in the remedial strength of its utterance, feeling vulnerably impotent, or fearfully flee from its presence, confessing some defilement. Lacking the literate wherewithal to reflect on the experience, the Bemba are more likely to try to reproduce it in myth and ritual. They may also induce others to actually attend to it, if it is a permanent occurrence, like a waterfall.

Bemba traditional religion can thus be typed as manifestation. Its authenticity as religion lies in the experience of wonder, which orients its votaries toward some wholeness, for which the radical depths of their intelligence pines. This is the decisive character of the truth of Bemba religion: its fundamental recognition of the whole, uncannily manifesting itself and rallying a community of adherents around that experience in appropriate symbols and rituals. The flaw in that religious character lurks in the ability of those powerful images of the whole to seduce the Bemba with the promise of a comfortable participation in the whole. They feel no need for reflective attention to its claims of meaning and truth. Without the technology of writing, the Bemba do not have the means for the differentiation of self, and are not moved to critical reflection on their experience (See below, Conclusion). They recognize that the experience belongs to a wider and deeper reality than the community can achieve of itself. At the same time they do not reach beyond that uncanny experience to a higher level of understanding and formulation adequate for systematically communicating its meaning to others in words alone. In order for others to experience the whole, they must be brought to the time and place of its occurrence. This may be done either by actually reproducing its intensity and particularity for them, or by catching them up vicariously in myth and ritual (Tracy 1981, 200). In summary it may be said that, orality favors the participation and saturation of religious manifestation; literacy sponsors the alienation and distanciation of religious proclamation.

Five Characteristics of Bemba Religion

It is an Africanist's cliché, popularized by John Mbiti, that the whole of the African world is permeated with religion. It would be more inclusively accurate to remark on the African tendency to conceive of every aspect of their universe, including its religious dimension, as a whole.

This conception is the theme and variation of every religious belief and practice, and will be amply exemplified throughout this work. Bemba (1)tradition shares this proclivity to conceive of the universe, in which the (2)community of (3)humans is the consummate part, as a (4)vitally dynamic (5)whole.

Several ideas in that last statement require elaboration, since they are the basic characterstics of Bemba religion, as (1)traditional, (2)communal, (3)anthropocentric, (4)vitally dynamic, and (5)cosmically holistic.

The discovery of these five characteristics of Bemba religion is not original to this treatise.[7] But their application as a whole to a particular African religion and their clarification in terms of an oral-aural worldview are its concern and contribution. Studies in the phenomenology of sound, like those of Walter Ong (1967) and Don Ihde (1976) show that there are oral factors, which correspond to and give supportive evidence for the five qualities of Bemba religion. These linkages are at least implicitly discussed in the lengthy section on orality, and will only be indicated in this section.

1) The designation "traditional" applied to Bemba religion carries, first of all, the connotation of a particular content and practice which existed before the arrival of Islam and Christianity. More importantly, it refers to the word of mouth transmission from generation to generation. Unlike a scriptural religion, whose locus of authority resides in historical documents and which can be learned-about by reading, oral religion must be directly participated-in by listening to the immediate words of living authorities. "Traditional" obviously implies sound, in that oral words are the means of transmission (Ong 1967, 1-35; Ihde 1976, 3-17). The tradition exists only when the community recalls it; and whatever the elders "recall," no matter how recently incorporated, becomes "the tradition."

2) The "traditional" therefore is also the communal: "True tradition is only that on which the community agrees" (Booth 1978, 93). The converse is also true: the community is formed when the tradition is shared. "Communal" is reenforced by the socializing effect of sound (Ong 1967, 121ff, 176ff and 192ff; Ihde 1976, 117ff). Generational relationships within the community are not just chronological; they are ontological and deontological. Listening to the community of elders recite the tradition is not just a way of coming to know what is meaningful and what is valuable. It is a religious act of a coming-to-be as well as a coming-to-be-of-value by ritually discerning and identifying with the traditional deposit of accumulated wisdom. The contemporary community celebrates the fact that it represents the continuity and completion of an ancestral community to whom a measure of ideal perfection is mythically attributed. Community and tradition are interrelated as contemporary dynamic and generational depth.

3) Bemba religion is also qualified as "anthropocentric," as it refers to the pivotal interaction and central control exercised by the human community. "Anthropocentric" correlates both to the Bemba sense of being at the center which sound confers on its hearers, and to their predilection for associating all sounds with personal communications (Ong 1967, 34-5; 111ff; Ihde 1976, 133ff).

Some writers want to conceive of the Bemba tradition in the Christian terms of human weakness and divine omnipotence. Gouldsbury (1911), for example, wrote of the Bemba person as a pawn in a game of the great gods. He centered traditional religion on a feeling of a lack of power and the desire to placate greater powers.

The evidence gathered for this essay converges on the conception of Bemba religiosity as the quest for communal realization. The means is not so much by involving divine aid, but by human exertion. Virtually every religious belief of Bemba tradition declares that the human community occupies a powerful, central position in the harmony of the whole. All Bemba religious practices seek to establish and maintain the central and regulative human place in the whole formed by the spiritual and physical universe. The Bemba are tenaciously terrestrial, and their vision of themselves—their life, their world and divinity—is determined by their earthly fixation. They are at once the image, the model and the integral part of the universe in whose cyclical life they are powerfully engaged but not overwhelmed. Satisfaction is not postponed to any other-worldly, future dimension. There is finality in this world now. The Bembas' destiny is completely consummated by mastering themselves in the discipline of tribal customs, the world by magical and technical manipulation, and divinity through cultic control (Cf Zahan 1970, chap. I).

The power of this mastery is acquired and exercised through the metaphoric knowledge (1) of these realms, (2) of the relationships between them and (3) of one's own status and responsibilities within them. The human community occupies a privileged position in the universe and exerts a centripetal force on all else. Order and harmony, as well as their disruption, are arranged around the human sphere. The rest of creation is made to coordinate with and relate to the human center which transcends them all. With their powerful metaphors, humans adjust the cosmic rhythms to human life-cycles, projecting their interior life into all that seems to be foreign. Thus, they domesticate and humanize their cosmos. All matter, nature, cosmos are anthropocentrically conceived to the extent that they are assimilated to the personal world of mind, culture and consciousness. For example, even "East and West" *Ku Kabanga na ku masamba* coordinates are valorized in human terms of life, health, prosperity, and death, sickness and evil, respectively (Komakoma XI). Through complex religious symbolism, which is anthropocosmic in structure, an almost mystical solidarity is established between the human, and the vegetable, animal, inorganic even spiritual worlds (Cf Kapompole n.d., passim).

In their charter myth (See below, chap. 2), the Bemba locate themselves at the interaction of the terrestrial and celestial coordinates. This is clear in their story of Mumbi Mukasa, their first queen, who came from the sky and married an earthly king (Roberts 1973, 39-43). In this hierogamy the sky itself is humanized and divinity itself is subject to human control (See Heusch 1958, 146-50).

As will be demonstrated in Chapter 3, Bemba traditional religion does not deal with a supreme divinity. Proper divinity is perceived as irrelevant to what is essentially a human endeavor--maintaining harmony in the cosmos. In the Bemba practice, divine roles and prerogatives disintegrate and diffuse into "spirits" *Mipashi*. The distance between the divine and the human creates the middle ground where spirits hold forth.

In rituals spirits seem to be caught up in a manifold of modalities, manifesting, radiating and emanating from divinity. Be that as it may, *Mipashi* "ancestral spirits" have a definitely human matrix. They were humans once, and they may be born human again. Human initiative effects the constant commerce between the spirit world and Bemba. It is humans who oblige them to communicate. Humans command them, and once empowered by their spiritual presence, humans dismiss them. Spirits are invoked not for their own sakes, but for what cooperation they can supply in human development. Though the spirits may be stronger than the humans by a greater realization of their innate powers, they nonetheless are susceptible to religious finesse. Like Judo experts, the Bemba turn powers greater than their own to their own advantage.

Thus, when the Bemba invoke spirits in a prayer or sacrifice, they do not seek to please the spirits. The concern is rather to enlist refined human powers in their efforts to become fully themselves, to realize the order in which they are implicated and to tap and exercise their own resources (Cf Zahan 1970, chap. I). The Bemba are saved not by grace but by works in their religious economy. The powers they rally, however, are not individual but social. Just as the Bemba rely on the human community in this life, they call upon the *Mipashi* "ancestral spirits," whose powers are continuous with the human. Spirits are former humans now incorporated into the spiritual community of ancestors (Chilubula III).

Affirmation of human centrality and mastery in the universe confers a feeling of superior power on the Bemba. Even death is not considered a permanent fatality. Its fearful consequences are rationalized away into a retreat. Death is an interlude, a fall back position, a higher rank from which the Bemba regroup their human resources for a new assault on terrestrial life (Chomba 1978). A *Ciwa* "evil spirit" is the extreme case, where, by suicide, the human gathers hostile forces of hatred and vengeance into death. These are then unharnessed with baleful intensity on earthly enemies (Labrecque n.d., 20). Instead of being removed from earth to a saving heaven, human spirits remain bound to earth, haunting cemeteries or "abandoned villages" *Fibolya* (Etienne 1948, 57). They may even be recycled to the living sphere: through the *Kupyana* "succession," they are returned to their clan, or through the *Kwinika ishina* "naming," they are reincarnated in the newly born (Shimwalule VII).

Spirit veneration in these rites is simply a means to ensure the cooperation of the accumulated wisdom and experience of generations of humans. It is directed to ancestors who preceded

and were successful in making a memorable mark on the earth. The
cult of the spirits of dead humans is an extension of the
exaltation of the human spirit and its fulfillment in the living
community.

4) Bemba religion regards everything as "<u>vitally dynamic</u>."
"Vitally dynamic" identifies the capacity of sound to signal the
present use of power and the inclination of its hearers to
attribute animation to the source of any sound (Ong 1967, Ihde
1976, 149ff). This other community, formed by all that is non-
human in the cosmos, is modelled on the field of human
relationships. A primordial example of the Bemba assimilation of
non-human realities to the human community would be their
"totemic clans." These have a special, though now faint,
religious charge attached to them, because they symbolically
incorporate every sector of the universe. All Bemba persons
identify themselves according to some matrilineal clan-- *Mfula*
"rain," *Ngombe* "cattle," *Kani* "grass," *Mbulo* "iron," *Isabi*
"fish," *Nguni* "bird," *Nkalamo* "lion," *Kashimu* "bee," *Bowa*
"mushroom," *Ngoma* "drum" and many others (Cf Etienne 1948, 109-
11).

Every ceremony, belief, magico-medicinal practice, and
divination proclaim how all the ideas in the Bemba conceptual
universe interpenetrate and intercommunicate. They have the same
agility as the totemic metaphors of their human world. The
primary focus and ultimate concern of Bemba traditional religion
are for human fulfillment in community. Still human
relationships can be enhanced or diminished by the use or abuse
of the potential and kinetic powers available throughout the
cosmos. It is believed that the dynamism and life of the whole
of reality can be made to ebb and flow in relative calm or in
tempestuous and destructive turmoil. Human harmony and
environmental peace are ineluctably connected.

The religious task **par excellence** of the human community at
the center is to maintain an equilibrium of the vital forces
within the whole. Schneidau (1976) ascribes the conception of
such a "cosmic continuum" to "mythological consciousness." Each
and every element and compound, out of which the Bemba universe
is constituted, are potentialities which can be brought to bear
on any human problem. Even curing a toothache, as Goody (1977,
5) points out, involves a readjustment of relationships not
simply with one's physical environment but with the moral and
supernatural universe.

Cosmic congruences are used in ever escalating combinations
of force. Anything that bears the valences of two or more worlds
is an especially powerful metaphor. This may be marginal
animals, such as elephants with wing-like ears as if for aerial
flight and living both in water and on land, or crocodiles with
skins like the bark of trees and likewise amphibious. Liminal
persons, mutiliated or handicapped, are seen as having one foot

in the spirit world.   Bats haunt the night, fly in the air and
live in the bowels of the earth.   Crossed paths in the forest
with their intersecting lines of human force coordinate with the
powers of the undifferentiated landscape.   Tall and majestic
trees draw together the celestial vertical forces with the
terrestrial horizontal forces and span past and present.   All
participate in the religious notion of the whole.   In short,
there is a perpetual osmosis between the many interfacing and
interlinked realities which religious rites and symbols draw on
and intensify.

The Bemba "healers" *Ng'anga* exult in the art of creating
metaphoric linkages to the whole.   They muster and juxtapose all
the various and intrinsically transferrable properties of nature
(Cf Etienne 1948, 2-4, 111-14; Tanguy 1954, 246-56).   For
example, connatural linkages are employed in Bemba "magico-
medicinal constructs" *muti* where the various powers of herbs and
organic materials are augmented by any number of *Chishimba*
"catalysts."   An empty cartridge case may be used to accelerate
the effect of the remedy, or a piece of magnifying glass to focus
and intensify its power, or a length of string to tie up and thus
guarantee the desired effect.   Oftentimes, in this oral society,
the association of like sounds is enough to qualify a "piece of
the universe" for its *Chishimba* efficacy.   Thus the scale of "an
anteater" *Nkaka* would be used for its power to tie off a disease
or to frighten it away.   (The verb *Kukaka* means "to tie" and
Kukakabala "to tremble" (Tanguy 1954, 255).   Since the verbal
sounds are similar, they surely have power to produce similar
effects.)   Again, the obviously fertile "mother of twins" *Nampundu*
will be asked to sow seeds, the habitual drunkard to cast poison
on the river to stupify the fish (Richards 1969, 337), and the
short-armed man to plant gourds lest the vines grow at the
expense of the fruits (Etienne 1948, 3).

In contrast to this use of *Bwanga* "magic" for beneficient
purposes--appealing to the harmonies and correspondences of the
universe--"sorcerers" *Muloshi* (Cf Tanguy 1948, 261-68)
deliberately confound the dynamic vitality of the whole.   They
violate the traditional order, by setting the affinities of the
universe in conflict and creating the type of discord hell-bent,
as it were, on their malevolent metaphors.   For example, incest,
using erotic powers for erratic purposes, is one of their
effective energizers.   There are also nighttime violations of a
cemetery and the affectation of an eccentric, even bizarre lifestyle.   Such play to antimony is calculated to alarm normal
sensitivities and conjure up evil influences. The *Muloshi* might
also use otherwise salutary energies, but pile them up so that
they reach a critical mass.   In reaction they are ruinous.   For
example, by over-eating or over-drinking, by dancing into frenzy,
even by over-working a garden into surplus, they signal their
accumulation of explosive energy.   The *Shinganga* deals in the
virtues inherent in every sector of the harmonious universe;
viciously the *Muloshi* seeks to grind them into cacophony (See
below, chap. 4, 134ff).

5) Finally, as perhaps already clear, Bemba religion is "cosmically holistic." Bemba religion conforms to what Africanists are nearly unanimous in affirming of African religions in general: the universe is conceived variously as a "seamless web of relationships" (Booth 1978, 90), "a rapport of forces" (Tempels 1945, 68), "an organization of diverse relationships . . . as a whole" (Parsons 1964, 176), an "immanent occult vitality" (Obiechina 1975, 38), the "fundamental unity. . . of reality as a whole" (Theuws 1964, 15) and a "comprehensive whole" (Nurnberger 1975, 174).

In brief, the African cosmos manifests what V. Turner calls "communitas." Elements are not hierarchically arrayed, but possess a

> . . . common substratum beyond all categories
> of manifestation, transcending divisible time
> and space, beyond words, where persons,
> objects and relationships are endlessly
> transformed into one another . . . the
> corporate identity between unique identities .
> . . (1975, 22).

It is our argument that the Bemba, as an oral people, conceive of their experience of the universe as a unified whole in analogy with an auditory harmony. Phenomenological support can be cited for this thesis. Ihde observes that the first gain of phenomenology in regard to sensory experience is a recovery and reappreciation of the fullness and richness and global character of experience (Ihde 1976, chap. 2). He believes that the plenary quality of the complex flow of experience is most "comprehensively apprehended," when phenomenology takes "its auditory turn" (Idem, chap. 3). In the "plenum" of experience, "the global, encompassing surroundability" and "omnidirectionality of sound" are constantly copresent (Idem, chap. 6). This "plenum of sound is full and penetrating" and produces a Parmenidean sense of "continuity" and of "the whole" (Idem, chap. 6). Thus, "holistic" matches the plenary and global dimensions of auditory experience, as sound seems to immerse, surround, permeate, penetrate and totally encompass its hearers (Ong 1967, 128ff; Ihde 1976, 49ff). As Levi-Strauss succinctly states it: "the savage [i.e. oral] mind totalizes" (1966, 245; see Ong 1982, 175).

An Extended Example of Bemba Limit-Symbols

Tracy comments that "the study of metaphor may well provide a central clue to a better understanding of that elusive and perplexing phenomenon our culture calls religion" (1979, 104). Each religion is grounded in certain root metaphors, he argues, forming a network of dominant metaphors, which organize and diffuse subsidiary ones. These metaphorical clusters describe the mystery and hope of the human situation and prescribe means

for its possible renewal (1979, 89). Furthermore, Tracy
identifies "the contemporary understanding of metaphor not as a
substitute for literal meanings but as an emergent meaning
occasioned by the tension or interaction between various
`literal' words" (1975, 122).

It lies outside the purpose of this section to analyze the
various interaction theories of metaphor, which abound in recent
scholarship.[8] At the same time, it is appropriate to note Ong's
view that the oral mind is preeminently metaphoric, with more of
a poetic than a scientific thrust. It orders the whole of
reality into a mosaic, where discourse about one thing must needs
include several others at once (Ong 1962, 30-1). This metaphoric
mind indulges in a "metaphysics of metaphor" (Ong 1969a, 589)
exhibiting the "endemic binarism" of all human knowing, which
functions only by twinning or doubling of concepts in predication
(Ong 1969a, 478). Metaphor, on Ong's definition, generates
meaning by fusing sensory apprehension and abstraction in a
moment of experiential plentitude. As such it remains
contextualized in a virtually inexhaustible array of concrete
relations (Ong 1948, 173). As the Africanist Fernandez explains,
metaphor suggests correlations between the corporeal external
world and the inner world of social experience; its purpose is to
temper the analytic tendencies of human thinking with a "return
to the whole" (Fernandez 1974, 129). Tyler combines elements
similar to both Ong's and Fernandez' into a unitary view of how
we creatively use metaphor's revealing and obscuring power. It
serves

> . . . (a) to call attention to or focus on a
> relation by exaggeration and disproportionate
> comparison, and (b) to make the ineffable
> effable by (c) breaking down the taken-for-
> granted structure of concepts that imprison
> our thought and by (d) bringing into contact
> concepts normally distant from one another in
> order to (e) extend the domain of a central
> structure of concepts, gradually establishing
> a universe of perfect knowledge in which the
> smallest event occurring even in its most
> remote hinterland was known, anticipated
> planned for, and duly noted long before it
> actually happened . . . (Tyler 1978, 336).

The following examples of Bemba limit symbols all partake in
some measure in the nature and function of metaphor. Of course
water, blood, sex and fire are in themselves quite natural
realities. As basal religious symbols, the Bemba use them to
redescribe their own mode-of-being-in-the-world, likening their
form of life to certain normative characteristics which are
traditionally predicated of these elements. All together, they
comprise the Bemba central network of root metaphors which Tracy
finds in every religion. These metaphors are functionally

integrated by a fundamentally homologous body of beliefs, which attributes spiritual power to their configuration (Cf Richards 1956, 30). All Bemba rituals declaim water, blood, sex and fire as contact points, the tangents along which the Bemba set in motion their most sacred values.

These root metaphors symbolize in fact the limit-character of the situation they qualify as crucial for either positive or negative consequences. If these potent elements in any combination are not ritually pure and proportionately balanced, they can quickly reach a critical mass that chain reacts and destroys. The pivot around which their ambivalent powers revolve is the spontaneously operative notion of the whole, which uncannily discloses itself "in a limit-situation" or "at a center." In sum, the root metaphors interactively affirm the basic Bemba belief in the radical coherence of their world: somehow everything "holds together," "makes sense," is "of value," is "of a whole" (Cf Conclusion).

So far only random and disparate examples have been used to illustrate the metaphorical processes of such religious discourse. Now they will be more cogently exemplified by examining the Bemba root metaphors of water, blood, sex and fire.

Menshi

"Water" can give life or destroy it, refresh or drown, cleanse or muddy. In a controlled combination with fire, it cooks, warms and purifies; "oil" *Mafuta* is its vegetable counterpart. Through ritual both are metaphorically capable of "quieting and cooling" *Kutalala* the spirits. Oil mixed with *Mpemba* "white clay" signifies spiritual cleanliness; mixed with *Nkula* "red camwood powder" it means strength and courage. A new born girl is anointed with *Mpemba* , for there is joy in continued matriliny. The boy is anointed with *Nkula* , for he will be the protector and provider (Etienne 1945, 116). The newly installed chief cries *Ifwe tuli malabwa nkula no bunga* "we are anointed red and white," for he is the hero endowed with the matrilineal spirits. Marginality characterizes all three--the infants and the neophyte chief.

Only water can purify and cool the heat of sex. The first sexual contact of newly weds requires the purification of "a river-swim" *Kuowa* (Etienne 1948, 44). Solemn ceremonies involving the chief also require his ritual purification in the river. The main mourners at a funeral are purified from death's pollution at a river. The temporary succession rites, which ensure the spiritual continuity of a dead person, are affected by a child-successor "drinking water" *Kunwa amenshi* ; later a permanent successor is chosen for the sexually effected *Kupyana* "succession rite" (Etienne 1948, 66-7, 72-5). Lustral waters, heated in the ritual "marriage pot" *Kanweno* (Tanguy 1954, 22-3), can purify a married couple from their sexual taint. So, too, water, as a metaphoric substitute for purified sex, can ensure the unbroken continuity with ancestral spirits. Each of these situations is at the limit.

Mulopa

"Blood" can be a metaphor of life's power or of life poured out. Blood marginalizes people. The murderer, like the warrior and hunter, who shed blood, or the witch who deals in blood, and the menstruating woman, are all hot and dangerous people to the community; many of the same fire and sex taboos surround them (Tanguy 1954, 243-45). Matrilineal blood of members of the ruling Ng'andu clan gives them a measure of the life-force of the all powerful royal spirits. The man, who cannot transmit blood, acquires rights of access to his own matrilineal spirits by the hazardous route of marriage (Richards 1956, 155, 159). In this case he is in contact with the blood of a woman.

Sexual intercourse is thought of as a "mixing of blood" Mulopa wasakanya . If ritually purified, it can produce new life. But, as polluted by promiscuity, adultery or incest (three bloods are mixed), it can be perilous to the lives of all concerned, especially the innocent partner or unborn child of the triple relationship (Richards 1956, 134-35).

Just as water tends to cool and calm the spirits, so blood is used to arouse and incite them. This is the case, for example, when it is sprinkled on a Lufuba "shrine" (Tanguy 1954, 116) or painted, in its symbolic form Nkula, on people entering or withdrawing from the threshold of a dangerous enterprise.

The menstruating woman is said to be a "hot" medium Akuba na mpepo , and should "avoid fire" Atina mulilo ; it would only intensify her heat. Metaphorically she is a "smelting furnace" Mutanda, a womb-like structure, full of fire, which pours out its molten metal like a "child" Mwana. This Mutanda , built by prepubescent children under the supervision of a ritually purified adult, is honored with white cloths and beads and sprinkled with blood. Like a woman, it houses spirit power. Another metaphor of the uncanny is linguistically related: a menstruating woman is one of the Mitanda "temporary garden cottages" set apart from the community. Her blood represents a fertility uncontrolled by marriage, an unpurified sexuality (Etienne 1948, 46ff).

Many of the same taboos are in effect during pregnancy, when a woman's blood is thought to be extremely hot (Etienne 1948, 5 and 46 ff).

Mulilo

"Fire" symbolizes the life of the people, and it must be kept scrupulously free from contamination. Through the food it cooks, it could infect the whole eating group. Spilled outside the family hearth, like sex, fire can consume a home, village, garden or forest. It, too, must be ritually handled and protected. It is a metaphor of life's continuity with the ancestors. For example, if a child dies at birth, it is thought to be the uncanny result of the father's adultery and is called *Kumwipaya mulilo* "murder by fire." A proverb describes a dead person as "one who sleeps without fire" *Nalala citutu* (White Fathers 1954, 138).

Old polluted fires are extinguished and their ashes thrown to the West. New fires are lit for all ceremonial "boundary situations": a new village site, a new chief, a marriage, a birth, a death, at the time of sowing and harvest, or hunting and fishing. New fires are "lit by friction" *Lushiko* with an upright stick of hard wood called *Kalume* "the little man"; this is inserted in a notch of soft wood called *Katoba* "the little woman," and twirled to generate a flame which is called *Kamwana* "the little child." The act metaphorically links sex and fire (Corbeil IV).

Fire cooks food and beer which unite all sizes of community. Fire warms water in the *Kanweno* for purification, and burns branches to prepare "the gardens" *Citemene* for agricultural fecundity. A fire of her own is formally given to a woman with several children as a sign that her marriage is complete during the "entrance ceremony" *Kwingisha* . "A burning fire brand" *Cishishi* is thrown out of the nuptial cottage by the bridegroom as a sign of his potency and the successful unity of the marriage (Labrecque 1931, 219). The woman, chosen for the ritual intercourse of "succession" *Kupyana* after death, is also called *Cishishi* "the firebrand" (White Fathers 1954). "Hearthfires are exchanged" *Kusansho mulilo* , when polygamist's wives are reconciled (Etienne 1940, 52 & 75). The first sign of a troubled marriage is when the woman throws all of her "cooking pots" *Nongo* out of the cottage (Richards 1939, 173).

Fire is a central metaphor of Bemba social life: it lights up the dark of night and invites people to share and celebrate together. As the riddle says: *Akamana tusambila mumbali? Mulilo!* "The pool in whose periphery we all swim? Fire!" (Kashoki n.d.).

The sacred apex of the Bemba hearth fire is the *Kamitembo* "the royal kitchen fire and pantry." Its flame, never extinguished, is guarded religiously by celibates against any, even royal, sexual contamination. Fire is the symbol of Bemba tribal unity and political authority. Part of the reason is that organization and distribution of food is essential for the security and well-being of the tribe (Richards 1939, 148-49). In fact a most solemn ritual is used to establish the *Kamitembo*, when a royal village is moved. The *Kuteka ishiko* "the setting of the royal fireplace," on the axis of the East and West constitutes a symbolic sun. The ceremony centers on the ritual intercourse and sexual purification of Chitimukulu and his main "councillors" *Bakabilo* with their wives (Richards 1968, 29-31).

Cupo

"Sex," too, is an ambivalent force needing ritual social control to keep its naked power from fiercely exciting and accelerating life to a wild and dangerous level. Spilled outside of the humanly sanctioned precincts of the home, it can destroy the very life, which, in its ritually pure state, it can generate.

As fire heats food, so sex is thought "to heat a person's body to dangerous potential" *Umubili wakaba ne fibi* . It needs ritual purification with the cooling effect of water, gradually warmed over the marital hearth. Unpurified sex can pollute the fireplace of a home, impair agricultural productivity, sour the beer for the village community, soften a blacksmith's metal, kill a child of the next generation or scare away game, contaminate the prayers and offerings to the spirits (Etienne 1948, 6, 13, 15, 28, 34, 44, 46). Hence, the sexually active person, a pregnant or menstruating woman, an adulterer, indeed any promiscuous person, whose sex is not socialized and sacralized in the purification ceremonies possible only to married persons, are terribly dangerous contaminants of fire. Any of these may threaten the life of the group that gathers there for communal food. A sexually impure chief can "pollute his whole territory" *Kuonaula calo,* and adversely affect the fertility of gardens and people. Positively his sexual virtue with the "wife of the land" *Mukolo wa calo* imparts blessings to the land by contact: *Umulandu wa bufumu ico mfumu ilelelapo* "because the chief has slept on top of her (it)." To sex is attributed the uncanny power of a religious metaphor.

Sexual relationship produces a mystic "union of life-blood" between partners *Mulopa wasakana* and includes their "spirits" *Mipashi* . Children can "play at sex" *Masansa* . However, as soon as a girl's periods begin, there is danger that sex and blood would mix to produce a "child of ill-omen" *Wa mputula* , born outside socially and ritually sanctioned precincts. In this case, the young parents would be driven into the bush away from their community (Etienne 1948, 9). The ritual, which symbolizes sex sanctioned structures, is that of the *Kanwemo* "marital purification pot." This *Kanwemo* is a ritual form of the *nongo* "cooking pot" which symbolizes the union of those who eat together. Through it the force of fire for cooking is controlled and distributed. The marriage pot, the sign that effects the union of husband and wife, turns the ambivalent force of sexual heat to advantage (Labrecque 1934, 219). Sharing of food and unity are so interconnected that the Bemba believe that the adulterer, the one who violates the family hearth and cannot be purified, will vomit the family food. *Ifyakulyo bushiku* :

Fitulikila ku malushi "What is eaten at night (secretly) is revealed in vomit" (Hoch 1966). Here eating and community are linked; sex and food are cognate metaphors and socially sanctioned.

The union of blood, sex and spirit is so binding that it endures through death itself. In the "succession rite" *Kupyana* , the surviving partner must sleep with the social equivalent of the dead spouse from the same clan. The intent is "to chase away death" *Kutamfya mfwa* from the survivor's clan, and "to bring back the life-spirit" *Kubwesha mupashi* to the deceased's clan. Without this purifying ceremony, the survivor would remain too hot a medium to remarry (Cf Labrecque n.d., 68-9). Accidents of birth are attributed to unpurified sex and the offending spouse is said "to carry away the life-spirit of the child" *Asenda mupashi wa mwana* (Etienne 1948, 8-9).

These doctrines interrelating sex, fire, blood and water are what Audrey Richards calls "an ideological obsession," "the idée maitresse behind most of the ritual behavior of the Bemba" (Richards 1956, 30, 35 & 141). Symbolically they extend the central norms for the Bemba mode-of-being-in-the-world into an organized network of the creative metaphors of religious belief and practice. By the twists of "semantic impertinence" which metaphors imply (Cf Tracy 1979, 99), they disclose the distinctively Bemba religious form of life. In short, they proclaim that every Bemba community, residing at the interfacing limits of nature and culture, can discern its relationship to the whole. Each can articulate and manipulate the vital constellation of forces between them. Each is the arbiter and facilitator of the messages and powers from "the whole," which the complex configuration of root metaphors represents.

A Concluding Reflection

The summary statements of this chapter are also projective of the task for fuller explanation in the following chapters.

Bemba culture is resoundingly an oral-aural reality, employing the spoken word as the primary means of transmitting its tradition. The oral word, as sharing in the nature of sound, situates its audience in the center of an engulfing power. This power is both present as a personal interaction and effective of what it intends. The Bemba's highly tonal and concordial language, their pleasantly instructive singing, dancing and drumming, and their rich rhetorical resources, all illustrate the people's ingenuity in exploiting the particular properties of the sounding medium to convey their cultural heritage. The sound of the spoken word contributes to the special conditioning of Bemba persons as markedly socialized and extroverted selves. Bemba knowledge and norms are formulaicly conformed to recollections of "the tried and true," and Bemba social structures are conservatively operative in the inherited power of those officials who embody the ancestral will.

Bemba religious experience and expression share the acoustically affected processes of socialization, extroversion and organization of persons, principles and powers. The oral character of the religion renders it traditional, communal and anthropocentric, and orients its adherents toward a vital and dynamic participation in the cosmic whole in its peculiarly Bemba manifestation. The esoteric maneuvering of sex, fire, blood and water promotes this religious goal. These serve in the Bemba belief system as the root metaphors of the religious dynamism contained in the notion of the whole and its uncanny disclosure in limit situations and at the center. Through this complex network of analogies that attach humans to the whole of the universe, people become both a part of it and a reduction of it. Humans assert their responsibility over the universe and set it in the order which the notion of the whole enjoins.

The media shift that writing introduces among the Bemba, from an oral culture to one organized through a more visualist sensorium, is played out in the transformation of the traditional religion. Traditional religion, composed of sound and the oral word, encounters Christianity inscribed on texts (Cf Ong 1967, 265). For the oral religion, the encounter leads to the disjoining of the sacred symbiotic relationship of the cosmic continuum between human culture (community of selves), nature (the world) and the realm of the spirits (the whole). Writing makes the world knowable, dispassionately and disinterestedly, from the outside. Its analytic, perspectival mode dehumanizes, devocalizes and depopulates the natural cosmos. The oral synthesis of the Bemba universe is broken down (Cf Schneidau 1976, chap. 1). Writing increases the likelihood that the root metaphors will be literally scrutinized for their conceptual and ethical meanings, and their creative artistry and interactive potential discarded as mere decorative ornaments substituting for their real ideas (Cf Tracy 1979, 95-9). Writing facilitates the introduction of the dialectic religious expression, typed as proclamation, to the manifestation-oriented religious expression.

Bemba religious experience will expand, not so much by a renascence of the tradition, as through its transformation by Christian proclamation. Through the literate medium, Christianity has already managed to differentiate the notion of the whole from any of its temporal manifestations, to liberate the self from the tyranny of the tribal traditions and to understand the world according to its social, historical and natural dimensions. Christianity's symbols and doctrines, refined by literacy's reflective capabilities, authentically and adequately articulate the original revelatory event of the whole, as the powerful, decisive, self-relevation of God. Its conception of the whole explicitates the nature of both the self and the world as well as the order of their coexisting internal relationships (Tracy 1982, 429-39).

CHAPTER ONE FOOTNOTES

[1] This whole book is obviously indebted to the scholars, like Ong, Goody, Kelber and Ihde, who comprise the Anglo-American school for most of the ideas and many of the expressions used to discuss orality. General acknowledgment is made here for any of their specific coinages, which may have inadvertently crept into the author's own thinking and style.

[2] Biesheuvel and Wober both agree that auditory perception is favored by African cultures, but neither agrees with Hudson's genetic emphasis (S. Biesheuvel, **African Intelligence**, Johannesburg: South Africa Institute of Personnal Relations, 1943; M. Wober, "Sensotypes," **Journal of Social Psychology**, 70, 1966, 181-89). Hudson even postulates an evolutionary factor, where, by a process of natural selection, auditory perceptual organization becomes more characteristic of sylvan cultures.

[3] Sometimes, however, *Ulutambi* clearly indicates a certain impatience with the enquirer, who is asking about something too obvious for explanation. Thus, one hears in this context the proverb *Ulebusha mbwa, nga ifwele* "You ask about the dog's sex as if it were clothed." A silly question! (Shimulamba IX).

[4] In all of this discussion there are echoes of Tempels' famous ontological resolution between the Christian and the African view of self. The Bantu view the universe dynamically as the turbulent ebb and flow of powerful forces, while the European sees it as stark and structured. Hence the Bantu self is a dynamism in rapport with the universe, containing varying quantities of these powerful forces, the possession of which one seeks to maximize. The European self is a container with a relatively constant quantity of power, whose quality must undergo redemption (Placide Tempels, **La Philosophie Bantoue**, Elizabethville: Lovania, 1945).

[5] Tracy, like his colleague and mentor in the history of religion, Eliade, writes of Manifestation as an event in visual terms and of Proclamation as applying primarily to a sense of hearing not vision (Tracy, **The Analogical Imagination**, 269ff). Neither Tracy nor Eliade advert to the fact that, for an oral culture, the sense of hearing and sound itself can be correlative to a manifestation-oriented religious experience. Indeed, in the case of Christian proclamation, distanciation from and denial of any participation in the manifest whole are requisites of the protestant principle (Idem 386ff); the **heard** word, of which Luther and Tracy write, is primarily the **scriptural** word as normatively codifying the manifest-event (Idem 249). This written word is **read** from a biblical **text** and only secondarily preached about and listened to by a Christian audience. Therefore, this book's correlations of Manifestation with sound

and hearing, and Proclamation with text and sight, are legitimate, corrective extrapolations from Tracy's typology.

[6]The task of determining the hermeneutical criteria for the adequacy and appropriateness of religious language in general, and then the critical investigation of the cognitive claims of a specific religious tradition, are the proper problematics of theology. According to Tracy, theology as such is the attempt "to correlate certain specified meanings and truths in our common human experience and language with the interpreted meanings and truths of a specific religious tradition" (Tracy "Metaphor and Religion" 1979, 91). The present task of this treatise is to describe the facts of Bemba religion from a historical, oral-aural and phenomenological perspective, employing the limit language of the Bemba themselves. The Conclusion will move into the more value-laden horizon of theological hermeneutics, exploring how second order, reflective and conceptual language may apply to the Bemba religion.

[7]At least two are explicitly treated by N.S. Booth, "Tradition and Community in African Religion," Journal of Religion in Africa IX, 1978; one or two others may be implied in Booth. Certainly, this section is deeply indebted to Booth's insights.

[8]See, for example, Paul Ricoeur, The Rule of Metaphor: Multidisciplinary Studies of the Creation of Meaning in Language (Toronto: University of Toronto Press, 1978); and Sheldon Sacks (editor), On Metaphor (Chicago: University of Chicago Press, 1979; and Max Black Models and Metaphors (Ithaca: Cornell Univ. Press, 1962, esp. 25-47).

CHAPTER TWO

ORALITY, MYTH AND RITUAL

This chapter will present a précis of the Bemba charter myth. It will then discuss its religious and oral characteristics. After examining the relationship of oral ritual to myth, the chapter will detail the mythic themes, the religious dimensions and the oral features of one particular Bemba ritual. It will serve as a paradigm of other rites wherein the special ethical lessons of the tribe are orally transmitted. The chapter will conclude with a reflection on how literacy adversely affects traditional oral values.

The Bemba Charter Myth

In our discussion of the Bemba charter myth, we try to appropriate an attitude of serious and respectful attention commendable to all students of culture:

> We little care if our object of analysis is a myth of modern science or of ancient religion, for we find in both the same structures of thought, the same dialectical movements, the same metaphors, and the same exalted pride that tempts us to see the order of things in the order of our language (Tyler 1975, 112).

The myth summarized in this chapter is a construct of many partial and varying renditions. All the extant written versions are, admittedly, redactions of several oral performances into a synthetic abbreviated edition.[1] As such they participate in the plurality of all oral recountings of the "same" narrative according to the reciter's purposes and the audience's circumstances. Just as the oral word is, not an item, but an event, so is the charter myth, not a verbatim recital, but a performance narrative.

> A. "Silly little one, wander not from the path your ancestors followed / Forget not your origins / Forget not how you came to the land of the paramount."

> B. Long ago in the land of Kola, there lived white and black people, who were baptized Christians. After a quarrel, the white people sailed away to get rich in Europe, and the black people remained under their chief Mukulumpe Mubemba.

C.   One day while the chief was hunting in
the forest, he met a beautiful woman, Mumbi
Mukasa Liulu,   with ears as large as an
elephant's.   She said she was a queen fallen
from the sky.   She belonged to the "crocodile
clan" Ng'andu.   The earthly chief and the
heavenly queen married and had three sons,
Katongo, Nkole and Chiti, and a daughter
Chilufya Mulenga (Bwalya Chabala).

D.   The   royal   sons built a great tower to
their mother's chambers in the sky, but it
fell down and killed many of the tribespeople.
Their angry father blinded Katongo, who then,
using a talking drum, warned his brothers
Nkole and Chiti to flee from their father's
murderous intentions.   Chief Mukulumpe also
dismissed his wife back to the sky and
imprisoned his daughter in a hut, which had no
doors or windows.

E.   Chiti   led Nkole and a band of partisans
in a journey to the East.   A white magician
named Luchele Ng'anga appeared at crucial
times   to   guide the migrants with his
divination.

F.   When they crossed the Luapula river, at
Kwisandulula,   Chiti claimed the land, by
throwing his lance into a large tree and
singing a song of triumph.   Then he sent his
half-brother   Kapasa back to rescue their
sister Chilufya Mulenga from their father's
darkness. During the night, Kapasa, erected a
ladder and lifted Chilufya Mulenga up through
the roof to the sky.   In the flight from their
father's land, Chilufya Mulenga carried the
insignia of chieftainship and the seeds in her
hair for the exiles' future gardens.   Because
Kapasa later seduced and impregnated his newly
nubile sister, Chilufya, he was shamefully
banned from the royal totemic clan by Chiti.

G.   The travellers conquered many tribes in
battle like the Lunda, or simply intimidated
others, such as the Lala in the South.   Near
the end of the migration they crossed the
Chambeshi river, where, Chilimbulu, the wife
of the hospitable Senga chief, Mwase, seduced
Chiti with the elegant scarifications of
chevrons, which adorned her stomach.   They
were caught in adultery by the hunter husband,
who killed Chiti with a poisoned arrow.

H. Nkole succeeded Chiti and avenged his
death by killing both Mwase and Chilimbulu;
after carefully preserving the seductive
Chilimbulu's tatooed stomach skin, he
dismembered their bodies, immersed them in
water jugs and finally burned them. The
poisonous smoke asphyxiated Nkole, but before
he died, he had Chiti's body embalmed with
lentil beans, dessicated in the rays of the
sun, wrapped in a cow hide and buried in a
white termite mound at Mwalule's village.
Then Nkole himself died. Shimwalule prepared
his funeral in the same way, burying him in
the same white termitiary atop his younger
brother Chiti.

I. The Bemba settled for a while at
Mulambalala. Later they established their
capital at Ng'wena, 'the place of the
crocodile.' They called their kings
Chitimukulu "the great tree" after their
original ruler, from whose heavenly mother
they all trace descent.

J. From that time until the present, the
Bemba were ruled by over twenty-five
succeeding paramount chiefs. By war, they
expanded the Bemba control over conquered
territories, and by intrigue, consolidated the
control and political authority of the
crocodile clan over rival tribes and clans.

The following sections will discuss both the religious
dimensions and the oral features of this Bemba charter myth,
taking each pericope in alphabetic order. Then there will be a
transition section, linking myth to ritual in general. Finally,
the themes of the charter myth will be related specifically to
incidents of the Bemba girls' puberty rite.

The Religious Dimensions of the Myth[2]

Although the story does bear testimony to certain
independently verifiable historical propositions, it is clearly
more of a narrative account of the origins of the basic features
of Bemba culture (Roberts 1973, 56). Its juxtaposition of
praeternatural elements alongside familiar tribal geography and
genealogy underscore its aetiological character as a Bemba
charter myth. This is also evident from its incorporation of
Central African mythological cliches--the hierogamy, the tower
motif, the incest themes, the white magician, the seeds in the
hair.

While this charter myth is not a religious classic for all peoples, it certainly is the Bemba religious classic. It will bear some resemblances, worth noting below, to the **functions** and **form** of religious classics described by Tracy (1981, 154-230).

The religious meaning of the charter myth is readily described in several **functions**. a) It promotes tribal respect and loyalty to the divinely ordained rule of the crocodile clan with its hierarchical system of chiefs (See below, chap. 3, 80). b) It maps out as sacred the tribal territory, which the ancestral migrants traversed in the beginning (See below, chap, 3, 80). c) It articulates those archetypal values enacted in ancestral lives, by whose reenactment in myth and ritual the present generation can verify and justify their own existence (See below, chap. 3, 69ff). These religious messages are greatly enhanced by the **form** which the limit-language of the charter myth imposes on them.

All those events symbolic of the uncanny, involve liminal characters, such as the heavenly woman and the white magician. They are engaged in marginal activities, like marriage (positive), incest (negative), leadership and war. They depict limit-situations occurring at the intersection of heaven and earth, at the river crossings. The net effect is that they disclose the whole, elicit fright and fascination and reveal meaning and value to the listening Bemba community. The peoples' participation in the recital and ritual reenactment of those primordial events ensures a religious response. They feel either dependence on an integrated reality greater than their individual selves, or alienation from that whole and gratitude for proffered reunion.

This section now proceeds in alphabetic order to examine how each pericope of the myth illustrates these religious dimensions.

(A) The exordium, which usually precedes the myth's recital, is performed in an antique Luba language--a ploy, which serves to carry the olden days forward for contemporary listeners. They are exhorted not to become like *Keluba* , (a teknonym from the verb *Kuluba* "to forget"), the stock comic character in fables, whose confused and asocial demeanor is typically attributed to a lack of roots or grounding in the tradition. The oral audience is reminded that they must constantly recall to mind the recital of their origins or they will suffer disintegration for their forgetfulness (See below, chap. 3, 89). They are admonished to become empathetic participants in these foundational events. Only then can they retain their identity with the whole, represented by this fabulous adventure.

(B) The inclusion of white people and Christianity in this myth of Bemba origins is clearly an intrusion into the traditional tale. The Bemba, in accordance with their oral economy of knowledge, simply redact successful new ideas or inescapable realities into the tradition. Such novelties can only make sense, if they can be brought into contact with the beginnings (See below, chap. 3, 85ff). In religious terms, the whole, represented in the myth of origins, is the touchstone of all truth and value, even those recently appropriated.

(C) Mumbi Mukasa is portrayed as an inhabitant of heaven and earth, astral and chthonic, a divine and human citizen capable of mediating between the two worlds. She reveals herself. This "give-ness" of her character associates her with the numinous. It is not just her descent "from heaven" *Liulu* that establishes her divinity. It is her being found in the "forest" *Mpanga* , a mysterious realm of the uncanny and spirituality in the Bemba mind. Mukulumpe finds her in the primeval animal world, and feminine game at the end of the ritual hunt is always a good omen (Etienne 1948, 77). Her "ears like an elephant" *Matwi nge nsofu* further enhance her liminality at the animal and human worlds. As elephantine, she participates in the ambiguous character of a water and land creature, with her feet on the ground and her head high in the skies. She has wing-like ears to transport her back and forth between her several realms. Her clan totem is the *Ng'andu* "crocodile," another marginal creature of the land and water. True to her ambivalence, she introduces fortune and misfortune, harmony and discord into the story.

Her association with the animal world deep in the natural forest, gives her the untrammelled freedom of the divine beings. Unfettered by human law and civilization, they sport in the chaotic realm, where human standards and conventions are broken with impunity.

Obviously the daughter of the divine ("fallen from the sky") and the animal ("ears like an elephant"), this first Bemba ancestress is not of human origin. All ancestral spirits will share in her divinity and animality. Bemba matrilineal totems reflect this cultural rule. The more general religious principle of the interpenetration of all realms is also established at ths outset.

In a classic hierogamy (Cf Heusch 1973), this ethereal woman marries the earthly prince and establishes the sacred character of marriage, sex (especially feminity), and procreation. All three touch closely on the divinity of the primordial mother. Matriliny becomes the genealogical rule of the Bemba, and is of especial importance for the royal crocodile clan's descent from the heavenly queen. The myth initiates the kinship and clan systems, which undergrid Bemba polity. Despite their finitude, the Bemba can trust in the gracious healing promised by this remedial action from the whole.

(D)   The marriage of heavenly and earthly elements not only procreates a princely progeny, Chiti and Nkole, but issues in destruction for the kingdom.   For in building their tower to the heavens, they seek immortality and presume to ascend to the world of divinity, thus violating the heavenly chambers of their mother.   The symbolic incest of the attempt, implying a demotion of paternity in conception, provokes paternal jealousy.   The tower's collapse destroys the kingdom.   Mukulumpe, as the wrathful husband, chases away his wife Mumbi Mukasa. As an angry father in inverse Oedipal tragedy, he plucks out the eyes of one of his offending sons, and drives the others into exile.   The project's failure is the mythical explanation for the dispersion of peoples and cultural diversity.   It symbolizes Bemba estrangement from the whole.

More significantly, this first attempted incest expresses the Bemba anxiety over their human contingency and dependence. Sexual union with their mother would make the brothers self-engendering.   Now they will be forced to seek immortality elsewhere.   The disjunction of heaven and earth, symbolized by the tower's collapse, introduces cosmic discontinuity.   This is reinforced by the divine mother's reascent to heaven in her divorce from the earthly prince (Cf Heusch 1973).

The radical religious formulation of the myth suggests the withdrawl of the divine from human affairs, but leaves the hopeful remedial link of blood and life in the maternal lines of ancestry traced back to Mumbi Mukasa.   The basic structure of Bemba traditional religion is grounded in her person. The figure of Mumbi Mukasa has descended from the divine world and mated, however briefly, with the earthly prince Mukulumpe.   She bequeaths forever the tenuous relationship of life and blood in the mother's line to the divine.   She is the archetypal form of ancestral mediator, establishing the influence of matrilineal ancestral spirits and validating the pattern of their veneration in Bemba institutions.   That she figures not at all in future religious mythology does not diminish her significance as the initial contact point to the whole.   In fact, the myth itself narrates her dismissal from the scene, effectively rejecting divine help.   Humans, momentarily but forever touched by the divine, are left to work out their religious completion within their own social dimensions and spiritual resources. While their divine mother is assumed back into her heavens, Chiti and Nkole continue their quest for immortality by setting out on their exodus to the unknown lands in the East.

(E)   The topography of the journey is a mythical cosmography (Cf Heusch 1973). The East is cosmologically analogous to heaven in the story; the vertical ascent to the sky is transposed to the horizontal $_3$ journey to the orient, where sun and earth are conjoined. ^{3} The Bemba trust that, at the limits of their world, surely they will re-establish contact with the transforming power of the whole.

From the Bemba perspective, the sun itself duplicates this vertical and horizontal movement. In its diurnal East/West movement and in its annual high/low oscillation between the tropic extremes, it circumscribes a double spiral, corkscrewing around the earth (Cf Zahan 1970, chap. 5). When this helix is projected onto a flat surface and schematized into a zig-zag line, it forms the omnipresent Bemba decorative motif of the chevron (See below, 51). This familiar emblem is found on drums, utensils, facades, pots, beadwork, mats, ironwork. Chevrons are also "tatooed" onto the skin *Lubemba,* produced in open "reed fences" *Lusaka,* and woven into nets (Brelsford 1937). Since the solar region in the East is also the direction from which the rains come and from which the Bemba river *Chambeshi* flows, the chevron has symbolic connotations of those falling rains and flowing river. It also represents mounded gardens and feminine and masculine sexuality. The chevron represents the hearth's flames as the earthly counterpart to the solar fires. The multivalent symbolism of the twofold movement of the sun centers here on the wandering journey of the Bemba people toward their new home in the East, the farthest limit to the whole.

It is no accident that the search for immortality in the land of the sun is guided by the white magician Luchele Ng'anga. He appears at critical moments of the migration. His color and name associate him with the sun, *Luchele* "the dawn," and with the spirit-world, *Ng'anga* "the healer-diviner." He is a mythical sun-hero whose theme was introduced a thousand years ago by the Sudanic migrations into central Africa (Hall 1965, 13).[4]

The journey-motif symbolizes the moral striving of the people, a communal quest for what is authentically Bemba. As they move toward and constantly extend the horizon of their experience, they impose order and law on the land they traverse and develop those cultural parameters, which will distinguish them as a people.

(F) The river-crossing is another significant threshold experience in the Bemba odyssey. The chief Chiti lays claim to the land in the East by hurling his spear into the tree. The land is considered the "wife of the chief," and its life and fertility depend on the well-ordered sexual activity of the chief. This latter point is reenforced with the incestuous insinuations of the episode of Chilufya Mulenga. She is the prisoner of her royal father's darkened love and jealousy. His kingdom lies in the havoc wreaked upon it by the illicit, filial quest for the primordial mother and by his own excessive love for a daughter. Her imprisonment in the perpetual night of the decadent land in the West is contrasted with the light-giving potential of her rescue for the journey to the East. At the moment of her (Bemba!) liberation, she carries "the sacred insignia of the chieftainship" *Babenye* as a sign that she is to be the matrilineal source for generations of new chiefs. The seeds in her hair hold the promise of agricultural prosperity in the new land. Her brother Kapasa effects her escape with a brief ascent by the ladder to the "divine realm" *Ku mulu* , but brings her terrestrially low again by the sexual betrayal of his sister.

The threefold incestual rupture of the normal order--by the brothers with their mother, the father with his daughter, and now this brother with his sister (Cf Heusch 1958 & 1973)--provides the point of departure from the patrilineal system of the Luba people. In this new people, the Bemba, dynastic blood-lines are entrusted to the mother. The father's life lines are penalized to the extent that "the Bemba believe that the child is entirely formed from the physical contribution of the mother" (Richards 1956, 148). The father has very limited rights over the daughter in the matrilineal system. An important corollary to this dogma of descent is the legal and ritual relationship, pivotal for matriliny (Idem 82-3), obtaining between Bemba brothers and sisters, who are born from the same womb (Richards 1940, 96-7); the brother is responsible for his sister's welfare and her children are his heirs (Richards 1956, 40). The banishment of Kapasa from the royal family, because he erotically violates the sacred trust of his sister, solemnly sanctions fraternal obligations for the Bemba.

(G) The myth recounts the destructive consequences of adultery for Bemba society. Not only are the accomplices in the act destroyed (Chilimbulu and Chiti). According to the Bemba taboo sanctions called *Cilolela* "the danger of seeing blood" (Etienne 1948, 49), the innocent partner of the violated marriage (Mwase) is also slain by the triple mixing of blood (Richards 1956, 34, 157). Thus the myth underscores the inviolable integrity of husband and wife, father and daughter, brother and sister relationships within the Bemba family.

(H) The succeeding chief, Nkole, displays Bemba loyalty to even erring chiefs. He inaugurates the priestly functions of the royal office by a post-mortem purification of sexual pollution, by the ritual preparations for the gardening cycle, and by the funeral arrangements to ensure the royal spirits of immortality and veneration.

Chilimbulu and Mwase are physically and symbolically disjoined. Then, in a ghastly parody of Bemba ritual purification after sexual intercourse, they are immersed in a water pot and cremated over a polluted marriage fire--warning commoners against adultery.

Chiti dies (with appropriately sexual symbolism) from the poisoned arrow from the bow of the angry husband, warning royal adulterers that their unpurified sex is a pernicious threat to the whole tribe. He is to be purified in the rays of the solar fire.

The solar fires that mummify Chiti's corpse symbolically introduce "the season of the great sun" *Lusuba* . The waters corrupting Chilimbulu and Mwase mark the presence of the rains. The chopping up of their bodies, their aquatic immersion, and cremation signify the violence with which the gardens are prepared. The agricultural activities include *Citemene* "the lopping off of tree-limbs," *Kuoca fibola* "the firing," and *Mainsa* "the watering by rains." The preserved stomach skin of Chilimbulu, whose cicatrisations are in the chevron design of a garden fixed for sowing, is a fertility symbol used in the planting ritual each year at the chief's court. It is fitting that the priestly chief Nkole presides over this agrigonic episode.

In the funeral ritual for his brother, Nkole sets the pattern for the appointed office of Shimwalule, the priest and royal undertaker. The Bemba leader, at the extreme oriental point of the migration, mummifies the corpse of the first sovereign in the rays of the sun. Symbolically, the founder of the Bemba kingdom is granted his immortality by being united with the sun, completing in death what he failed to accomplish in life. He <u>thus</u> joins heaven and earth, but not through his construction of the tower nor through his journey to the land in the solar East. Nkole, too, as co-constructor of the tower and successor chief of the eastern migration, is assured of the same immortality. In death, he sits, as *muchinshi* "the prerogatives of age" demand, <u>above</u> his younger brother at the summit of the termitiary, whose whiteness reflects the sun. This termite mound, which forms their mausoleum, is the natural replica of the cosmic tower they constructed in their ambition to be immortal like the sun. Together in their cosmic termitiary, uniting heaven and earth, they represent the immortal Bemba kings who touch on the sun itself, assuring the mystical survival and divine character of their sovereignty. Their immortal ancestral spirits mediate the divine and human worlds and guarantee the permanence of Bemba society and the ruling crocodile dynasty as descended from the heavenly queen mother.

(I) and (J) The peroration of the charter myth is actually a rather prosaic recall of famous heroes and deeds, with exceptional flashes of praise poetry in the genealogy of some twenty-five paramount chiefs. Very little of the limit-language is retained and the narrative is no longer of the uncanny legend of migration that stands as the Bemba charter myth. The <u>structure</u> seems not yet to have been developed to integrate the genealogy into the richly woven and complexly embroidered character of the previous sections of the charter myth. The <u>content</u> of the genealogy, however, is essential to the religious purpose of the myth and establishes the divine right to rule for the legitimate matrilineal successors to the original crocodile clan.

Thus the charter myth, "from the beginning," ordains, inaugurates and validates both the Bemba religious system, centered on the veneration of "royal ancestral spirits" *Bashamfumu,* and their political structure, based on the divine right of the Chitimukulu to rule. The Bemba search for wholeness is at an end.

The Oral Features of the Myth

The length of the charter myth makes it the "roomiest repository" of Bemba lore. Organized into an eminently repeatable narrative, that mass of traditional knowledge is made durable (Cf Ong 1982, 140-41). The Bemba charter myth thus advertises the principal accents of an oral performance, which Ong enumerates in overlapping, yet serviceable headings: "(1) stereotyped or formulaic expression, (2) standardization of themes, (3) epithetic identification for 'disambiguation' of classes or individuals, (4) generation of 'heavy' or ceremonial characters, (5) formulary, ceremonial appropriation of history, (6) cultivation of praise and vituperation, (7) copiousness" (Ong 1977, 102; Cf 1982, 37-57).

These assertive strains are taken up in order here. They instance oral strategies, which the Bemba charter myth employs to gather, store, retrieve and communicate knowledge and history.

(1) Some of the formulaic and stereotypcial expressions are:

a) The set songs, which are interspersed throughout the narrative to organize the material and to prompt the memory of the performer. For example, the opening song used as an exordium to the listener (A), the drummed message warning the brothers (D) and Chiti's song of triumph at the river crossing (F).

b) The set phrases and cliches attached to some of the more popular incidents, such as the discovery of *Mumbi Mukasa Liulu aponene ne fimatwi fikalamba nge nsofu* "Mumbi Musaka fallen from the sky with ears as large as an elephants" (C).

(2) Some of the standardized themes that organize the thought are:

a) The journey-motif itself, propelled by arrivals and departures and river-crossings, provides a mnemonic map for the story, through the familiar territory of the Luapula and Chambeshi rivers and the forest at Mwalule.

b) The description and manipulation of the actors' implements, which are still kept as "sacred relics" *Babenye* in ancestral huts, punctuate the story--"the talking drum" *Lunkumbi* (D), "the royal lance" *Mulumbu* (F), and Chilimbulu's "tatooed stomach-skin" *Nkanda ya pe fumo iyalipo inembo* (G).

c) The controlled set of mythic themes, whose dramatic imagery memorably encapsulates central cultural principles, such as "the heavenly origin" of the primordial mother *Aponene ku mulu* (C), the building of "the tower" *Lupungu* (D), "the mystical sun hero" *Luchele Ng'anga*(E).

(3) Some of the epithets used to disambiguate the typical heroes and groups are:

a) Certain praise songs attached to ancient chiefs, such as Chubili *Kaseke* "the little basket," referring to the basket of severed enemies' heads as a sign of powers in war, or Salala *Bana-bonke* "let the children suck," referring to his peaceful reign while mothers nourished children (I) (Cf Tanguy 1948, 20-1).

b) Epithetic explanations for the origin of various clans and tribes, such as the *Mwine Membe* "phallic totem," contemptuously given to Kapasa, who violated his sister (F), and the *Balala* "the sleepers," a name given to the southern tribespeople, who submitted so timidly to the Bemba conquerors (G).

(4) Some of the heroic figures, with their burden of ceremonial accouterments, around whom the cultural lore is organized and moral truths are typified are: Chitimukulu, whose toss of a spear into the tree signifies the royal powers effecting tribal transitions from nature to culture (F); Chilufya, whose portage of seeds in hair and of sacred relics in hand signifies the Bemba woman's fertile powers over agriculture and matriliny (F); Shimwalule, whose presidence over the solemn burial rites of the Bemba founding fathers, signifies the immortality of their spirits (H).

(5) Some of the oral devices used for the ceremonial appropriation of history are:

a) The nomenclature of persons and places serves as an important focus for the noetic organization of historical material. For example, the first chief is functionally, not properly, named as *Mukulumpe*, a Luban word for "a worthy person, a chief;" his name bears the eponymous addition *Mubemba* , after which the Bemba tribe is supposedly named (B). Mumbi Mukasa is teknonymously identified as *Liulu* "originating in heaven" (C). Chilufya, etymologically from the verb *Kulufya* "to mislay or forget," refers to the fact that she was at first left behind by her fleeing brothers; her pseudonym, Bwalya Chabala (from the verb *Kubala* "to begin"), bills her in the role as the first sister in the matrilineal dynasty (C).

The names of places used to forward the story line are: The ford for the Luapula river-crossing is called Kuisandulula from the verb *Kusandulula* "to divide and enlarge;" it refers to the dispersal of tribes and the growth of the Bemba (F), which is the main theme of the next section of the myth (G). After the critical crossing of the Chambeshi river, the village is named Mulambalala from the verb *Kulambalala* "to stretch out on the ground;" it refers to the Bemba need to rest, regroup and consolidate after the adventures and mishaps of their trek.

b)   The genealogical recitation which concludes the charter myth (J), reenforces its political purpose by justifying the present administrative order "from the beginning." For example, the rounded figure of twenty-five or so paramounts, who appear in the genealogy, will not noticeably increase as generations pass on; mnemonic capacity will restrict the number to that couple of dozen. Oral techniques diplomatically make room for recent rulers by dropping those whose lineage are no longer so politically influential. Thus, the genealogy collapses long periods of events and telscopes long lists of chiefs into the virtually manageable reigns of more memorable paramounts (Roberts 1973, 26-8; Cf Goody 197). In another example, the legend of migration itself actually represents a prolonged process of recurrent migration of small bands lasting many centuries. Another example is the praise name given to Chitimukulu Mukuka as *Wa Malekano* "of the separation;" it attributes to this individual the responsibility for a division of royal power in the Bembaland, which actually occurred for a variety of obscure historical circumstances throughout the eighteenth century (Cf Roberts 1973, 94-5).

c)   The anachronistic recitation of recent changes as occurring long ago (an oral tendency which Goody calls "homeostasis") (See below, chap. 3, 106) serves to realign inevitable historical alterations with the more desirable cultural continuity of a conservative tradition. For example, the novel intrusion of European and Christian elements into nineteenth century Bemba society is narrated in the charter myth as archetypically posited (B).

(6)   Principles of knowledge and behavior are embodied in the narration of adverse events. Polarized contrasts are memorable. For example, the abhorrence of incest is registered in the destructive familial conflict between the primordial father and his sons and between the royal brothers (D & F); the prohibition against adultery is rooted in the lethal consequences of the hostilities amongst Chiti, Nkole, Mwase, and Chilimbulu (G & H).

(7)   The charter myth exults in an abundance of things to say and ways to say them. Its verbosity and redundancy give a boost to memory and pause for thinking. For example, incest is a symbol marking the evolution from a naive state of

irresponsibility amidst the primordial simplicity of a fantasy
land to the maturity of dutiful knowledge amidst the actual life
world of the Bemba (Roberts 1973, 47-8); it is at least implied
in three episodes (D and F). One river crossing of the Luapula
symbolizes the transition from the Luban land of darkness in the
West with its unfamiliar terrain to the Bemba land of light in
the East with its well known geography (F); and a second river
crossing of the Chambeshi symbolizes the threshold between the
errant life of nomads and the stability of a tribe politically
organized under Chitimukulu (G). Parallelism is another
reduplicative agent. For example, there is the correspondence
between the cosmic tower's vertical ascent to heaven and the
horizontal quest by terrestrial tour for the East (D & E). In
like manner, the several interventions by Luchele Ng'anga
punctuate and coordinate the story's episodic sequences (E).

In summary, the most telling feature of oral story-telling
is the fact that the charter myth plunges immediately and
episodically into the middle of the action. It does not evidence
a grand design of building tension to a climax followed by an
exquisite resolution. It has the progression of steady plodding
through episodes not the composition of tight plotting through
intricate involvements (Ong 1982, 140ff).

Our discussion now moves from the particulars of the charter
myth to the more general question of how myth and ritual are
interrelated.

The Relationship of Ritual to Myth

Oral ritual is connected to oral myth insofar as both are
basically a narrative elaboration of symbols. Ritual, according
to Eliade (1959b), is their dramatic reenactment. For Eliade,
the most important discovery of the human spirit, disclosing its
essential destiny, occurs when archaic consciousness initiates
the quest for reality, value and significance ("The whole" in
Tracy's terms). These will orient human life. The human spirit
then construes that the heterogeneous realities of the world can
be integrated into a coherent system and the seeming antinomies
of life can be comprehended as a unified whole. Furthermore, the
power of nature, and the existential "angst" and "peak moments"
of human life are experienced and celebrated as "hierophanies."
They reveal the substance and form of that "transcendent other,"
that "whole" at the depths of reality (Cf Tracy 1975, 105-09).
Symbols are devised to express the multivalent dimensions of the
cosmos and to articulate the holistic character, which is
immanent and operative in all human reality as well as all
modalities of nature. The symbols, which invite and promote
reflection, become saturated with tradition and authority, as the
community traces the notion of whole to its origins. Myth
narrates the actions of the heroic founders of the cosmos ("the
whole") who, in the very beginning, established its principles

and dynamics.   The sacred time and place of these mythic origins lie, not so much in the past, as at the very center. Indeed they are the constitutive substratum of present reality (See below, chap. 3, 85ff).[5] Contemporary people, thus, can participate in those archetypal events at the cosmic foundations by a ritual repetition of the myth.   The rite places them in intense contact with their center, where the power of the whole is disclosed and released to them.   It recreates their sense of what is really meaningful and ultimately valuable in everyday life. Through the rite, representing and realizing these ideals, the present community reorients itself and reaffirms its solidarity with the primordial words and deeds radiating from within its perfect center.

Since an oral culture lacks a script for its rites, it is difficult to get a precise and definitive account of any ritual. There is no prescribed liturgical format, complete with marginalized rubrics. Willing informants, even though experts, are not used to the type of mental operations which abstract required procedure from an actual performance and classify facts in a way convenient to a literate enquirer.   Consequently, they tend to dwell on dramatic, public and pleasurable events which are readily recalled and described, and to neglect the esoteric aspects as perhaps offensive or irrelevant to an outsider (Richards 1956, 135-36). More importantly, as Tyler argues, the ethnographer's intention is to scrutinize a ritual's transcription in the hope of arriving at a complete set of symbolic elements; those seem to constitute an explanation for the rite, involving the universal truths and motivations operative within the culture.   It is likely that the oral informant's description "does not implicate an exposition that goes beyond the rhetorical circumstances of its performance;" it intends only to persuade people of the correct way of getting through the rite (Tyler 1981, 18). An act is correct because "it comes next" *Cakonka*   (Sampa XI).

Descriptions given by informants outside actual rites tend to be terse and sparse, detailing only the amount of food and beer and familiar acts.   These second-hand acts are often little more than unreliable reminiscences (Cf Chikoti na Bwala 1957, 15-23).

During an actual ceremony, certain events may be left out, because they are simply forgotten.   Others may be abbreviated because of the unavailability of certain props or the varying interpretive emphasis of a particular leader.   But even during the ceremony the oral ritualists are not entirely extemporaneous. They are correctly guided by the event in progress; the sequence of episodes and the unravelling of symbolic acts carry them through the drama without confusion.

Actually, there is considerable fluidity and spontaneity in oral ritual, as the specialist's genius for the impromptu adds a measure of creativity to the tradition as the occasion demands. Just like the oral story teller, Bemba ritual officials manipulate the fundamental components, transmitted from generation to generation in a continuum of structures. Accordingly, they create a unique celebration for the tribal participants, who are both critically aware of the traditional parameters and desirous of an artistic surprise. Dissonance in the tradition has itself become ritualized; for example, arguing and bickering between the official and the bereaved over the correct details of a funeral rite function to provide some relief to the grief and guilt-feelings of surviving family and friends (Mpundu XI).

Obviously, rituals cannot in principle be so thoroughly extemporaneous as to lack all commonality. The repetitive and formulaic character of oral tradition, which has been discussed in chapter one, is the primary means of assuming continuity and stability amidst profuse oral variability. The visual and auditory symbols used in rituals operate culturally as storage bins; they perform as power points of information, through which oral society's deep knowledge and cultural axioms are transmitted. Moreover, the liminal situations, which rituals induce, provide not just an opportunity for society to take cognizance of itself and reflect its social structure. There are also periods of anti-structure, wherein a momentarily egalitarian community is given the time and space for creative transformation and reformation of out-moded social norms and practices. Chaos briefly reigns as the tensions necessary for maintaining general order are relaxed and experimental innovations introduced for assessment (Cf V. Turner 1974). For example, ritual is felt to be an occasion for excess, for exuberant singing and dancing and for consuming food and drink in quantities over and above those normally consumed. This excessive expenditure of material and spiritual resources is paralleled by the risky relaxation of the culture's regulations. These limit symbols signal: (1) the threat of nature's chaotic intrusion into a well ordered culture, and (2) the need for occasional relief from the pressures of conforming to social standards. At the same time, by the rules of the rite and the fixed time which limits the ritual antistructure, human dominance over natural chaos is reasserted; the need for reinvestment of and recommitment to the social system is clarified by temporary human chaos (Leiris 1958).

Obviously, the total value system of the tribe can not be presented in any one myth, nor does any one ritual exhaust its capacity for reproduction. Each ritual will dramatically evoke some of the basic values narrated by the charter myth. For example, the rites for the agricultural cycle, for the founding of a village, for the succession and burial of chiefs, etc., will all symbolically represent those archetypal episodes of the charter myth, selectively appropriate for their function. Through each ritual, the sacred time and sacred actions of archetypal personages are re-presented in order to explain the

world as it ultimately is and to renew the natural and human
order according to the holistic ideals of the charter myth (See
below, chap. 3, 68ff).

Finally, let us insert here a salutary reminder about the
hermeneutical differences between the texts, transcriptions and
written descriptions of these myths and rites and their actual
oral performances. This caution is necessary lest we become too
sanguine about our assignment of various meanings and
interdependent allusions in their oral execution. Quite
disturbing to literate interpreters is the fact that oral
performers and participants are often unable to verify the
understanding of symbols which ethnographers ascribe to oral
myths and rituals. Does this not mean that oral celebrants are
mindlessly parroting words or aping empty forms? In answer to
this problem, Stephen Tyler (1981, 13-25) espouses a modified
deconstructionist perspective for interpreting certain Hindu oral
performances, which is somewhat applicable to the Bemba case. He
explains that performers and participants alike oftentimes do not
look for significance beyond the assigned role which the words,
acts and artifacts play in the rite or myth as a whole: "They
are not means of knowing what it means but means of knowing how
to do it" (Tyler 1981, 25). Tyler argues that the secret world
of hidden meanings and structures of esoteric knowledge which are
discerned in symbols could actually be products of the objective
observer's imagination (Idem 24). That syntax of symbols often
exists only in the texts and transcriptions not in oral
performances (Idem).

Tyler's sensitivity correctly highlights the different
hermeneutical potentials of texts and oral elocution. Texts can
alienate meaning from the function of words and deeds and things
and cross-reference them into unintended and unattended schemes
of theoretical speculation. In live performances symbols are
intimately tied to "the appropriate way or standard method of
doing something" (Idem). They may not convey knowledge about the
extra-ritual or extra-mythic world. Symbols may simply be ways
of organizing that knowledge (Cf Sperber 1975).

It may very well be (if we may be allowed to continue our
paraphrase of Tyler) that in many Bemba rites and recitals the
words and deeds themselves constitute the whole aim; they need
not be indices to the structures of knowledge and behavior which
impel the culture as a whole. Our position will grant to Tyler
that the nexus of interpretation we ascribe to symbols may be at
a level removed from indigenous intention and interest. But we
will also maintain with Ong that the texts and transcriptions we
offer in evidence retain an originating relation to their oral
substratum (Ong 1982, 164).

Cisungu: The Puberty Rite for Women[6]

After these general remarks on the relationship of myth to
ritual, our discussion will now return to the specific episodes
of the Bemba charter myth, exemplifying how a particular Bemba
ritual--*Cisungu*--dramatizes mythic themes.

The Mythic Themes of *Cisungu*

As a rite de passage, *Cisungu* initiates the young girls
through the archetypal symbols of life and death, established in
the charter myth, in order to give social form and meaning to
their sexuality. The transformations induced in the candidates
follow the classic pattern. They consist of rites of pre-liminal
separation, liminal transition and post-liminal reincorporation
(Cf Van Gennep 1960 and V. Turner 1969). The special themes
ritually enacted in *Cisungu* are those recounted in the charter
myth: the sacrality of feminine sexuality, the centrality of
matrilineal descent, the honor owed to seniority, the wisdom of
listening to the tradition, the fidelity of marriage, the purity
of family life, the duty of wife and mother, the womanly
responsibility for agriculture, and the veneration due to chiefly
spirits. The Bemba symbols, which enshrine these meanings, have
a "fan of referents" which allow a penumbra of interpretations
(Richards 1956, 164-65). All interpretations center on, are
tangential to, or draw from the limit-character of the young
girls' status and the uncanny, revelatory and salutary power of
the whole.

The *Cisungu* rite draws on the episodes of the charter myth
whose themes relate to the dignity and duty of women in Bemba
society.

First, the puberty rite returns to the hierogamic episode
of Mukulumpe hunting the elephant-eared Mumbi Mukasa in the
forest. At their first menstruation the initiates, sometimes
called *Cisofu* "the big elephants," run into the forest (Etienne
1948, 27). Their unbridled sexual fertility will be rescued from
chaotic animal needs and brought under social control. Later,
their fiancés sing *Kanonde nama yandi* "Let me follow my wounded
prey," while they shoot a small bow and arrow into a target,
claiming the initiates as their wives. The symbolic associations
with the heavenly archetype imply the sacredness of feminine
sexuality, of marriage and of matriliny.

Next the rite returns to the achetypal episode of Mukulumpe
imprisoning his daughter in his lightless hut. The initiates are
warned against incestuous disorder: now that they are nubile,
their approach will pollute their fathers' hut. So their fathers
are chased away, and they are locked up in the huts for ritual
seclusion prior to the marital ordering of their fertile powers
(Richards 1956, 121; Etienne 1948, 29).

The rite has several symbols, which both depict the wandering path of the journey to the East and associate that quest for immortality and wholeness with the twofold movement of the sun. First of all, there is the ever-present symbol *Liyongolo* "the sacred snake." It forms either an angular or a circular chevron design, ornamenting *Mbusa* fired pots, like *Liyongolo lyapinda ng'anda* "the snake stretches across the house,"

and mural designs, like *Bufyashi* "motherhood."

These have sexual connotations obvious to the Bemba. The first *Liyongolo* stylizes male genitalia and signifies the male as provider and protector of the household. As *Bufyashi* , it stylizes female genitalia and signifies the female as the source and nurture of continuing life. The senior woman at the ceremony sometimes refers to these chevrons as *Mashindo eya itengo* "the rays of the sun," or "the flames of the hearth" (Richards 1956, 82).

The sun-motif is picked up, when another dramatic presentation of *Mbusa* evokes the solar symbolism of the charter myth. The unfired clay sculpture called *Mupeto* "the hoop" is fashioned by a frame of two branches bent into circles at a right angle over each other and fastened to the ground. It is plastered with clay, studded with seeds and painted with red dye. A round ball of clay is stuck on top. The initiates are forced to jump over the structure, and then to crawl through its loops, biting off the seeds and spitting them off in blessings. The *Mbusa* is uprooted and thrown into the river on whose bank it is erected. As a badge of honor to those who have passed through mortal danger, the initiates are daubed with red dye, signifying the blood of birth (Richards 1956, 95, 97-8).

The symbolism is complex. The throwing of the *Mupeto* into the river represents the ritual act of purification after marital intercourse. The ball of clay represents the sun at its zenith and the two bent branches delineate the twofold path of the sun. The girls jump over the solar structure (a traditional way of exposing sex organs to another influence (Etienne 1948, 113-14)) and then trace the diurnal and annual movements (See above, 40) of the sun by passing back and forth through its hoops. The passage represents the period of pregnancy, which the Bemba traditionally think lasts about the year that a garden takes from preparation to harvest. The connection of the sun symbolism to pregnancy is now made explicit: the fired clay pot, called *Mwanakashi* "pregnant woman," is presented to the girls with the song *Kasuba kawa / Kasuba kaeli aya / Nshiku shafula / Kanshindama Musuku ila /* "The sun has fallen. The has already passed on. The days are fulfilled. Let me go and honor the woman's fertility tree" (Richards 1956, 210). The underlying theme of all these episodes proceeds from the charter myth. The immortality, which the first chiefs found in the suns' rays, is continued in matrilineal recycling of Bemba spirits through the mediation of feminine fertility.

This episode climaxes with the coming of the "bridegroom" *Shicisungu.* He claims the girl as his wife by shooting his model bow and arrow into the *Mushintililo* "bullseye." The latter is set into a mural *Mbusa* surrounded by chevron designs with paintings of the sun (male) and moon (female) on either side. The accompanying song calls him *Mwine walasa* "the owner of the wounded game" and *Cikulu mwaume mu Ng'anda* "the pinnacle of the house," (recalling the sun at the peak of "the hoop" *Mupeto*). Early the next morning comes the rite of the "cocks of the dawn" *Nkoko ya ncela* with its primary song *Walele cisungu* "you have slept with the *cisungu* -child" (Richards 1956, 96-9, 105-8).

The gesture of the bridegroom shooting a bow and arrow ritually evokes two of the charter myth's episodes: when the hunter Mukulumpe marries the elephantine Mumbi Mukasa in the forest, and when the first Chitimukulu throws his spear into the tree to claim the new land as his own "wife." The fact that this same mythical scene is repeated, as the initial act of the *Citemene* "garden rite," accentuates the agricultural allusions of this frankly sexual imagery. Bemba marriage is also described in such agricultural terms: "She is my wife because I make her a garden" (Richards 1939, 190). And because the woman is the sole source of human life in the Bemba matriliny, she is made responsible for more than half the agricultural work of the year (Richards 1939, 100).

The puberty rite is full of such symbols, ambiguously associating purified human sexuality with agricultural prosperity and identifying the earth's fertility with that of woman. At one point, the initiates carry pots of grain-seeds on their heads, as Chilufya Mulenga, their primeval sister, carried seeds in her hair. They are reminded that her incestuous violation endangered agricultural fertility. Amidst the several garden mimes, the initiates are presented with the *Mbusa* "fired pots" named *Mputa* "garden mounds" and *Amabala* "gardens." Then their paternal aunts, the seniors in a matriliny, give them two model *Mbusa* : *Kalonde* "a hoe," symbolizing their garden duties and the conjugal rights of their husbands, and *Kanweno* "a purification pot," signifying that every sexual act must be purified within the confines of a loyal marriage. The tragic scene in the charter myth of the deaths of Chilimbulu, Mwase and Chiti, serves as an admonition against adulterous unions.

Finally, the *Ng'wena* "crocodile-shaped pottery" is shown to be girls with the song *Mutwale umwana kuli ng'wena* "You take the girl to the crocodile." This episode evokes the charter myth narration of the crocodile as the royal totem, representing Bemba authority and tradition. It also associates their sexual powers with the divine origins of the primal mother, Mumbi Mukasa, who was from the crocodile clan.

All in all, the fragmenting potential of sexual power is averted by the ritual turn toward the whole, whose uncanny revelation reintegrates and restores the social elements.

The Religious Dimensions of *Cisungu*

By most definitions of the term, any rite can be properly deemed religious, which gives symbolic access to the transcendent whole. The previous chapter showed how the Bemba religious system revolves around the cardinal notion of the whole. Richards in effect agrees with this analysis. She produces a chart exhibiting how each ritual of the Bemba metaphorically expresses their essentially homogeneous body of beliefs, "which links authority with the exercise of supernatural power based on access to ancestral spirits by those who have correctly handled sex and fire" (Richards 1956, 141). The *Cisungu* ceremony is singled out for the outstanding capability of its symbols and limit-language to communicate a powerful sense of participation in the polyphonic whole by which those beliefs are harmoniously integrated (Cf Idem, 141-53).

In *Cisungu* , the drumming, dancing, singing and drama serve to create the kind of acoustic uproar, which the oral Bemba associate with the whole of cosmic and human forces. The young women are understood to be entering the sacred space of ancestral authority, where they will **both** learn what it is to be women **and** be transformed from giggly girls into thoughtfully mature women (Richards 1956, 202-04). There is an uncanny power, emanating from the whole and tapped-into by the rite itself. As the ceremony progresses, the initiates are "magically changed . . . by supernatural means": they are "**made** clever" *Kubacenjela* and they are "**caused** to be nubile and fertile" *Kubakusha* (Idem, 121-25).

Cisungu is profoundly religious, despite Garrec's (1916, 78)
Tabalelasha ku cisenshi yoo ni ku bupulumushi fye "They engage
not in religious paganism but only in obscenity." During the
month-long ceremony, the young girls and their society are
promoted from experiencing their sexuality to the effort to
understand it, and to make right decisions regarding its use. It
is a conscious effort mediated by symbolic action. For, in
Cisungu, the girls' vision of their worth is transcended by the
communal horizons of their new status and role. They come to
feel themselves as the tribal trustees for the vital potentials
within their bodies. They transcend their girlish world by being
inducted into the extra-familial life of the tribe and join a
sorority of women, banded together with an **esprit de corps** of
having undergone initiatory trials. *Cisungu* emphasis on the
transcendent origin and dignity of matriliny prepares them as
women to endure life graciously in a patriarchal society.
Through their fertility, their parents succeed in transcending
their own lives, their community extends its limits for growth,
and the ancestral spirits achieve an immortality in the cycle of
life continued in their progeny (Kapwepwe VIII).

The ancestral spirits are venerated explicitly only in the
opening and middle moments of the rite, when there is a brief
"invocation" *Kulumbula* and "spittle blessing" *Kupala amate*
(Richards 1956, 63 & 88). A couple of days later, the "emblems"
Mbusa are tied to a *Musuku* tree and handled with the women's
mouths. There are thus religious associations with this tree
which bears much fruit and symbolizes matrilineal fertility
(Maier 1976, 5-7). The women's spittle is the means by which
ancestral blessings are conveyed (Richards 1956, 164). The
representative ancestral spirit, *Lesa*, is mentioned only at the
midpoint and then in conjunction with the *Kupala amate* and
Kutotela "blessing and veneration" of the ancestral spirits. For
example, while the young women, bathed and whitewashed, swing to
and fro over a pool imitating the act of birth, they sing
Kucilingana Lesa / Tupashana mayo "In following the ways of *Lesa*
/ We imitate our mothers" (89 & 196). Lesa clearly represents
the ancestor **par excellence** of all the ancestors in the
matrilineal line from whom all traditions and life flow to, and
on through, the young woman (See below, chap. 3, 90ff).

Thus *Cisungu* effectively incorporates the whole of Bemba
belief, to which their notions of sexuality, authority and
spirituality are cognate. It shares in and celebrates the Bemba
ultimate religious concern--the continuaton of human existence in
community with all else.

The Oral Features of *Cisungu*

The initial episode of *Cisungu* recreates a sacred space,
reminiscent of a cave, which echoes with the voices of ancestral
wisdom (See below, chap. 3, 84-5). The initiates are concealed

under a blanket, representing their passage into the dark cave, wherein *Mipempe*, "a cloudless dawn," will reveal secret knowledge. In fact, the rest of the ceremony could be conceived as Havelock's (1978 passim) oral cultural "echo system." It virtually reverberates with the tribal deposit of accumulated wisdom, reinterated in vocal, mimetic, poetic, instrumental and choreographic rhythms in order to ensure its retention and validation (Cf Ong 1967, 204; Havelock 1982, 116-19 and 132-36).

Oral mnemonic devices. The preparation, presentation and ritual handling of *Mbusa* "sacred emblems" occupy most of the time in the ceremony and are the most important activities.[7] In an oral equivalent of writing, a good deal of tedious labor goes into crafting the designs carefully, painting them exactly, and precisely spacing the decorative beans. The didactic intent and mnemonic function bring *Mbusa* into the vicinity of words. Since all human artifacts are utterings (outerings) of human interiority, *Mbusa* bear a relationship to the oral word as prime analogate for the knowledge and communication (Cf Ong 1962, 49).

Unlike the written word, whose exactness of form contributes to an exact meaning, the words associated with *Mbusa* exult in ambiguity.[8] In an oral society there are no dictionaries "to look it up" (Ong 1982, 14, 31-2). Meanings of speech are negotiated and renegotiated in the very act of speaking (See below, chap. 3, 77-8). The meaning-event is as complex and polysemous as any life-situation. The diversity of place, time and social setting of the vocal exchange enters into the hermeneutical transaction between speaker and listeners (Goody 1968, 29).

Therefore, the stereotyped formulations of the lesson are highly allusive and evocative of multiple meanings (Richards 1956, 106 & 112). But, because *Mbusa* are traditionally crafted, everyone believes that the meanings are always the same. This is enough to ensure that *Cisungu* maintains its charter function for transferring roles to each generation. The *Mbusa* are, then, "ocular equivalents of verbal formulas" (Ong 1967, 25).

The words of the lesson are formulated in short poems set to music and stylized in dance. This poetry should not be considered as a luxury or a sophisticated embellishment of the oral culture. It is a necessity. Oral poetry has the rather prosaic function of preserving cultural information. "In an oral culture," as Havelock notes of the Greeks," metrical language is part of the day's work" (1982, 189). Hence each *Mbusa* is mnemonically associated with doggerel rhymes and mimetic dances.

It is significant that the truths and moral precepts sanctioned by ancestral spirits are entrusted to musical genres. Besides being aesthetically and mnemonically capable, music is a privileged medium of truth and value in Bemba oral epistemology (Mapoma 1980, 46 & 60; see above, chap. 1, 11). In the lyrics and rhythms a central cluster of common meanings and sentiments possesses enough of a moral charge so that a woman can merely hum a line of a *Mbusa* song or pirouette a step or two to rebuke a negligent wife or mother (Richards 1956, 162). They serve as formal, quotable expressions of public morality, triggered by the *Mbusa* images. During the ceremony, each song is intoned by the "initiator" *Nacimbusa* and repeated by the attending women and initiates, until its moral has been drummed in over twenty times. The dances' drum beat, too, serves as a formulary device of abstract fixity for the various word groupings, much like versification in songs, which also has a neurological effect on the community's memory (Ong 1968, 285ff). In the absence of writing, there is nowhere to store inherited cultural information, save in living memories (Ong 1967, 204; 1982, 33-6).

The lesson that the winged words of the tradition, which are not mnemonically retained, are irretrievably lost, is dramatically demonstrated: each day, the beautifully sculpted and painstakingly decorated wet-clay *Mbusa* are scraped away to leave floor space for the next round of teaching (Sampa XI).

Thus, *Mbusa* guarantee that the intricate succession of ritual songs and dances of *Cisungu* are more or less exactly repeated, and that the established wisdom is rigidly formulated. Still the range and depth of interpretations may vary from year to year and from individual to individual (Richards 1956, 147). The exact meaning is not so important as the duty to pass them on (Richards 1956, 164).

Mbusa literally means "things handed down" (Richards 1956, 59). The rite of handing down *Mbusa* has its own meanings, which are symbolically conveyed. The women arrange themselves in an order of precedence, and honor the *Mbusa* with "a royal ululation" *Kutotela* . Then the senior *Nacimbusa* "initiator" picks up the sacred emblem and passes it on to the woman in the next rank of age, who receives it and so on down the line in passage to the initiates. After they are offered and received in the order of seniority, they are placed on the girls' heads. The girls then do a dance out of respect for the traditional wisdom and for its transmission through the elders. The handling down in the order of seniority among women symbolically emphasizes the prerogatives of age among the living, the veneration of matrilineal spirits and the transmission of traditional wisdom through authorized channels.

Every episode with *Mbusa* is considered a ritual submission of the girls to authority *Kunakila ku bakalamba* "to be soft/pliant to elders," and a test of their *Mano* "good sense" to attend to the traditions (Banapenge IV). The Bemba criterion of intelligence is not originality, but familiarity with the tradition (See above, chap. 1, 13). Compliance with the traditional wisdom enshrined in the formal songs and dances of the elders is a sure sign that one "understands" (*Kuumfwa* , literally "to hear"). *Munshumfwa sha bakulu* "the one who does not obey / listen to the enders" is the proverbial butt of many jokes in the culture (See below, chap. 3, 88-9). This lesson is explicitly rehearsed in the *Cisungu* song *Tumfwe mafunde* . "Let us listen to the teachings." Its accompanying *Mbusa* pot is slashed with dozens of small curved slits "like ears bent to hear" (Corbeil IV). The girls are to listen in silence, and not to be heard. So when the girls sit down on stools, they are immediately and dramatically chased away by senior relatives, as the stools are signs of traditional speaking-authority.

The authorized channels for handing down traditional wisdom is, of course, the mouths of tribal seniors. Appropriately enough, the handing down of *Mbusa* is itself effected orally. They are passed from mouth to mouth by the women in that order of precedence.[9] The song, which accompanies the handing down of *Mbusa* goes: *Tolela na mulomo* "let me pick it up with my mouth." The mouthings and songs are repeated endlessly and punctuate the ceremony (Richards 1956, 64, 71-4, 76, 78, 81, 82, 84-6, 89, 90, 93-5, 97, 101, 107, 108, 153, 163, 193).

Richards either ignores the symbolism of all this oral handling (eg. Idem, 78 and 193), or confesses that it is "obscure" (64, 90, 95), "incongruous" (154), "curious" (82) and "esoteric" (130, 165). In the argument of this treatise, the mouthing of the sacred emblems is meant to signify the Bemba appropriation of their oral culture. Bemba society's knowledge and ethics live in its oral cavities and will slip out of cultural consciousness unless they are constantly verbalized. Another mouthing-exercise emphasizes the fleeting nature of the oral tradition: from pots filled with water, the girls are made to catch *Njelela* "darting water-insects" in their mouths and spit them into the hands of the *Nacimbusa* (Richards 1956, 76). The words of the tradition will flit across the community's consciousness and dash away, like darting insects across water, unless someone orally imbibes them in memory.

The mouthing of the tradition rises to a higher level of meaning in another distinctive metaphor, that of seeds. Each of the unfired wet-clay *Mbusa* is elaborately decorated with seeds (Richards 1956, 87) and the stylized *Nsaka* "village speak-easy" is covered with seeds. Although Richards finds the symbolism obscure, it is clear that the seeds are a metaphor for traditional words of wisdom. The ritual *Nsaka* has a "roof-peak" *Nsonshi* frayed out, clearly resembling *Ngala* "the feathered headdress" of traditional speaking authority (Idem, 97-8). Both the *Mbusa* , which function as words, and the *Nsaka* , which is the place of words, are appropriately covered with such seeds. The kneeling girls pluck out the seeds with the mouths (Idem, 89) and spit them in ancestral blessing. The ceremony continues with the *Nacimbusa* passing on baskets of seeds with her mouth, and then later a cob of cornseeds is passing along orally as if by word of mouth.

In another very dramatic episode, the girls' mothers sow a small garden with "sorghum" *Masaka* and "millet" *Male* seeds, signifying the planting of ancestral wisdom. The girls are then made to lie down and put their heads against the seeded mounds (Richards 1956, 74). The millet is the traditional food and sorghum is the royal food. The practical lesson is for the girls to provide food for the family and to submit to royalty. But there are also connotations of the passing-on of oral knowledge. As the proverb has it--*Amano ni mbutu balondola fye* "wisdom is like seeds: both are on loan only." Borrowed seeds must be returned at the food-harvest and so must traditional wisdom be passed from one generation to another along authoritative channels.

Food as a variation of the seed metaphor for orally transmitted authority and wisdom also features prominently in the rite. For example, the seeds are cooked up into "food" *Bwali* over the new fire (Idem, 78-80). *Mbusa* , decorated with seeds, are hidden in bowls of this food. Then the girls touch the bowls all over before handing them to a senior woman. She in turn picks up the lid with her mouth, revealing the food which hides the *Mbusa*. She now begins passing along the bowls from mouth to mouth in order of precedence. Finally, when the food is ritually tasted, the secrets of the hidden *Mbusa* are revealed by mouth.

Later in the rite, when the girls are made free to offer food (Richards 1956, 767), they learn that food, like knowledge, is highly socialized. Food and knowledge are never procured, owned or consumed by an individual, but are supplied by elders to be shared with contemporaries and successors, and remain subject to elders' special rights (Richards 1939, 199-200).

Food and knowledge are implicated in another incident. While climbing up the *Musuku* tree, the symbol of matrilineal descent, the girls sing of "the way monkeys eat everything" *Kolwe kulya kwakwe* and "learn from their mothers" *Kolwe ita nyina* (Richards 1956, 72 & 192). So the girls are to devour the traditions and imitate their mothers.

The oral consumption of the tradition is also symbolized in a drinking incident. A hole is scratched at the foot of a *Mwenge* female tree, which has been honored by the application of red and white anointings and white beads. The latter signify veneration of matrilineal spirits. "Beer" *Bwalwa* is poured into the hole and lapped up by the women, who in hierarchial order lie on their backs and drink from the left and the right sides. Clearly, they are drinking in ancestral wisdom at the treefount of tradition.

Even sexual fertility is symbolically transferred orally. There is a "lighting of the new fire" *Namushimwa* , which is described as *Kulomba bufyashi* "begging for parenthood." It clearly represents the handing over of procreative sexual powers by the old women to the next generation. This is effected in oral symbols. The young girls attempt to make fire by friction on the thighs of their fathers' sisters. Then they are led by these women crawling together to an actual new fire and, <u>with their mouths,</u> place a marriage purification pot on the fire (Richards 1956, 77-8).

In the "firewood fetching" *Kuteba*, a bundle of firewood, hiding some domestic *Mbusa*, is opened with the teeth (Idem 107). With this episode, the lesson is brought home a final time. The secrets of *Mbusa* are opened and revealed orally by the initiates mouthing the *Mbusa* and their accompanying songs.

All this constant eating and communal mouthing of *Mbusa* in the *Cisungu* may seen quaint, bizarre and even unhygenic to observers unable to grasp the oral implications. An oralist appreciation provides the key. The pioneer student of oral culture, Marcel Jousse, wrote of the mouthing of formulas and its "verbomotor" effect:

> . . . cette repetition en echo s'est cependant specialisee et transposee sur les muscles de la bouche, dans les gestes de l'articulation qui sont, sinon identiques, du moins grandement analogues aux gestes de la manducation. D'ou le perpetuel va-et-vient semantique: articulation-manducation, manducation-articulation . . . de bouche en bouche au cours de generations innombrobles, jusqu 'au jour ou la formule a acquis comme une perfection souveraine . . . (Jousse 1975, 46-8).

Speaking makes the traditional words of cognition and behavior palpable and palatable. The spoken word is not passively assimilated, but chewed on, eaten, mouthed by its hearers and ruminated over by repetition. Oral knowledge must be tasted and savored (Ong 1977, 258-60). This is the import of a frequent proverbial admonition which Bemba parents give to their children: *Ulepela matwi ubwali* "You must give food to your ears" (by attending to the elders).

Oral ethics. The contents of *Cisungu* -teachings recapitulate the ethical lessons already learned by the girls growing up in the village (Sampa XI). Richards (1956, 140) produces a numerical chart of the specific morals ratified during the ceremony: 10 Pure Fire Taboos, 19 Social Obligations for the Husband and Wife, 3 Obligations to in-laws, 10 Domestic Duties, 7 Agricultural Duties, 7 Maternal Duties, 3 Mother-Daughter Obligations, 12 Sex & Fertility Rules, 7 Affirmations of Royal Power, and 9 General Ethical Principles. However, the main interest here is not in the actual content, but in the oral media for transmitting the ethical norms and how they influence the character of the ethical message.

An oral ethics tends to be situationally and existentially bound to here and the now (Havelock 1978, 213-21). Without the benefit of writing, oral wisdom cannot be arranged according to fixed principles but is programatically embedded in folklore exemplifying "ad hoc" procedures (Idem, 36-37). Orality consequently indulges in a bewildering lack of uniformity in moral guides as well as in cognitive tendencies. There is little systematic control when the rules are preserved in a prolixity of proverbs, stories, rituals, songs, etc. (Idem).

The Bemba are adept at ageric and iconic presentations of their own culture. Their traditional ethics, like the rest of their religious and social wisdom, finds its authentic expression in constructs of the creative imagination rather than the abstractions of reflective intelligence. The Bemba endow their ethical tenets with symbolic complexities which express a semantic melange of feelings, notions and values. The asethetically pleasing and easily recallable *Mbusa* trigger the ethical information. The highly imaginative quality of the oral process makes this information dramatically and memorably active in the ritual. The attendant commotion invites participation and imitation (Havelock 1963, 187-89). Some of the imagery of the songs and dances associated with the *Mbusa* is mildly salacious, enhancing their mnemonic capability.

The songs' archaic language also serves a special purpose. By employing *Luban* words, like *Mundu* for *Nkalamo* or *Tota* for *Mpemba*, the songs have the ring of ancestral discourse and ancient wisdom. They claim the mysterious past and all its authority as underlining the importance of their message (Kapwepwe VIII).

The *Mbusa* become mnemonic metaphors and the young listeners are emotionally caught up in the values and aspirations they represent. By participating in the dances and songs associated with them, they become rhythmically tied into the ideals the society communicates. Combined with the *Cisungu* -emphasis on the correct observance of ritual rules and reliance on elders (Richards 1956, 156), these oral factors greatly influence the content of Bemba ethics. The metaphorically delivered lessons are interactively appropriated.

The highly socialized and dramatized lessons inculcate a sense of "propriety" *Mucinshi* --what Bemba society deems fitting --as the oral ethical goal (Cf Havelock 1978, passim). There is no question of personal morality. Social propriety--what Durkheim (1965) calls "conscience collective"--is at issue: what is seemly and appropriate, what is accepted by the group. "An oral community is incapable of conceiving of a personal morality apart from the communal" (Havelock 1978, 35). The cultivation of personal moral virtue and the performance of good deeds are not as desirable as adherence to public norms. Thus, Richards identifies Bemba culture as "a 'shame' rather than a 'guilt society'" (1956, 156).

Nsoni "shame" is what the Bemba feel for misdeeds. Oral morality issues not so much from interior motivation as from public pressures to ensure conformity with proper tribal behavior and public penalties for non-compliance with social norms (Ong 1967, 134-35). Bemba behavior is determined more by taboo, where the outer constraints of command are imposed by feelings of affection and fear. There is a less developed sense of moral obligation, which arises from the inner implications of personal judgment.

Tanguy (1954) states as a general principle that for the traditional Bemba an act has no morality, if no publicity ensues and if the wrath of the spirits is not aroused (Idem, 183 and 203). Even virtue is public. Power and prestige are won from its recognition. A person's whole identity and character are publicly defined. As the proverb says: *Munshifika ku bwingi tapelwe shina* "Whoever does not mingle with the crowd is not given a name (i.e.) remains unknown" (White Fathers 1954, 348).

To be caught out in misdeeds and exposed is to be avoided at all costs. In the tradition, publicly humiliating punishments are meted out, like being tied naked to a pole in a village, or being ostracized from the community by mutilation, where one's eyes are put out, or ears, lips and nose cut off (Etienne 1948, 49-50). Malefactors are subjected to public insults, which abound in the language and are perversely prized: *Abaletukana e bakali, e balecindama* "Those who can hurl insults cleverly are fierce and are to be respectfully feared" (Tanguy 1954, 191-92). The Bemba exult in the oral art of insult (Cf Richards 1939, 173, 187, 190).

The public hurling of insults and the agonistic antagonism of extroverted peoples are characteristic of an oral culture. Oral peoples indulge in what Ong calls "oral fliting" (Cf Ong 1967, 207-22; see above, chap. 1, 13-14). During *Cisungu*, there is just such a period called *Kushikula* , when the silent initiates sit in submissive shame to be subjected by the elders and vociferous reproaches for their past behavior and stern counsel for future conduct (Richards 1956, 109-10). A high quotient of verbal combat is rhetorical and interactively necessary. It gets the audience's attention, arouses their interest, involves them and insures that what is said is retained (Cf Ong 1967, 237; 1982, 43-5).

Propriety, then, is socially enjoined and publicly enforced as the ethical pattern. It is embodied, for the most part, in a series of obligations to kith and kin,[10] promulgated with a deep sense of respect for elders' authority and celebrated in the veneration of ancestors (Cf Mpashi 1947).

Zahan (1970 and 1963) treats of African ethics almost exclusively in terms of speech and silence. Silence for the African, he says, is a sign of self-mastery. To control one's speech is to dominate one's passions and behavior. The mature African has a great facility for inhibiting reflexes of affective sensitivity and African reticence indicates personal integrity, temperance and interior peace. Hence, the best of African speech does not reveal one's inner self, but is restrained and artfully indirect (Zahan 1970, chap. 8).

Zahan's treatment of ethics in terms of reserved speech and silence would seem to be a boon for the oral-aural interests of this treatise. But his analysis makes too strong a case for the control of speech as a desire to preserve personal integrity and deepen individual interiority (Zahan 1963, chap. 6). These virtues reflect literate concerns, perhaps even French philosophical ideals. Oral people, as already discussed (See above, chap. 1, 12ff), are public persons and much given to extroversion. Reserved speech, as we saw in the preface, is indeed a much cultivated art. But it is not out of any introspective discipline for fostering serene, subjective rumination. Theirs is a desire to maintain the public accord. While describing the fragility of village bonds, whose very existence depends on good human relationships between the mostly kinsfolk who comprise its population, Richards (1939) remarks on how apprehensive the Bemba are of any actions likely to disrupt the group. Their conversations are constantly emphasizing the value of peaceful relations. They are afraid of persons whose quick tempers and sharp tongues make them liable to give or take offense easily. Prospective husbands inquire anxiously about women, whether they come from quarrelsome families or "make offensive remarks" *Ikusose fibi* . Reputable persons are those whose hearts do not get hot quickly and who ignore insults and give up rights in order to avoid friction. It is not just a mark of good breeding and good sense to be tolerant during a clash of personal interests. This traditional cultural attitude *Kusula* "to take no heed of insult," is religiously sanctioned. The Bemba are anxious lest a publicly aggrieved person die and become an "evil spirit" *Ciwa* (Richards 1939, 267-68).

So silence and speech control are publicly oriented disciplines and are more indicative of submission to social pressures than of personal dominance over one's behavior. Ritual silence, enjoined on initiates, reenforces social controls. For example, the marriage ritual dictates silence for the couple, lest their speech dissipate their fragile unity. The funeral rite enjoins silence in the bereaved lest speech communicate the dissolution of death to others. The *Mako* customs forbid speech between in-laws lest the great potential for clan quarrels be given voice. Loud speech is taboo in sacred places (*Chileshe XI*): tenuous links between the human and spirit worlds may be disrupted. In *Cisungu* , the girls observe silence, except to repeat the songs. They are often even tucked away in the corner of the initiation cottage, to impress on them further that they are of little consequence. In *Cisungu* as throughout their lives, they must properly submit to what is being done to them and to the traditional obligations imposed on them authoritatively by elders and husbands (Richards 1956, 126-29). They sing *Napelwa na mulume wa nkalamo* "I am given to my husband as to a lion," to be destroyed or smashed up (Richards 1956, 189-90). In each case, the concern is for communal order and compliance with social proprieties.

The Demise of *Cisungu*

In the old days *Cisungu* lasted from six months to a year (Richards 1956, 61-2). The ceremony continues to wane as it did in Richard's day, and for basically the same reasons which she enumerates (Cf Idem, 134).[11]

There are a couple of additional reasons for this demise, related to message **and** medium, and connected with the growth of literacy.

First, school-learning for girls has become their new rite de passage, where they are isolated from their families, achieve a new identity in a new group, learn an insiders' body of knowledge, assume a new responsibility in extra-familiar society. All of this is undergone in an atmosphere of hard discipline imposed by new authority figures (Cf Ong 1967, 251 and 1974, 5).

Secondly, in the schools, the girls learn biological facts of human reproduction. These are at variance with some of the traditional lore proffered by the *Nacimbusa* in *Cisungu* such as the Bemba dogma of descent. The latter holds that the child is entirely formed from the physical contribution of the mother and not the father (Richards 1956, 148). Thus, the content of *Cisungu* teaching is suspect in their schooled minds.

Thirdly, the girls, by reading and writing, develop a deeper sense of self-hood and individuality. They gain a sense of their own worth as persons, which belies much of the male attitudes perpetuated by *Cisungu's* teaching on accepted sex roles.

Fourthly, the authority of the oral representatives of the tradition has been undermined by the shift to the literate medium. Books are the new sources of learning and the written word is the new criterion of truth (Cf Snelson 1974, chap. 1).

Cisungu in the final analysis is an event of sound. The drumming, the clapping, the dancing, the singing, the shouting, the general uproar, which are supposed to last for weeks, create a *Musumba* , "a royal sacred village" (See below, chap. 3, 80ff). For one shining moment of their lives, the young women

inhabit this enchanted place. But the villages are smaller   now
that   many of the young and middle-aged are off in the towns   for
employment.   It   is   hard   to   raise a   noisy   quorum.   As   the
clamorous   world   of orality is quelled,   so   *Cisungu*   loses   its
hold.

Richards   remarks   near   the   end of   her   study   that   "the
frequent oral handling of the   *Mbusa* and other objects . . . may
also be significant from a psychoanalytical point of view" (1956,
153).   This   review of her data,   it is hoped,   has   shown   that
Cisungu symbols--emblems,   songs,   and   ritual   acts--declare   a
profoundly   oral   nature.   Their   oral coefficients affect   the
distinctive   development   of   Bemba   culture   and   the   social
differentiation of Bemba consciousness.

A Concluding Reflection

Through   their   myths and rituals,   the Bemba pose their   own
limit-questions   and posit their own partial,   tentative,   broken
experiences   of the whole.   Their discovery,   that the ultimate
meaning   of   Bemba   existence   is   internally   related   to   an
encompassing   whole,   is   an   existentially and   fundmentally
religious   experience (Tracy 1982,   257-58).   Bemba   mythic   and
ritual   symbols more or less appropriately enshrine the truth   of
their   more   or less adequate apprehension of the   whole.   Their
approximation   in experience and expression of the notion of   the
whole is endemic to all religious systms.   What   makes the   Bemba
religious   is their recognition of the decisiveness and   ultimacy
of   the   event,   which discloses and conceals the   power   of   the
whole.   What   makes their   religious system less   adequate   and
appropriate is their inability to distinguish what,   in   fact,   is
disclosed   from   what   is   concealed.

There   is   no   literate   technology   to   facilitate   Bemba
reflective   capacities.   Its   penetrating   tools   for   critical
analysis and consequent distanciation are not available to   Bemba
oral selves.   The powerful sounds of oral myths and rituals give
their   symbols an aura of **immediacy**,   of actual participation   in
the event they do in fact only **mediate**.   The meaning and truth of
the   symbols seem to be "already out there now real" (Tracy 1970,
122)   immediately   available   to   sense   for   recapture   and
reexperience.   Without   the technical capability to   distinguish
between   the literal and non-literal meanings of symbols'   double
intentionality,   the   Bemba cannot demythologize and deritualize.
They   cannot avoid the incoherence,   vagueness and   ambiguity of
symbolic   discourse.   Literacy   would herald a new level in   the
differentiation   of   consciousness and the evolution of   culture
(See below, Conclusion).

With   the technology of writing,   the Bemba could   explicate
the   existential   meanings   of   their   symbolic   system,   using
conceptual   categories   and precise criteria for determining   its

cognitive character and claims (Trach 1982, 268ff). In fact, literacy, with its books of abstract science and morality, is alienating the Bemba communal audience from the myths and rites. All the compelling paraphernalia of symbols, songs, drama and narrative, are emphatically associated with manifestation-oriented religion. But tribal celebrations are becoming less adequate and less appropriate for mediating the meanings and values, which must inform and motivate the lives of individuals. The more proclamation-oriented religion of Christianity has the greater chance of success in the literate economy. Its notion of the whole is conceived as a monotheistic, personal God, calling free individual selves to responsible action in history in order to build a world of justice and peace. This Christian God's word-event is normatively codified in texts named scripture (Tracy 1982, 248ff). The oral world and its divinity fade like distant sounds.

CHAPTER TWO FOOTNOTES

[1]The Bemba Charter Myth is recorded and/or commented on in the following resources: Luc de Heusch, *Myths et Rites Bantou,* Paris: Gallimard, 1973; E. Labrecque, "La Tribu des Babemba," *Anthropos* 28, 1933. P.B. Mushindo, *A Short History of the Bemba,* NECZAM, 1976. A. Roberts, *A History of the Bemba,* Madison: University Press, 1973. F. Tanguy, *Imilandu ya Babemba* , London: Oxford Press, 1949. White Fathers, *Ifyabukaya*, Chilubula, n.d.

In addition to these resources, the author has recorded and transcribed performances of the Charter Myth (Shimwalule VII; Chanda Mukulu IV).

[2]In preparing this section, Luc de Heusch's *Essais sur le symbolisme de L'inceste Royal en Afrique,* Brussels: Universite Libre de Bruxelles, 1958, and *Myths et Rites Bantou,* Paris: Gallimard, 1973, were especially helpful keys for decoding Bemba narrative symbols.

[3]The Bemba have another old tradition linking divinity and the sun. It is a domestic ritual for petitioning the sun in the cold season: the grinding-stone *Mwanawelibwe* or the stirring-spoon *Mwiko* is "inscribed with interacting lines" *Bashilapo Musalaba* , indicating and effecting the convergence of two forces (Labrecque, "Croyances des Bemba," 7).

[4]There is a certain amount of interesting historical discussion, which would identify Luchele Ng'anga as the fading tribal reminiscence of Portuguese missionary priests, who evangelized the Congo basin area in the late fifteenth century. They were no doubt adept in the medical arts and skilled in medieval technology, hence the name Ng'anga, which carries the connotations of religious magic, medicine, and craftsmanship. Perhaps one of these priests accomanied a migrating band in their wanderings across the plateau. Tanguy entertains these notions ("The Bemba" 1954, 7). Such a historical explanation would be further enhanced with the consideration of the *Babenye* kept in the "relic huts" of the Chitimukulu. Some of these relics accompanied the migrations and reportedly include, among other things, a very large book which could be a **Missale Romanum** for Catholic mass ritual, three statues of bearded men (saints?) and a statue of a woman with a baby in her arms (Tanguy, "The Bemba," 221). Since Bantu women carry babies on their backs, this latter could be, so the theory goes, a Catholic statue of the virgin madonna. Even early Scottish missionaries to Malawi in 1800 heard Africans singing hymns to her which had been imported in the 1600's by the Portuguese (Schoffeleers, M., "The Interaction of the M'Bona Cult and Christianity," in Ranger, **Themes in the Christian History,** 1975, 14-29).

The name Luchele would then be a Bantu rendition of a Portuguese name, like Lacerda, who passed through the region in the first half of the nineteenth century. Since he promised to come back to the Bemba, several subsequent Europeans have been greeted as Luchele Ng'anga Redivivus, notably Dr. David Livingstone, Bishop Joseph Dupont and even Chirupula Stephenson. The mystery of his unexpected arrival and disappearnce is preserved in idiomatic Bemba where to declare *Nafika Luchele Ng'anga* "I arrived Luchele Ng'anga," means to surprise someone with a visit (Bantungwa X).

But it is not necessary to establish Lucele Ng'anga as a historical figure in order to make sense of the narrative. There is even a sense in which such a task distracts from the structural meaning. It is as fraught with difficulty and dubious returns as the quest for the historical Jesus.

[5]This is a significant departure from the Eliadean model, which because of its linear conception of time in terms of "behind" and "in front of," considers ideals and origins as lying in the past. The African oral model is cyclic, not simply as an eternal repetition, but more precisely as a centering. What is past in a literate sense is what is perfect in an oral sense, and this lies at the center, to which everything else is tangent and from which all else radiates. This divergence from Eliade is more amply discussed below (Chap. 3, 85ff).

[6]In preparing this section, the following sources were especially helpful: A.I. Richards, <u>Chisungu: A Girls' Initiation Ceremony Among the Bemba of Northern Rhodesia</u>. London: Faber, 1956; N. Garrec, "Croyances et coutumes religieuses des Babemba," Chilonga, 1916, 77-90; L. Etienne, "A study of the Babemba and the neighboring tribes," Kasama, 1948, 27-37; J.J. Corbeil, "The Sacred Emblems," Mbala, N.D. Interviews with *Nacimbusa* "women initiators": Banapenge IV, Sampa XI.

[7]*Mbusa* are of three kinds: (1) over eighty fired-clay pottery models, painted red, white and black representing domestic objects, animals or historical characters, some realistically portrayed, others conventionally designed. Some are small enough to be handled; about a dozen others, made of unfired clay, are large enough for two or three of them to take up the floor space of the cottage. There they are sculpted, elaborately decorated with beans, soot and chalk each day and then replaced with new ones for the next evening's rites; (2) over thirty intricate wall designs of conventiona patterns on the inside of the cottage; (3) small bundles of real objects like food, firewood and tobacco (Richards, <u>Chisungu</u>, 59-60).

[8]Take, for example, the song: *Pali Mayo wandi / Epo amateye yafunika/ Pali Mayo wandi* . "Oh my mother / That is where the reeds are broken / Oh my mother" (Idem, appendix: Song #9). To the "uninitiated" *Bacipelelo*, the meaning revolves around the mother's happiness that so many young men are vying for her daughter's attention. To the initiated, however, the reed *itete* represents a phallus, whose power is released by even a young girl, humbling the greatest of men (I. Mwesa Mapoma, "The

determinants of style in the music of Ing'omba," Ph.D. thesis, University of California 1980, 45).

[9]For example, *Cisungu* opens with the *Nacimbusa* picking up in her mouth two small bowls of seeds and passing them on in the manner described. During a dance mime, while the women actors pretend to sow seeds in a garden, the *Nacimbusa* picks up a corn cob with her mouth and gives it to the initiates to bite. Later, white beads are tied around the twigs of the *Musuku* traditionally a feminine tree since it bears wild fruits. These beads, symbolic offerings to the matrilineal spirits, are bitten off in the mouths of the initiates, who hand them back along the hierarchy of women, who kneeling and ululating out of respect, receive them covered with the saliva of the previous women. The saliva recalls the spittle blessing of the spirits *Kupala amate*. All the while they are singing: *Kwapa takacila kubea* "The armpit is not higher than the shoulder." This song is repeated very often during *Cisungu* in order "to honor the elders" *Kucindika bakalamba* and impress on the initiates that youth is never as important as age (Richards, Chisungu, 72).

[10]Richards notes that once the tight bonds of traditional village-life are loosened and there are no kinship connections to keep a person in line, a highly demoralizing dynamic sets in. The agglomeration of peoples around a mission, or a town, or a city, does not provide the kinship setting, where ethical principles are acquired and enforced by public censure. In a milieu out of touch with this communal compulsion, strangers can become fair game for unlicensed behavior (Richards, "Anthropological problems in north-eastern Rhodesia," Africa, 5, 2, 1932, 134-36).

[11]The initiation rites were curtailed for a number of reasons: (a) the absence of productive men in the villages makes for food stores too small to provide a sufficient feast for the festival; (b) in a wage earning economy, male dominance is given a new emphasis and *Cisungu* is entirely organized by women; (c) traditional authorities, like chiefs and village heads, do not promote the rites, since there is nothing in it for them; (d) it was for a long time forbidden by missionaries and its boisterous drumming and dancing could hardly be carried on in secret, like the traditional rites of venerating the spirits (Richards, Chisungu, 134).

CHAPTER THREE

ORALITY AND DIVINITY

This chapter will open with a brief, general reflection on the role of fiction in religious discourse. This will set the context for a specific examination of Bemba oral performances and their religious function. Then, we will turn to a consideration of Bemba spirits. They are the prime protagonists in many traditional narratives and common rumors, whose constant repetition partially accounts for the reality attributed to spirits. We will portray these spirits as oral linguistic constructs in the Bemba world. This chapter will show how this social construction of reality is reenforced by the Bemba oral-aural propensity to conceive of even inanimate things in personalist terms and to verify their ideas in terms of what they traditionally hear. The spirits then will be understood to be leading linguistic lives as they are conjured up by the ontological power of the oral word. They may function as vehicles of Bemba moral lessons and as coordinants of their spatio-temporal organization.

Our discussion will then seek to expand the understanding of the reality of spirits by explaining their cognitive relationship to limit language and the notion of the whole. In this way, we can argue for the religious significance of spirits. In their oral capacity, they refer to and re-present those intimations of transcendence and ultimacy identified by historians of religion (Cf Van der Leeuw 1963, vol. 1, chap. 18; Eliade 1963, chap. 2). The chapter also advances the idea, contrary to most previous pious and scholarly opinions, that the Bemba tradition evidences profound predilections for polytheistic expressions of the transcendent and the ultimate. In addition, we will proffer the controversial view that the Bemba tradition retains traces of a primordial Mother-earth spirit. Finally, we will describe the spirit Lesa as one, who has been emancipated from the polytheistic trajectory of oral religion and conveniently set on a monotheistic track, primarily by the missionaries of literate Christianity. Lesa has also been stripped of Mother-earth imagery and elevated to the Christian position of Father-sky God.

Oral Performances and their Religious Function

This section will briefly reflect on the religious function Tracy assigns to fiction and then discuss Bemba performance of oral fiction against that background (Tracy 1975, 201-11). Like other forms of symbolic discourse, fiction satisfies the human need to imaginatively explore new possibilities for authentic living. Fiction does not simply provide an escape from the demands of ordinary life, but it gives refreshment to the minds and hearts of harassed people, transforming them by a creative reorientation. A society's cherished stories recapture and represent its essential meanings and values in the appropriate symbolic actions of heroes and villains as narrated by fiction.

Stories can have a powerful psychological influence. People are trained from childhood to pay attention to storytellers. They learn that storytellers are those who can be trusted and believed. Interesting and well-told stories hold and focus the attention of those who listen. Messages that have a specific and important cultural intent can be subtly embedded in stories so as not to alert and engage the resistance of listeners.

When such stories do not consciously advert to the character-forming action of their narratives' dramatic depiction of social mores, they can be said to have an implicit religious dimension. This is the case insofar as they impact positively on the readers' (listeners') behavior and thoughts. The readers (listeners) can be said to be caught up unawares in fundamental questions and responses relative to the whole of their lives by the disclosive power of the truth and value claims of the story.

When such stories consciously recognize and acclaim the ultimate rational and moral criteria of a tradition, they can be said to serve an explicit religious purpose; they narrate some limit experience of the whole in the limit language conventionally associated by their readers (listeners) with their culture's appropriation of the transcendent. In this case, the readers (listeners) can be said to be willingly celebrating their religious realities and reflectively committing themselves to the style and quality of life those ultimate ideals imply.

Bemba oral performances evidence both these implicit and explicit religious traits and fulfill the purpose of true fiction. Stories redescribe ordinary events in Bemba lives with an extraordinary flair. Tribal meanings and values are so radicalized and emphasized that seemingly concrete actualities are reworked into ideal possibilities. It is as if the very essence of what it means to be Bemba were distilled from reality and disclosed in imaginative narration for the audience's appropriation. The authentic way of being Bemba is vicariously reintroduced to be idealized for emulation or criticism.

Bemba oral tradition distinguishes between two major types of stories, *inshimi* , which normally include songs, and *imilumbe* , which conventionally teach explicit lessons. These performances begin with a formula, which emphasizes how present-day reality is rooted in the past, as ancestral wisdom continues to enliven and evaluate Bemba society: "A little thing was told, and that little thing remained, and people lived long ago as we lived" *Patile akantu, na kantu kalikele, na abantu balikele, balikele nge ifwe twikele* (Frost 1977, passim). The liberal use of proverbs, which distill the cumulative experience of Bemba society, reinforces this ancestral connection. Proverbs assure the listeners that the social message is being delivered from deep within the culture, and that the narrator is credibly versed in that tradition (Lutato 1980, 169). Then the performers continue with certain other formulae, set songs and traditional structures. Each oral performer draws upon them in presenting an unique creation, artistically consonant with the expectations of the audience gathered at the *Nsaka* ("palaver cottage"). Besides their entertainment value, the traditional stories symbolize and evoke feelings, concepts and actions sanctioned by the society (Meyer 1973).

The narratives do not leave the judgment of an action or situation to the audience. Instead, the performer, while subtly adjusting the story to maintain the participational interest of the listener, will inject the judgment of the ancestral tradition (Lutato 1980, 34 & 205). For example, the Bemba scholar Lutato judges it a literate misinterpretation of oral material (effected by the distanced relationship of writer and reader), when the trickster in the transcription of a traditionally oral narrative is written up as getting away with impunity for evil deeds. The copresence and interaction of performer and audience would prevent that apparent approval of socially unacceptable action in the oral forum (Lutato 1980, 34 and 205; for a discussion of literate mismanagement of oral proverbs, see below, 102ff).

The social utility of the stories is integral to Bemba aesthetics. They demand that "a beautiful moral lesson" *ubusuma bwe funde*, either to promote social harmony or to preserve cultural values, be implicit in the conception of characters (Lutato 1980, chap. IV). Each character, whether animal or human, displays one single trait determining its behavior for good or bad. Complex characters would not make a clear cut moral choice for the listener. The contrast of such polarized characters focuses the intended ethical message as unambiguously as possible (Cf Ong 1967, 203-04). Each character represents only one moral metaphor.

Although named characters are rare in oral tradition, sometimes a significant teknonym is used as a mnemonic device to underscore the moral point of the narrative. *Fololowa* may be the name given to a greedy person, since *kufola* means "to eat in great quantity" and *Bowa* is "a mushroom seasonal delicacy." Some characterizations briefly retard the narrative flow, while the listeners sound out the moral nature of the metaphoric agent.

Abstract moral qualities are frequently made concrete in the physical appearance of the character, "big headed" pride for example. Or the guilty conscience of a character may be animated, projected outwards and finally cast as other harrying figures (Lutato 1980, 197).

Good and evil are erected into metaphoric personifications of actions and agents, laudable deeds and abominable ways, in traditional narratives. Moral prescriptions and traditional wisdom cluster around their typical characters, who embody public concerns and command communal attention (Ong 1967, 203-04; 1982, 69-71). Some characters are traditionally stereotyped, such as the Rabbit as the conventional trickster, or the Jackal as the conventional dupe. Opposing patterns of desirable and undesirable behavior can be immediately established (Cf Frost 1977, passim).

The purposes of these stories derive from their general genre as didactic legends. They entertain, teach problem solving, correct social conduct, and instill proper speech patterns and orthodox religious belief and behavior (Mapoma 1980, 59; Lutato 1980, 204-05; Frost 1977, passim). Ethics and asethetics are united in the oral medium (Cf Leach 1965).

But the function of these highly structured oral performances is not totally circumscribed by their construction and maintenance of the Bemba cultural universe, which they share with conventional etiological narratives like the charter myth. Raymond Firth (1961), Edmund Leach (1965) and Jan Vansina (1965) have demonstrated that oral traditions provide models for change and variation as well as stability. In the religious parlance of this discussion, symbols created by religious imagination need **both** a negative denouncement of whatever actually ails a society **and** a positive articulation of however possible a society intends to reform (Tracy 1975, 210-11).

When the stories play to their audiences' expectations, they make the Bemba cultural world a whole and encourage participation in its social certainties. Thus, both *Nshimi* and *Milumbe*, as fictional performance narratives, generally focus on *Mucinshi*, the respectful mode of behavior which represents the basic values of Bemba social propriety (Richards 1939, 128-29). A character, for example, may be dramatized with a tragic flaw disregarding these basic laws and values of social life. It thus offers vicarious suffering to a Bemba audience, sparing it the risk of communal dissolution in reality (Frost 1977, chap. 1).

When these same Bemba genres carry values in defiance of traditional practices and norms (Cf Simukoko 1978, 13), they do so within certain tolerances. These tolerances do not totally subvert conventional logic but they experimentally introduce prudential qualifiers to the inherited wisdom. *Milumbe* are more likely to indulge in this slightly perplexing and threatening deconstruction of the cultural contract than *Nshimi*. For *Milumbe* (a term applied to imaginative performances as well as to other symbolic art forms like sculpture and painting) represents a continuum of conundrums, predicaments, trickster tales and riddles. Tales of this sort center around reversals. The resolution of a dispute occurs, when illogic is transformed into logic, disadvantage is turned to advantage, the weak become strong, and stupidity reigns over cleverness. The famine/food, village/forest, male/female, life/death, inside/outside and similar polarities are prominent structural features (Frost 1977, chap. 2). A *Nshimi* tale, for example, may dramatically present the need for "in-law avoidance customs" *Mako* . That bit of cultural reenforcement may be immediately followed by a rebuttal in a *Milumbe* tale, where the *Mako* silence is carried to such an extreme that an in-law fails to warn another of some impending disaster, destroying the very relationship *Mako* is intended to preserve (Idem, chap. 5).

Although individual stories may construct or deconstruct the Bemba cultural world, they are in fact performed dialectically for a listening community from counterbalancing viewpoints. An equilibrium of conflicting values is reestablished or an obsolescent tradition is amended for contemporary circumstances. For example, another cultural value--the Bemba loyalty to a hierarchical system of autocratic chiefs--is vigorously promoted in heroic legends, such as the charter myth, (See above, chap. 2, 42-44), and in *Nshimi* . Yet, in *Milumbe* , the cherished figure of the "trickster rabbit" *Kalulu* uses irrepressible cunning to outwit the high and the mighty. *Kalulu* represents the Bemba egalitarian tradition, paradoxically asserting the dignity of common people (Frost 1977, chap. 4). In this way, the oral tradition as a whole reflects a proper respect for figures of authority. At the same time it affirms a proper regard for those who lack any status (Idem, chap. 7).

The *Milumbe* and *Nshimi* do not merely tell a pleasant story to evoke a moral maxim. They are fictions. Like all good fiction, they are endowed with a transformative power in the Bemba world. By their limit-use of metaphor and narrative, Bemba traditional performers so intensify and typify the norms of proper behavior that they transgress their audience's expectations. They jar their complacency into a recognition of the exceptional exertions enjoined for authentic Bemba living (Cf Tracy 1975, 204ff; see below, 85ff).

The Rumors of Spirits

Besides the highly structured, formal narratives, which for the most part, tend to be rather conservative by nature, there are less formal genres. Common gossip, rumors and simple stories are constantly bandied about in Bemba concourse. These informal genres operate under the same oral dynamics that give credibility and stability to existing information. They encode and enforce some of the same cultural concepts and are emotionally imbued with the same religious ideals. But, since they thrive on multiple meanings, they are more amenably manipulated to accommodate new situations and interests. They provide an agreeable climate of changed communal opinion, which then can unconsciously assimilate the homeostatic adjustments (See below, 106ff) in the formal genres. What is of true value in the community's new experience can be made to share the respect owed to the tradition (Booth 1975, 89-90).

In addition, by instilling a little fear and motivating listeners to follow traditional behavioral prescriptions, these innumerable "ghost-stories" and rumors of spirits provide a float of evidence on which belief in spirits rests. Such informal genres (as well as the formal genres!) enjoy a remarkable success in eliciting popular credulity in sometimes preposterous tales. Their efficacy is directly dependent on two propensities operative in the oral-aural economy of knowledge. First, everything is conceived in personalist terms, and secondly, the ear, not the eye, is the organ of truth.

Orality and the personalist paradigm. It is not particularly helpful to talk of animism in characterizing Bemba religion. There is a better explanation for what is happening when the Bemba point to a waterfall and declare *Kwabe Ngulu* "a personal spiritual force is acting there" (Kalonga XII). The key lies in understanding the oral proclivity to accommodate the knowledge of everything else to what is known best--other persons (See above, chap. 1, 2-3). The phenomenology of sound and the ontology of listening support this claim. Ihde (1976) observes that sound penetrates, "obliterating inner and outer distinctions" (75), making things "come alive" (82). Through an "imaginative mode of auditory experience," listening becomes "polyphonic" and imputes voice, language and personality to the sounded presence of the world of things (Idem, chaps. 9-11). Vision objectifies. Sound personifies and gives voice to the environment, implicating things, persons and gods into the same life world (Idem, chap. 2).

Ong agrees (1982, 71-4). After contrasting the psychodynamics of sight versus sound, he concludes: "Knowledge of things . . . is more immediately assimilable to knowledge by sight; knowledge of persons . . . is more immediately assimilable to knowledge by hearing" (Ong 1977, 140-41).

Since the Bemba mental mechanism is driven predominantly by sound, human behavior is the paradigm for their knowledge. The Bemba are great observers and judges of human character, a fact dramatically brought home to any outsider attending a village's evening entertainment. In marvelous mimicry and wonderfully apt nicknames, private idiosyncrasies and peculiarities of personality are gently and humorously revealed. Bemba conversation revolves around persons, partially because the mechanics of oral noetics prevents them from finding out much about things (Ong 1967, 307). Horton (1964, 85-104; 1967) sees this as the primary difference between African and scientific thought systems, which otherwise have much in common. Both patterns of reasoning develop models to explain and predict, in order to control the diversity of experiences in the world. Since explanatory models must exhibit a regularity and order familiar enough to qualify as prototypical, argues Horton, the more socially astute African chooses the human world and likens nature to people.

For the Bemba, persons are better known. But there is error in Horton's characterization of the personal world as qualifying for the African archetype of knowledge on the grounds that it fulfills the requirements of "regularity and order." On the contrary, persons are the most unpredictable of creatures. The oral person, alert to the world of sound, thinks of it as a world of querulous voices. This type of person, enveloped in a confused, fearful state of excitement, and under duress, projects hostilities and anxieties outward onto the natural world and other persons (Ong 1967, 131-34). Later it will be shown that this unpredictability of a personally wrought universe provides the background for witchcraft (See below, chap. 4, 121ff).

Ong would contend that the Bemba "choice" of a personalist rather than a naturalist paradigm is based on an oral feeling: somehow, nothing, like no one, is completely objectificable into precise and distinct definition. Indeed such clarity is somehow even devastating. Persons and thngs are not entirely unlike each other and are best known by a sort of intersubjective exchange (Ong 1977, 139-41).

Cause and effect relationships are relevant to Bemba conceptions of the world, but only as personally construed: if something happens, it is because somebody has done something. Some perverse or benevolent will is acting. Personal decisions and human motivations are familiar to oral society, and so events are ascribed to personal action and things are conceived as persons. Havelock observes that the gods of Homer's and Hesiod's oral precursors are not so much objects of cult as they are necessary ingredients in the vocabulary of oral description and orally preserved records of causality:

> If all our knowledge of our environment . . .
> and all the moral directives we give our
> children have to be reported and preserved as
> a narrative series: if the facts have to be
> stated either as things that happen or as
> things that are done (and the latter form of
> statement is in fact preferred), then the
> preserved record must be populated by agents
> who perform acts regarded as important or
> produce the phenomena which require
> explanation . . . they have to be super-
> agents, that is, divine, in order to be
> everywhere, in order to cover the territory
> (Havelock 1982, 227ff).

Havelock's statement should be a sobering qualification to any sweeping generalization about Africans' supposedly inherent religiosity, which is based on the pervasive presence of divinized beings in oral narratives and in popular conversation.

The habitual oral synthesis of cause-effect relationships in personalist terms produces another important religious corollary. As effects are diverse and plural, so too are the personal beings who cause them. An oral religion thus forms a decently populous pantheon, which can provide opportunity for multiple personal conflicts and agreements. They become a convenient explanation for everything that goes on in the world. It is more plausible that the melange of good and evil, which is the human lot and nature's issue, is motivated by many powerful spirits than by the inscrutable will of a single God (Ong 1967, 206-07; see below, 77 and 90ff).

There is also a poignancy about the oral propensity to populate the relatively unpeopled world around them, and a desperation about their imputation to inanimate nature a life-like glow (Ong 1967, 296-304). The Bemba live in isolated villages scattered in the vast forests and savannahs. They conjure up numerous personal presences, symbolized by "nature-spirits" *Ngulu* haunting marvelous forest phenomena and by "ancestral spirits" *Mipashi* , inhabiting the "abandoned villages" *Fibolya* (Labrecque n.d., 8-11). These provide plenty of comforting retreats for personal communication and social feelings to dispel loneliness and alienation. Rumors of spirits are rife, firstly, because the Bemba tend to and need to populate their world with personal presence.

Aurality and the criterion of truth. Secondly, the criterion of reality in oral hermeneutics is whether something is consonant with an auditory synthesis. The ear is the organ around which the Bemba sensorium is organized, and the mouth is the primary means of communication. In their folklore, the Bemba depict the "rabbit" *Kalulu* as the cleverest of animals. When asked what made the *Kalulu* so smart, Mpundu answered in narrative terms: *Amatwi ayakulu* "its tall ears" by which it has "the ability to hear the slightest noise" *Kukwatila ulutwi* . Since it hears much, it knows much. Its other physical feature, *Akana kalatikatika* "a mouth in constant motion," gives the impression of "speaking words all the time" *Kwati kalasosa utumashiwi tumo tumo* (Mpundu XI). This is confirmed by the proverb: *Icisosa cipa mano* "conversation gives brains."

What others say, what one hears--these are decisive evidence for truth and reality in this hearsay culture. (See above, chap. 1, 8ff). Thus, when the marvelous story of Ituta's easily catchable but uncookable fish was recited, one boy near Malole confirmed the story as emphatically true. He said, "I have heard that story two times now with my own ears" *Naumfwa ku matwi yandi miku inga? Ibili* ! (Chileshe XI). The indigenous evidence for the spirits is found to be a linguistically constructed world of spirits. Its only reference to reality is the sounds of endlessly circulated and elaborated accounts. These become evidence for themselves, emerging as variations on the theme and structure of spirit stories and returning to the traditional deposit as verification. Repetition is thus corroboration. The soundness of an idea is tested by sound. The Bemba seldom confirm in terms of what is seen but often in terms of what is heard: *Icumfwa matwi: amenso tayomfwa* "Understanding is a function of the ears; the eyes do not understand a thing."

In fact, another proverb *Cintu mu minwe, amenso yalabepa* states that "the eyes are the source of lies." All the sounds from their own experience of the world and from the telling of their elders converge on the fabulous construct of the spirit world (Cf Kacuka V). A place where rumors of spirits abound is called *Calo ca matwi matwi* "a territory of ears and ears" (White Fathers 1954, 299). The telling of tales rings true, setting up a sympathetic vibration with the community's conditioned expectations as with a tuning fork. The spirits are authenticated not in virtue of their historical or visual reliability, but on the authority of the speakers and in the receptivity of the hearers. To speak about the spirits is to feel their power. The stories create a reality in which the hearers can partake. This is possible not just by vicarious participation limited to imaginative identification with the story, but by the lively interaction, which oral communication entails.

Such is the active forum in which the orally created spirits are encountered. Oral words are powerfully effective in arousing images in the listeners and fixing for them the emotions and ideas with which they will associate events. People perceive and remember not ony what the sense organs deliver, but what linguistic and cultural habits and past experience predispose for them (Allport & Postman 1965, 143). Factual details, which might be used to disprove a rumor, are lost in transmission, and only the core-matter—the "fact" of the spirits—is retained. A rumor, finding ready reception in the listeners' minds, becomes its own verification (Idem, 105). Spirits occupy an important and ambiguous role in Bemba psychology. Rumors about them circulate freely as they explain uncertainties or vent anxious tensions in terms of them (Cf Idem, passim). The Bemba penchant for copiousness and elaboration of instances are the oral equivalent of logical connection and reasonable evidence (Cf Havelock 1963, 175). What is repeated by rumor is reinforced. The oral mind hoards like-experiences into dense clusters of plural reports, and, by this habit of associative thinking, rests its hearsay case for the reality of spirits (Cf Ong 1982, 37-41).

The Reality of Spirits

Is there, then, no reality of the spirits outside of the language and the stories about them? First of all, there is a certain psychiatric reality which Jaynes (1977) attributes to spirits; this will be discussed later in a section on "spirit-possession" (See below, chap. 4, 132ff).

Secondly, there is another dimensional reality assignable to spirits. Spirit-language can be legitimately described as a limit-language. It conveys certain limit experiences which fundamentally affect the Bemba horizons of meaning and value. Listeners to these stories feel that a disclosure of the ultimate truths and values is offered to them, making a claim for their total acceptance and complete trust. They find themselves at that limit, as they perceive a radical wholeness to the universe and believe in the adequacy of their communal traditions and customs to be in touch with that whole. They are brought to that limit, as they strive to live lives in conformity with what, in story-form, the tradition sanctions as socially proper. They participate in that limit, as they try to cope in ritual with the negative boundary situations of witchcraft, sickness and death, or when they ritually celebrate the positive high moments of life. The births of children, the coming of age of young women, and bountiful harvests--all are traditionally narrated as the blessings of the spirits. Language about spirits is the Bemba symbolic articulation of the limit-experience of the whole. In the surprisingly odd stories about spirits, normal speech is belabored to the limits of language and ordinary scenes are strained to an extraordinary scenario (Cf Ramsey 1957). The Bemba performers try to repeat that uncanny experience of the whole by making the limit-situation linguistically available to others. Imagine, for example, the audience's startled reaction to the uncanny conclusion of the odd story about a country-wide famine. A young man, whose family has been fed by the *Mipashi* "spirits," insists, against their wishes, on seeing what the spirits look like. When he breaks into the spirits' cottage, an "evil spirit" *Ciwa* rushes out to be reincarnated as a person and "the young man just becomes a skeleton (walking along with his bones clanking against each other) *Sokoya, sokoya, sokoya, sokoya, sokoya*" (Frost 1977, chap. 2).

In answer to this section's opening question, we may say that the reality of spirits is related not to the literal meaning of their limit-language, but to its cognitive content referencing the notion of "the whole."

Orality and the Plurality and Definition of Spirits

Before we can turn, in the next section, to a discussion of the several kinds of spirits, two prior matters must be considered. We will give an accounting in oral terms (a) for the plurality of spirits, and (b) for the lack of precision in distinctions between them.

(a) Ong postulates that an oral religion will favor polytheism and animism, for the reason that a culture needs a convenient explanation for its plurality of personally construed capricious causes. He also surmises that an oral people with a sparse population, isolated in a vast forest, would spawn a spiritual multitude just for the comforting presence of these religiously fictitious companions (Cf Ong 1967, 206-07; see above, 74). The plurality of Bemba spirits is partially accountable to these oral factors.

(b) There are several distinctions between kinds of spirits, which the Bemba would appreciate, but which they would not enforce as hard and fast definitions. The various accounts written by missionaries and social scientists tend to set out precise parameters for usage, according to the dictionaries of the Bemba language which they compile. As a matter of fact, the Bemba themselves are not so rigid in their speech.

The meaning of a word cannot be determined by appealing to a dictionary.[1] An oral culture settles the meaning in the speaking. The meaning is negotiated in the dialogue and renegotiated if the circumstances warrant it. The Bemba habitual "meeting place" *Iteko* is often called *Nsaka* when it refers to the physical structure. But *Iteko* also refers to the meaning of a word, as in the phrase *Basose shiwi ilyabule teko* "they speak a word with no meaning," i.e., lacking the warranty of common usage. (White Fathers 1954, 350). In oral cultures "the meaning of each word is ratified in a succession of concrete situations" (Goody 1968, 29). The oral word is very pliable and merges with all that actually goes on in a speech situation to convey meaning (See above, chap. 2, 55). The Bemba are particularly partial to the profounder resonances and remoter implications of their vocabulary, whose symbolic overtones are often overlooked by the literal meanings assigned by dictionaries.

Ngulu, Milungu, Mipashi . Those cautions are germane to the distinctions made here between *Ngulu* "nature spirits," *Milungu* "divinities," *Mipashi* "human spirits."[2] Early literate accounts write of "semi-divinities," "demi-gods," "divine emanations" or "refractions," and "divinized forces of nature," when discussing *Milungu* or *Ngulu*; they leave the *Mipashi* on the more human level of quasi reincarnation (Labrecque n.d.; Etienne 1948; Tanguy 1954). The Bemba do not develop a taxonomy of spiritual powers and certainly do not, in the tradition, establish a hierarchy, where one or the other exercises central or supreme control (Garvey 1974, 35). An amorphous, indefinite and fluid belief surrounds them in the tradition--a fact which tempts the intellectual and emotional selection of data to fit the interpreter's perspective. It would be easy to enlist Bemba spirits as "mercenaries in foreign battles" over the theological nature of their cult as either worship or veneration (Okot p'Bitek 1971, 12).

Bemba oral tradition tends to discuss spirits by proper name rather than in generalities and to set out their attributes as

typical   qualities rather than as personal profiles (Cf Ong 1982,
151-55).   The reports from the tradition, taken as they are from
various times and places, are often contradictory and show how
futile and illusory it is to try to pin-down orally conceived
material to literate frames.[3] No category of spirits is really
distinct   from   the   other.   There are   considerable   oral
overlappings between them.   If extraordinary or hyperbolic
qualities are attributed to them, it is in the oral interests of
making them memorable and for the religious purpose of charging
them with a metaphorical potency to deliver meaning beyond
immediate apprehension.

Together the spirits form the primary religious reality of
the Bemba, dominating their ordinary and ceremonial life, because
Imilungu e Itupela fyonse "the spirits are the ones who give us
everything" (Tanguy 1954, 178). The cult of spirits, especially
those of royal ancestors, can be called the established religion,
incorporating all of its cardinal beliefs and practices.

The Bemba have absolute confidence in the efficacy of their
approaches to spirits.   There is no religious doubt nor is there
any religious "faith." As Horton (1967) shows, African oral
religion deals not so much in faith as it does in the pragmatic
techniques of designing symbols and metaphors for understanding,
predicting and controlling all that is extant.   Their religious
undertakings are accompanied by absolute certainty in their
successful outcome. The spirits cannot, will not, resist.   If
there is some delay, it is because the rite has been deficiently
carried out or the practitioner has not attended to the proper
order of things.   Living humans, not spirits, are actually in
control (See above, chap. 1, 20ff).

The term *Ngulu* or *Ngulu sha mushili* "spirits of the soil"
is used of the *Milungu* (Labrecque n.d., 8). It often is applied
to any natural phenomenon which surprisingly erupts into the
monotony of the ordinary woodland. *Ngulu* are also thought
capable of temporarily possessing people, who are in turn called
Ngulu (See below, chap. 4, 132). *Ngulu* properly speaking are
not "prayed to" *Kupepa*, nor "worshipped" *Kupupa* but are only
"invoked" *Kulumbula fye ngulu* . But when one characterizes Bemba
traditional religion as revolving around "the worship of tutelary
spirits" (Werner 1971), one refers primarily to the *Mipashi*
"spirits of deceased persons": "Somme toute la religion des
babemba consistait surtout en *Lukuko, kupale mipashi* " (Garrec
1916, 47).   Each human person has one of these *Mipashi* .   As
defunct ancestors, they are the principle of matrilineal clan-
life and are thought capable of being recycled permanently in
succeeding generations.

In   accordance with the anthropocentric principle of Bemba
religion (See above, 20ff), the power of *Mipashi* is an extension
and intensification of the very powers they enjoyed as human
beings. To qualify as worshipful ancestors (Cf Labrecque n.d.,

11-14), they should have achieved a longevity in life, ensuring an accumulation of profound experience and knowledge. They should also have lived in conformity with ancestrally sanctioned social propriety (See above, chap. 2, 59ff). At death, they are immortalized as oral constructs in narratives enshrining their virtues. That they are not actual historical personages endowed with such heroic proportions is not religiously relevant. It is enough that they have become symbols, cultural facts, representative of the transforming possibilities available to the community (Cf Tracy 1975, 215-16).

Fiwa . Another important group of spirits are those to whom responsibility for serious, persistent troubles is attributed. These *Fiwi* (*Fibanda*) are spirits of malefactors—witches, suicides, murderers, et al.—who die with bitter grievances and return to haunt and inflict injuries on the living from whom they suffered injustices (Labrecque n.d., 20; Etienne 1948, passim; Kabwe IV).

Fiwa are definitely oral constructs, "mainly associated with and belonging to the world of narratives (*ifishimi* and *imilumbe*), riddles (*ifishimbiko*) and proverbs (*amapinda*)" (Nkandu 1981, 10). Within narratives, they are further associated with the world of sound, where they are "sought out with barking dogs and beating drums" *Bafwaya nembwa no tuoma* (Chime 1980, 2). They are recognized "in their noisy conversation and loudly rumbling walk" *Filelanda no kulanda, fileisa filelula ifitali* (Idem, 3). Finally, *Fiwa* function in narrative as protagonists of the moral code (Nkanda 1981, 29-30; Frost 1977, chap. 2), dramatically reinforcing the moral lesson by showing that misbehavior never goes unpunished (Chele 1979). In funeral rites, oral extroversion tends to project *Fiwa* and transform the unconscious ill-will toward deceased relatives into the explicit ill-will of departed spirits toward bereaved mourners.

Spirits and the Oral Organization of Space and Time

There is another significant function which Bemba spirits exercise for their oral people. It has to do with their indigenous characterization as *E baleteke calo kale bashamfumu* "ancestral chiefs who ruled the land long ago" (Richards 1969, 241), *Bene calo* "owners of the land" or *Sha mushili* "pertaining to the soil," and as *Bene kale* "inhabitants of the previous time." The ancestral spirits and their shrines are bound up with Bemba notions of space and time. Rivers, mountains, trees, caves, waterfalls, water-sources, and abandoned villages—all places sacralized by the spirits of former chiefs and fixed in memory by the stories told about them—are the coordinates, wherein the Bemba locate themselves in space and to which the Bemba refer themselves in time. As the proverb says: *Ifikolwe ne calo* "Ancestors and territory are one and the same." Travel across such space can mean a transformation over time. In the

descriptive integration which a story effects through such
metaphors (Cf Tyler 1981, 17), landscape computes as an
articulate moral category, and temporal passage becomes a measure
of progress or decline. At the very limits of humanly habitable
space and at the farthest moment from present time abides that
reality tentatively alluded to under the spontaneously operative
notion of the whole.

Acoustic Space

Traditional Bemba places and ways form an intelligible unity
not through road maps and street signs, but through their
relation to sacred places that are their centers. Bemba
intervals of time are marked off not by calendars and clocks, but
by daily rituals and periodic festivals. These extraordinary
locations and durations are, in fact, the spatio-temporal
manifestations of "the whole."

By employing familiar tribal geography as the scene of
divine and heroic activity, the charter myth of ancestral
migration justifies the rights of living members of the royal
dynasty to rule over their present territories, precisely because
they were conquered and defined by the ancestors "in the
beginning" (Cf Roberts 1973, 38-56; see above, chap. 2, 37ff).
All Bemba space has been organized according to that archetypal
dispersal of the clans over the landscape. Locating themselves
in space gives the Bemba a sense of who they are as a society and
establishes as sacred the order they impose (Cf Levi-Strauss
1966, 10). The Bemba celebrate, as sacred, those places wherein
the ancestors lived and continue to inhabit as spirits. There
the spirits make their presence known--an event which Eliade
(1959) terms a "hierophany," a manifestation of other-ness within
the homogeneity of surrounding space. The space is experienced
as religious, because it is qualitatively different either in its
aspect or in its significance. Perhaps some great event took
place there, or a great person was born or died there. For
whatever reason, the revered space becomes a center to which all
else is referred as a criterion of reality and validity. It is a
point for orientation, a frontier, a "limit" of ordinary space,
and a measure of value or meaning in the culture. It is the
place wherein "the whole" is disclosed. The story of the place
is recited and celebrated in dance or ritual, so that the
participants can renew their contact with its sacred character,
while reflecting on the great moments associated with it. Thus
do spirits, already linguistically bound to story, become tied to
space as well.

Ong (1967) agrees with Eliade's analysis of sacred space.
But he emphasizes its acoustic character, a consideration which
applies to the Bemba oral life world. Sacred space is indeed
space-plus, for it is not possible to be reverent toward a thing
as a thing (Ong 1967, 163). But it is primarily the sound

associated with the place, which conveys the notions of presence, power and personality so indispensable for religious experience. Its sacrality is not so much a function of its hierophanic aspects (Eliade 1959, passim) as its hierophonic acoustics (Cf Ong 1967, 166ff). Space plus sound engenders an inkling of uncanny power that penetrates and reveals interiors without violating them. There is no physical invasion or collision by sound, and yet a sense of inwardness and interiority is insinuated by its resonances with the human voice (Ong 1982, 71-4). A space full of sounds is assimilated to a place of ringing personal communications. Habits of auditory synthesis, according to a phenomenology of sound, perceive space acoustically. It is not in fields of vision spread out in front, but diffused all around in a vast interiority, with the human person at the center of all the cosmic interlocutions (Cf Ihde 1976, chap. 6). Space apprehended by a sensorium organized around hearing is a space inhabited by personal presences in dialogue with human auditors (See above, chap. 1, 2-3). This space is endowed with sacral qualities. The personal, powerful, holistic presence it manifests by its sound has permanent religious possibilities.

In describing the interior of the royal burial ground of senior Bemba chiefs, the Shimwalule resorted to narrating what is heard therein:

> *Muno musumba mu mushitu mwaumfwa fye kwatampa*
> *ukubuluma ne miti yalakontauka. Ninshi*
> *inshimu kuti shakumana fye monse shatamfya*
> *na bantu mu ng'anda .* Here in this royal
> place (Musumba) inside the forest-grove there
> begins a lion-like roaring as if trees were
> breaking apart and bees were swarming from all
> sides chasing people into their homes
> (Shimwalule VII).

A *Musumba* is what the Bemba call such places. Formerly, Bemba travellers knew they were approaching a chief's village, the residence of royal ancestral spirits, from the great tumult that engulfed them:

> *Batesha ne ng'oma sha ng'omba*
> *ishingili shilelila ku isano . . .*
> *Na bakamangu, ne nitumba ilelila . . . ne*
> *mangu shilelila . . . na bantu bamo baleimba*
> *mu bwalwa no kulishe ng'oma no kucinda.*
> *Kwali icongo icapusanapusana mukati ka musumba.*
> *. . . No pano pene epo bubalilo kuca, nga*
> *abulalekelesha mu mbali monse.* They heard the
> drumming and singing of the royal poet crying
> out from the court, and the royal war drums
> pounding . . . and the people partying with
> singing and dancing to drums. Such a great
> din from various sources in the royal city! .

. . And right here, this is where the sun
dawns; where all roads lead (Mushindo 1958,
5).

Noted for its noise, the *Musumba* connotes life, power, and
throngs of talking, boisterous people in celebration. The chief
moves in an arena of sound sometimes supplied by the *Imishikakulo*
an almost incomprehensible verse, thought to be cognate to the
Luba language. It is cried out by the tribal elders in high
pitched and rapidly paced voices acclaiming the chief. These
beautiful songs flow along producing sound for sound's sake,
populating the royal presence with a crowd of voices (Chileshe
XI).

Any sacred center of the Bemba tribe must evidence the same
uproar, either in its own sounding or in the ritual and mythic
story assigned to it. A few of their sacred places are described
now in these acoustic terms.

Trees and forests. There are hundreds of sacred trees in
the Bemba tradition. But the tree's most significant religious
dimension is often overlooked by literate investigators, whose
trained eye for detail regard only its aspect and do not attend
to tone. The tree is sounding continually with the rustle of its
leaves in the breeze, or with the groaning and creaking of its
branches in the wind, its singing birds, humming bees, and insect
buzz. The tree is the vocal instrument of the spirits, who, not
surprisingly, are also called "winds" *Myela* (Oger 1972, 2).

Forests, too, are considered sacred, intensifying the
sacrality of the tree. There is a Bemba riddle (Kashoki n.d.),
which describes one of the elements of the forest's
attractiveness, not in its visual aspect, but,
characteristically, in its aural tenor *Akalimba tulishapo bonse?
Ciimpuusa!* "The thumb-piano (lamellophone) we all play on? The
shrubs grow out as shoots from tree trunks!" As a person walks
through the forest, there is a constant brushing against bushes,
making a sort of music.

The forest itself is, of course, full of its own sounds.
The winds, the cries of birds and animals, the crash of game
fleeing in the underbrush, the high pitched screech of cicadas in
the heated air, the rush of streams and rivers, the groan of
weighty trunks and branches, even its sudden silences, all
contribute to the sound effect of the sylvan experience.

The tales of uncanny events, like the appearance of fiery
lights at night, the sudden disappearance of villagers, or the
legend that caught fish cannot be cooked (Chileshe XI), are all
essential to the sacred character of the forest. The
transmission and articulation of the visitor's experience in the
limit-language of religious mystery and spirits make the place
acoustically awesome (Mpundu XI). The sound that the story

brings, with its attendant personal, powerful presence, transposes what otherwise would be only a beautiful, beneficial and oftentimes dangerous place into a space charged with sacrality. Therein the whole is manifest, an eruptive instance of the mysterium fascinans et tremendum.

Some forest groves, called *Mwalule* , receive their sacrality from their association with the deaths, funerals or burial places of chiefs. The most important of these is that original *Mwalule* near Chinsali, where the paramount and other senior chiefs are buried (Shimwalule VII). Since there are short historical myths associated with the chiefs' memory at the shrines in the forest, those memorable tales populate the otherwise empty space making it sacred with personal ancestral presences (Ong 1967, 168). Other historical sites, sacralized by memories of ancestors, are the *Fibolya* "abandoned villages," where spirits are said to linger. Narrative accounts of events and persons are constantly recited about these *Fibolya* . Warm feelings of affection and pride are retained by the living on their visits to pick a few fruits (ancestral gifts) from derelict gardens. From the depths of the forest, as from the hands of the ancestors, a veritable cornucopia pours forth blessings of game, mushrooms, medicines, etc. The reverence and respect are for a place linking the living to the dead, reenforcing the sense of continuity with the ancestors. Since villages are moved regularly and frequently, the whole *Mpanga* "forest" is warmed by human and ancestral habitation over the years. This enchantment of the forest by storied *Fibolya* helps to make it a fitting place of worship (Richards 1939, 237-39). Ancient battlegrounds everywhere in the forest as at *Kuli Ituta* , where many died and much blood seeped armies of Bemba warriors' and foes' spirits into the soil, are also venerated (Chileshe XI). Herein, the Bemba can feel at one with the whole of their tribal experience.

Waterfalls. "Waterfalls" *Cipoma* , too, are sacred places, "royal residences" *Misumba* of "spirits" *Ngulu* . The most notable of these sites is Chishimba or Camokoka Falls near Chilubula mission. Atop its cliff, at the dangerous edge of the falls, the mind can come peculiarly alive as at limit. From such a height overlooking the whole of the distant landscape, one's horizons expand dramatically. Any foreign observer marvels at all of its visual wonder--a series of three falls interrupted by placid pools and tumbling rapids, rich verdant banks of meadows, clusters of palm trees, flowing fields and towering monoliths. But two *Shimapepo* "priests," Kalonga and Mutoba, will direct attention to the voice of *Chishimba chiletuta* "the constant roar of the water," to the vibrations on the rocks, and to the reverberations in the cave below the main falls. Instead of "looking around" taking in all the wonderful sights of the falls--the colors of lichen and flowers, the silvery flash of the waters, the splendid rainbows, the soaring water-birds--Kalonga asks the observer to listen: *Bushe mukwai mwaumfwa ngulu* "Well, sir, do you hear the spirits?" Suddenly, the observer is alert

to how differently oriented is the predominantly oral-aural
sensorium of these Bemba priests (Kalonga XII; Mutoba VII). Once
again, the sound of the place, its concommitant tale of the Ngulu
and the visitor's own vertigo are the primary religious data.
What is merely an aesthetic experience for the literate observer
becomes a colloquy with the spirits for the religiously attuned
listener. Herein, the Bemba can feel harmoniously united with
the whole of their cosmos.

Caves. Finally, caves are considered sacred in the Bembaland. These sacralized lairs of powerful animals give them
access to the marginal world of their first totemic ancestor,
Mumbi Mukasa. Within their womb-like confines matrilineal
spirits are reborn (Cf Schneidau 1976, 92-3). For example,
Canga's cave near Kasama. There is an audible rush of
underground streams, the swishing of bats' wings, croaking of
frogs, whistling of wind, even the claustrophobic and the
reverberations of footfalls and voices in the cave. The echoes
in the cave are conceived as the voice of the spirit *Canga*, who
speaks from within the authoritative ancestral tradition. When
the priest Shimbulamba is asked about the echoes, he replies
Ciunda!? Tuleumfwa mashiwi ico balelanda "Echoes!?
We can hear words because they (*Ngulu*) are talking" (Shimulamba
IX; Namasala IX).

The phenomenologist Ihde could hardly improve on the
priest's formulation: "With the experience of echo, auditory
space is opened up." The echo resounds with "a sense of depth in
time and space," gives a detectable "voice to things," and
introduces "existential possibilities of listening" to otherwise
mute surfaces (Ihde 1976, 68-70).

The cave's hollowness is an essential part of the hallowness
and wholeness felt by its entrants. It delivers a chambered
revelation of interior mysteries to those like the Cisungu
initiates, whom the spirit leads along its labyrinthine approach
and guides into the depths of the Bemba ethos (See above, chap.
2, 55). Both chiefs Nkolemfumu and Mwamba make pilgrimages to
enter Canga's cave at their installment and order periodic
prayers and sacrifices of goats there for the ancestral wisdom to
rule their lands in peace and security (Kasama District Notebook,
65; cf Melland 1903, 388-89). In the cave, at the interior of
the mountain and womb of the earth, such marginal persons can
encounter the very "limits to" their reality and experience their
own ancestral recycling.

All in all, these places are sacred to the Bemba because
their engulfing sounds create a panharmonic center, which can
integrate and motivate the rest of their fragmented experience.
The wholeness makes them whole again.

Oral Time

Just as the ancestral stories of spirits are related to the Bemba acoustic conception and valorization of space, so, too, the spirits are related to their oral appreciation of time as an integral part of the Bemba cognitive map. The oral traditions about spirits represent an organized reservoir of normative information, for which certain spatial and temporal data serve as equivalents to mnemonic formulas. Where the concept of space provides an order to nature, the concept of time provides a way in which the moral universe is supposed to behave.

First, it must be noted that there is a certain sense in which one can agree with Mbiti that African cultures are essentially "oriented to the past" in a sort of "reversed teleology." Persons and events are conceived as moving backwards into the time of the ancestors (Mbiti 1971, 24ff). To a certain extent one can also agree with Eliade that archaic peoples tend to validate their present lives by a ritual return to origins (Eliade, passim). But there must be a precise clarification prior to this agreement. That "past," to which cultures are oriented, and those "origins," to which cultures return, do not have the true sense of pastness, "the past as past." This is achieved only by literacy, and orality cannot really know it (Cf Goody and Watt 1968, 321-26; Tyler 1978, 17-19). The journey into "deep posteriority," writes Ong, is better mediated by the retrospective character of literature than by the participatory nature of oral performance, "where the past lives at the surface of the present" (1977, chap. 9).

A sense of the past as history requires an explicit knowledge that the present grows out of a past, with whose vicissitudes there is verifiable contact. A writing culture appropriates the past analytically and appreciates its variety. It can move progressively farther away from past events without being victimized by the need to repeat them, mistakes and all. Writing effectively sponsors the discovery that every event is unique. It provides a method for probing far enough and accurately enough into the past to accumulate an extended record of the sequence of events in time, registering real changes in society and the world (Ong, 316-17; 1977, 107). Literate society carefully clocks its time on tables and calendars. But

> . . . in functionally oral cultures the past
> is not felt as an itemized terrain, peppered
> with verifiable and disputed "facts" or bits
> of information. It is the domain of the
> ancestors, a resonant source for renewing
> awareness of present existence, which itself
> is not an itemized terrain either. Orality
> knows no lists or charts or figures (Ong 1982,
> 98).

An oral culture can have a sense of the immediate or recent past, but its only contact with the distant past is mediated through the customs, memories and social institutions of its people. Oral culture, then, appropriates the past ceremonially, in themes and formulas, which tradition has made conventional, because they are memorably interesting (See above, chap. 2, 43ff). Orally delivered facts take on an accretion of fiction, as they pass from one generation to another. Singular events are transmitted into universals and archetypes, and human times are mythically imagined to be cyclic duplications of the cosmic rhythms (Ong 1967, 23; 1977, 74-5).

Time for the Bemba is conceived as a meaningful cluster of concrete events and activities. Because the Bemba live existentially in and for the present, their language reckons time around the present. It refers to the "near present" and "further from the present," just as the Luba language does (Beskitt 1951). The distant past and future are not really significant categories. The tense of a verb is more intent on determining whether a sequence of events is complete or incomplete hence perfect or imperfect (Cf Booth 1975, 88).

The notion of the past, as employed in the following discussion, has not the connotations of historical time, which literacy has developed. It refers rather to a timeless foundational period, whose events continue to influence the present, because they are complete. They thus share in the perfection of ideals. Bemba myths and stories use a perfect tense, in which elders narrate the basic values and absolute truths, which transcend all time. They reside not in the past but in the constitutive depths of the present community. Drawing on Gibson Winter's (1966) model for a social ethic, it might be said that the Bemba tradition is emergent from within the intersubjective matrix of communicating persons. Their identity embodies an approximate actualization of the ideals to which they aspire. Their integrity depends on a continual transformation, effected by intense recollection of certain values and meanings. These are already shaping the cultural world which their myths and rituals express. For what is structural and what is normative in the Bemba society are interdependent. The norms stand in judgment against a declining structure and in hope within a progressive structure. The Bemba notion, then, is not so much of a past time as of an ideal time. If anything, "the past" is a metaphor for "the ideal." The present, confronted with it oftentimes dark realities, paralyzes the past into a scenario of its more hopeful possibilities. The past is "at the limits" of the present and verges on "the whole," with its perfection and completeness.

The Bemba oral culture concentrates its cognitive processes on remembering what society has learned. In this sense, it is decidedly oriented toward the "past." This idealized past, preserved in myth and rituals, informs and reforms the culture.

This "past," wherein the standards are cast with a mythic perfection and completion, is the familiar norm for justifying all thought and action. What the ancestors are narrated to have done and thought "in the beginning" sets the standard. As previously discussed in Chapter One (9-10), this cultural attitude is often summarily expressed "It is our custom" *Ulutambi*. It does not reflect any notion of a historical time or of the "past as past." It betrays more of what Goody calls "a conservative or antiquarian bias" (Goody and Watt 1968, 315).

Only insofar as the present is related to the narrative perfect can it hope to have any meaning or value. Everything present is interpreted by, measured against, and likened to archetypal events and persons. On ceremonial occasions, this is accomplished by a symbolic reenactment of the myth of the ancestors (Eliade 1954 & 1959 passim; see above, chap. 2, 47ff).

But, this ritual process is not so much a "return to the origins," as Eliade would have it, with the inevitable connotations of "going back into the past." Nor do oral peoples, through their rites seek to "devalue," "abolish," "suspend," "annul," "reject," "escape from," etc. time and history, because of the strangeness and terror it evokes in them (Eliade 1954, passim). Why would an oral people desire to return to a time, which does not significantly exist for them? How could they be said to want to "ob-literate" history--literally "to erase the written letters from?" That is a problem which literacy later invents (Booth 1975, 91).

The ritual process is better conceived as a periodic renewal and recreation of the present by celebrating and participating in what is perfect and complete. In so doing, the rite affirms the essential identity of what literates distinguish as the past, the present and the future. For an oral people, the past, the present and the future are of a whole.

Indeed the primary medium of any "return to origins" would have to be the living oral world. But because of its evanescent nature, there can be no "return" to an earlier sound world. Once sounded, it is gone (Ong 1976b, 11). The past time is not "returned to" but is brought into the present. The present community is not ritually transported to the past. The mythical epoch, with the perfection and completion of its exemplary models, is, by a communal speaking-effort, made contemporaneous with the present.

What literates conceive as past is made coexistent with the present by the power of the oral word. The oral perfect is contemporized, which is to say, the world, as it is ultimately, is represented. In much the same way, because cause and effect are mutually interrelated, they are virtually present to each other; such is the case even though cause is logically prior to effect. Ideal originating causes are once again brought to bear effectively on the present, when contemporary people ritually recite the charter myth, articulating and validating their lives by the sacred contact of ancestral archetypes (See above, chap. 2, 47ff).

For example, to ask the Bemba for the time when Mumbi Mukasa came down from heaven is a senseless question. The mythical action is outside real time. It did not occur on a date in the past. It occurs continuously at the depths of the present community, where it maintains the link between the divine and the human world of the Bemba. Because the event lies outside time, its transcendence is accorded the reverence due to the sacred. Its priority makes it normative. Its essential character of being at the limits of tribal experience makes any mythical event contingent to and disclosive of "the whole."

All of these observations are well supported by the phenomenology of sound. Ihde refers to "timeful sound" and "auditory temporality." By these turns of phrase, he accommodates the already well known close link between time and sound: "Sound dances timefully within experience. Sound embodies the sense of time" (Ihde 1976, 84-6). But the regular repetition and wavering modulations of rhythmic sound register, not so much sequential or durational, as all at once, instantaneous and simultaneous (Idem, chap. 7).

Ong (1967, 32-3) writes in the same vein. Whatever is spoken is a sounding event, a happening going on now. The oral word advertises presentness and actuality. It connects person to person. It is of a piece with the reality of which it speaks (See above, chap. 1, 3). Because oral words have the ontological power to create, when the ideal is spoken about, it is made present to the interlocutors. Listeners are invited by the spoken word to participate in the myth not vicariously nor imaginatively, but interactively. The oral communication engages the speaker, the audience and the recited myth in an orally created living present. This is the only place in an oral society where paradigmatic events and people have any existence at all--in the memories of living people. The mythic epoch is preserved only by what people talk about now. If it is to survive, it must be made to live now, to be constantly assimilated by persons talking in the present. Thus the perfect and the present are simultaneous in an oral culture. Ancestors live coevally and companionably with contemporaries, and archetypal events coincide with the speech and social institutions of living people. The oral culture achieves a kind of timelessness, a praetertemporal, holistic existence. The constancy and unchanging continuity of the culture are ensured by an axis of time which revolves around the present, and whose meaning for life is found in its normative depths.

The distant future is an even less likely reservoir of Bemba human ideals. It is unreal since it contains no events, and it

is not humanized since so few human activities reach deeply into
it for their completion (Zahan 1970, chap. 3). The "future,"
like the past of history, is a construct that can be related to
consciously, only through the contact and detailed planning
possible in a literate culture (Ong 1967, 91). Bemba ideals,
then, are an ensemble of values ascribed to a mythic past and
presented for succeeding generations to realize. Each generation
acquires wisdom and experience by re-collecting the storied world
of the ancestors, whose tradition sits in judgment on the living
by what the living repeatedly say of them.

In his classic redaction of the Bemba oral narrative
tradition, S. Mpashi climaxes the tale *Pano Calo* with all the
Bemba people suffering from a mysterious amnesia.

> *Bonse fye balabile fye fyonse . . . .*
> *Leloline fye epela, kuli mailo wa ku*
> *numa tabaleibukishako iyoo . . . . Citi*
> *alasakamana sana ukuti aba bantu bakafwa,*
> *pantu tabaleibukisha fyakale .* "Everybody
> simply forgot just everything. . . . . They
> only lived in the present, that's all. As for
> the origins, they were not remembering a thing
> . . . . The paramount chief worried very much
> lest his people just die, because they were
> not remembering the tradition (Mpashi 1956,
> 36-8).

For Mpashi, an oral society is plunged into moral decline and
structural disintegration, when it ceases to recall and to set
itself in order according to the tradition. Forgetfulness of the
tradition is the mortal sin of an oral people. And so the
stories of the chiefs and legends of their spirits' powers are
repeated among the Bemba. These are the regional legacies
cognate to their organization of space and time. They also serve
as cultural coordinates integrative of their ultimate truths and
values (See above, chap. 2, 38).

Enter Literacy

The linguistic world of spirits is deconstructed by
literacy. The oral stories of ancestral spirits give the Bemba a
sense of tribal identity. Their emotional commitment to their
remembered dead and a sense of continued authority are enshrined
in their obedience to the tradition, as narrated by elders whose
seniority sets them close to the ancestral origins. The
immediacy of the oral word creates a simultaneity between
ancestral time and present time. Oral remembrance is an act of
oral contemporizing. When these stories are reduced to spatial
quiescence, the spirits gradually become immobilized and lose
their constant unpredictable life and ability to engage in active
communication. When the oral stories are written down,

inconsistencies can be highlighted and questions of literal truth arise. Individual literates depart from the oral construction of social reality, and the incongruities of beliefs and new categories of understanding are brought to consciousness. Their skepticism can assume a cumulative force, as traditions fall under critical scrutiny and permanent analysis (Goody 1968, 320-22). Massive supplies of fact and information can be marshalled as evidence against long held religiously unquestioned tradition.

Written history tolls the knell for the death of the ancestral cult. The Bemba literates can relate to a written history, and realize they are not coevals to, but successors of their ancestors. They surely bear hereditary marks but they have developed in the intervening years. Homeostatic tendencies are aborted, since elders' redaction of history in tune with present needs can be challenged by simply looking up the facts in the records. Writing gives them explicit analytic knowledge of their past, whose ghosts can safely be put to rest (Ong 1967, 320).

The Spirit *Lesa*[4]

The introduction to Bemba traditional religion (See above, chap. 1) did not open with the usual reference to the supreme God. This treatise argues, along with Ong, that the notion of "the whole" in an oral religion will most likely be located in polymorphic conceptions of transcendence. If there develops a focus on a singular personal embodiment of those ideas, it will probably have maternal and terrestrial features (Ong 1967, 206-07; 1977, 143).

So far this chapter has examined some of the many spirit forms of the uncanny and their narrative and locative residences. With these Bemba religion symbolizes the manifestation of some essential aspect of the whole or some essential human response to that aspect. Among the spirits in the traditional pantheon is one, *Lesa*, who has risen to an untraditional prominence in the Christian economy. Missionaries singled out this spirit for recycling as the decisive representation of the Bemba experience of the self-revealing whole. From elements traditionally deputed to a host of other spirits, they concocted a Lesa who best approximates the orthodox doctrine on the Judeo-Christian God. This chapter includes Lesa in the general discussion of spirit divinities in order to underscore its relative second class status in the Bemba religious world and to relativize the Christian revisionist reading of Bemba religious history. Lesa is discussed at length, not because Bemba tradition does, but because it is a prime example of what happens, when there is a literate overhauling of an orally fashioned idea.

Bemba History and Religious Change

Certain tendencies within the history of the Bemba prompted some religious changes. This first section aims to briefly interpret the facts of Bemba history in the light of Robin Horton's (1971) well respected theory concerning the history of African religious change. The significance of Horton's historigraphic approach is that it respects both the synchronic and diachronic dimensions of African systems of thought and value. It also rescues the study of their religions from the idiom of a timeless ethnographic present. Thus this section will indicate how the Bemba religious ideas and practices, manifest in their symbols and rituals, have themselves been in transition and constant change. Sometimes these alterations parallel political and economic fluctuations. Sometimes they respond to natural or human crises. At other times they undergo a self-transformation from within by the impetus of their own peculiar dynamics (Cf Ranger and Kimambo 1972).

So little is known about the Bemba religious past that we can provide only a tentative reconstruction. Horton (1971) argues that the field of African experience in recent times widened from the traditional microcosm of tribal village life to the more modern macrocosm of cultural interchange because of trade and war. Simultaneously, lesser local spirits, who controlled the microcosm, retreated in deference to a more remote powerful spirit, whose influence could be extended to the macrocosm. It is plausible to suppose, applying Horton to the Bemba case, that a monotheistic Lesa became acceptable as the traditional religion accommodated itself to the larger social structure intruding in the eighteenth and nineteenth centuries.

At first all the chiefs belonged to the same clan, and exercised undisputed sway in their own territories. Along with their counsellors, they were *Bene bufumu* "owners of the chieftainship." Gradually they were united in a quasi-federal system, with the paramount as a primus inter pares. Under Chitapankwa in the 1860's, the paramountcy assumed greater central control over the newly subordinate chiefs. He began to "delegate" territorial powers to them, while exercising a virtual monopoly over the wider external policy of ever expanding war and trade (Roberts 1973, chaps. 4, 5, 6). At the same time Chitapankwa lost interest in spirits and shrines. In a burst of inconoclastic fervor, he won for himself the title *Mukungula mfuba* "the one who sweeps away ancestral huts" (Milimo 1978). He got away with this heretical behavior probably because of the Bemba community's perception of the increasing inadequacy of local spirits to explain, predict and control events in the larger social universe they had entered.

The centripetal internal political evolution generated an ideological model for a hierarchy of subordinate spirits, even as the external imperial expansion created a religious need for a spirit not territorially limited.

At first, all the spirits participated in an undifferntiated divinity, whose executive functions were diverse, disparate and distributed. There was no monopoly or divinity. All were *Bene* "owners" of divinity. Gradually, as the metaphor of secular political authority took hold, spirits, who were limited in influence to a particular clan, like *Mipashi* , or to a particular area like *Ngulu* , would become subordinate to a central spirit-force exercising universal religious power.

Thus, as long as the Bemba remained a small scale relatively self-sufficient society, territorial and ancestral spirits were powerful enough for them to cope with their social environment. But trade routes, raids and wars opened them to outside cultural contacts. Alien ideas and goods circulated widely among the Bemba, as they adopted dances, etiquette, food crops, vocabulary, etc., from Swahili, Portuguese, English and other African peoples (Roberts 1976, 146-47). The Bemba also found themselves in alien territories, where neither the regional *Ngulu* nor the familial *Mipashi* were effective. In order to cope with the religious threat of the "owners of the land," they had (a) to placate them through the priests of the conquered people, or (b) to transport their own indigenous spirits into the alien area by means of possessed persons, or (c) to develop the latent powers of a remote and powerful spirit, who was not confined by cult to any particular region. It seems that all three religious developments did in fact occur.

(a) The Bemba conquerors encouraged their subject peoples to continue the veneration of local spirits, as in the case of the Bisa priest, Cingkalonga, of Pali Cembe under the Bemba chief Nkula (Cingkalonga XI; Harvey 1980).

(b) Werner (1972) argues convincingly that Ngulu spirit-possession is a late religious development among the Bemba. It can be added that a contributory cause was the Bemba need to reduce the hostile alienness of conquered territories by exporting familiar spirits from their homeland through human vehicles (See below, chap. 4, 133).

(c) And so, there was an internal and quite active religious revolution going on. The Bemba were casting about in their own internal resources for concepts, symbols and myths to accompany the rapid social changes. At this point the missionaries appeared on the scene with a manifestly successful religious apparatus appropriate for the Bemba needs.

The next section presents the Bemba tradition on Lesa and the spirits as the Bemba register their own uncertainty ("a" and "b" above). The third section will show how the early missionaries capitalized on the Bemba irresolution and imposed their own Christian solution ("c" above).

Bemba Traditional Religion: Monotheistic or Polytheistic

There is controversy among Africans themselves as to whether the traditional religions were monotheistic or polytheistic. Okot p'Bitek (1971, 47) suggests that monotheism in the African religions is due to their encounter with Western Christianity. Others, like Idowu (1973) and Mbiti (1970), argue for an indigenous monotheism, although Idowu is obliged to contrive the expression "diffused monotheism" in a tendentious effort to accommodate the African data (Idowu 1962, 63).

The great debate on whether the Bemba were polytheistic or monotheistic never took place, and now it is a moot question. But the discussion is renewed here in an efort to expose and exemplify the oral drives of the tradition. Bemba tradition is best conceived as a complex of competing tendencies, which arise from divergent spatial and temporal standpoints within a shifting oral system. These must be allowed to surface without the prejudicial dominance of a single tendency imposed to satisfy the interpreter's own over-systematic preference (Cf Ray 1976, 52-3). Gouldsbury (1911) wrote that the Bemba concept of God verged on a mystic formlessness that defied modern analysis. Lesa, he said, did not connote any defined idea of God, for this spirit's attributes were still in a process of evolution. The whole fabric of the Bemba religion represented not a doctrine, but a practice of sacrificial prayers to tribal spirits. There was no clear, free, fearless thinking, but only an obesssion with precedent and custom, characterized by the vagueness of its tantalizing thought (Idem, 80).

The very remoteness and vagueness of the traditional concept of Lesa must be respected and not too precise a definition demanded for this spirit (See above, 77ff). The focus of the tradition is not on Lesa so the spirit remains opaque and fuzzy (White Fathers n.d., 361).

The Bemba religious tradition at the turn of the nineteenth century could be better described as ambiguous. There is a remote spirit, Lesa, of little existential significance, amidst a plurality of other spirits. The Bemba tradition obviously involves elements, which are conducive, but not reductively so, to literate categories of monotheism (Lesa). The same can be said of its relation to polytheism (*Mipashi* and *Milungu*) and even to pantheism (*Ngulu*) (Labrecque n.d., 1-8). Our thesis is that it is not accurate to speak of the nature of Lesa as unique and consonant with the Judeo-Christian notion of God. Parenthetically it can be added that there is no need to justify Bemba religion according to Western or Christian standards. The oral tradition is a notable intellectual achievement on its own terms.

The Bemba themselves are divided on the theistic issue. There are emphatic denials of polytheism tinged with Christian rhetoric. Even the talk of *Mipashi, Ngulu* and *Milungu*, though often in terms pertinent to divinity, is filled with Christian disclaimers of precedence and control in the hands of Lesa. For example, the traditional priest Shimwalule, uneasily caught between his duty to the spirits and the Christian God's encroaching usurpation, said of the people of old:

> *Ukupepa imipashi balepepa na Lesa bena*
> *beletobeka. Nomba tulepepa fye Lesa, . . .*
> *Kwishina lya tata nelya mwana nelya roo*
> *mukatifu amen. Fwe bali mu mipashi nga*
> *fino fine Lesa tulepepa na kumipashi nefwe*
> . . . . They worshipped the spirits and Lesa.
> They just mixed them up. Today we worship
> only Lesa . . . in the name of the Father and
> Son and Holy Spirit. But we, who are
> concerned with the spirits like this, we pray
> to Lesa and to the spirits (Shimwalule VII).

The Komakoma brothers at Chikunga declared the original Bemba as worshipping many spirits with little heed of Lesa:

> *Milungu balikwete iingi, tabalelumbula bena*
> *ukutila mulungu ube umo tutile Lesa abe umo*
> *bashininkishe ukuti Lesa aba umo, awe chena*
> *tabaishibe iyo* . They had many spirits, but
> they did not pray to the one spirit as we do
> to one Lesa . . . they were certain there was
> one Lesa but they really did not know Lesa
> (Komakoma XI).

In an attempt to distinguish belief in Lesa and the spirits by their relative power and prestige, the Chikunga answered:

> *Abena kale basumine my ngulu ico*
> *tabashininkishe maka ya kwa Lesa e ico*
> *balesumina mu ngulu. Ico bamwene nga*
> *cakubafwalishako ku fyonse fintu balefwaya.*
> *Baletontonkanya ukutila ngulu ne mipashi na*
> *Lesa cimo cine.* The people of old believed
> more strongly in spirits, because they were
> not sure of Lesa's power. They say that help
> came from the spirits for everything they
> wanted. They thought that the *Mipashi*
> and Lesa were one and the same (Komakoma XI).

There is little doubt that the divine and the ancestral realms are conjoined. Chief Nkula and his *Bakabilo*, Chileshe Musonda of Kwa Mutemba, and others, repeated similar sayings: *Mupashi (imipashi) e Lesa Wesu* "The spirit(s) is our "Lesa" (Chileshe XI). (Lesa here used in the Christian sense of "God".) Tanguy (1954, 176-88) records such sayings *Mipashi e Milungu yesu* and even the startling pluralization *Balesa benu bengala-*

musunga "May the Lesas keep you." This cannot be dismissed as simply a plural of respect, since the idea is reinforced by: *Twatota apo bamalesa bakubwesho mutende* "We are grateful that the Lesas have brought you health." It is very clear here: *Abafwa bapilibukila balesa* "The dead are transformed into Lesas." In short, Lesa in the developing tradition is an extension and intensification of the values surrounding the ancestors (Cf Zahan 1970, chap. 3).

The tradition allows for a facile interchangeability between spirits. Etienne (1948, 92) has the expression: *Mulungu* or *Lesa obe akusunge*, where others, like Tanguy, say *Mupashi obe akusunge* "May your divinity, Lesa or ancestral spirit keep you." Even curses are interchangeable: *Mulungu* or *Lesa*, or *Kabwe*, or *Chishimba andye*. "May (any of the above named spirits) eat me" (Tanguy 1954, 193-94). Oger concludes that this interchangeability suggests an equality of Lesa and the other spirits (Oger n.d.). The Presbyterian Macminn records a saying which likens the *Mipashi* and *Fiwa* to the "winds" *Myela* and gives to them an "omnipresence" and "eternity" which other missionaries would rather restrict to Lesa: *Fili konse konse konse mu kashita kamo kene* "They are everywhere at the same time" (MacMinn n.d., a).

Trying to pin the Bemba elders down to the literate categories of monotheism and polytheism is to look for a precision not arrived at in the tradition: the question never arose. To confine the notion of spiritual power, so variously manifest, into a single name was not the goal of the tradition. The oral tradition lets its mysteries flow freely and flexibly, dealing with the dialectically and allowing polarities to stand together, even in contradiction and without comment. But a written text has an almost unlimited capacity to collect and digest oral materials, securing a single reading against oral pluralism, fixing it for dissemination apart from its former oral controls and qualifiers. Thus did the early missionaries pour new wine into old skins and sew new patches onto old cloth.

Lesa and other Spirits vs. the Christian God

The Christian concepts of God are not univocally applicable to the Bemba notions of Lesa. But it is clear that the evangelical strategy was to assume monotheism and then exploit the unknown, unconcerned, unattached, remote, hence unworshipped spirit Lesa as a "deus otiosus." The missionaries began, for proselytic purposes, to recreate a tradition for Lesa made in the image and likeness of the Christian God. The apotheosis of Lesa was not an easy task, but its successful outcome must be acknowledged. There is scarcely a Bemba person today, who will talk about Lesa in anything but strictly orthodox Christian terms (Musabandesu XI; Muselela XI).

Missionaries selected the spirit Lesa to carry the burden of Christian monotheism, probably for this reason: Lesa was so removed from Bemba religious centrality that the few indigenous conceptions around the spirit could be adjusted to the Christian model. This selection itself was not a foregone conclusion. For a while at least, the Swahili import "Mulungu" was used as a culturally extraneous, hence neutral, term to introduce the Christian idea of God (Cf Welfele 1920; White Fathers 1958, 364). Garvey (1974, 32-4) acknowledges that, while the existence of Lesa was a boon for Christian catechesis, there were elements in the traditional conception, which were difficult for neophytes to reconcile with the new theology.

To say there was no explicit Bemba concept of a monotheistic God does not mean that there were not resources within the tradition for responding affirmatively to such a religious development. So the earliest White Father remarks were a very positive appraisal of the Bemba belief in God and affinity toward Christianity. In 1895 Monsignor Dupont wrote of "tant de facilite a recevoir les principes de notre sainte religion" and "des idees assex exactes sur l'unite de Dieu" and of their lack of religious contamination "ni par les Musulmans, ni par les protestants" (Dupont 1895). In 1896, Father Guille writes of "une theologie assez exacte . . . un Dieu unique . . . des saints patrons" and of a religious system amenable to "les verites de notre sainte religion" (Guille 1896).

But despite an almost unanimous acclaim of this spirit Lesa with a dossier not unlike that of the Christian God, there is considerable misgiving about the nature of the cult paid to *Mipashi* and *Ngulu* : "mais malheureusement ils n'ont pour ce Dieu et ses patrons aucun culti, tandis qu'ils ne manquent pas de faire quelques sacrifices a leurs fetiches" (Idem). The cult of spirits was constantly condemned as pagan and idolatrous, and its practice by a convert led to excommunication (Cf Schoeffer 1910). By prohibiting the cult of other spirits and inaugurating the cult of Lesa, the missionaries hoped to curb very drastically spiritual overpopulation and despoil the Bemba pantheon, which the oral medium had spawned (Cf Ong 1967, 206-07). True worship, it was argued, could only be paid to the true God. But there was no cult, no "temple" *Lufuba* , no priest, no special observance, no adoration paid to Lesa (Labrecque n.d.,; Etienne 1948; Tanguy 1954; Ragoen 1935). For the ancestors and nature spirits, there was a cult that was "undoubtedly worship, adoration" (Etienne 1948, 95). Hence all rites associated with spirit-cult such as *Lubuko, Kupyanika, Kupala mipashi, Kusowa banda* were roundly condemned as "pagan" *Cisenshi* and idolatrous by each Bemba catechism from the beginning (Dupont 1900). So, if the cult of the spirits was understood as worship by the early missionaries, then the lack of a cult for Lesa and the attendant cult of spirits said something about the relative importance of spirits. In the general context of African religions, Idowu concedes that it is difficult to draw a line between "ancestor worship and the worship of God" (Idowu 1973, 180).

In the final analysis, none of the following Christian notions of God can be univocally applied to Lesa without doing violence to the authentic oral tradition.

Lesa: a supreme spirit? The word "Lesa" as Werner (1971) recognizes, has a wide linguistic distribution among Bantu dialects throughout central and East Africa. It also enjoys a very wide meaning ranging from legendary hero to high spirit. But to narrow the Bemba connotation to "supreme distant god . . . considered to be creator of men," as Werner does (1971, 7), is historical short-circuitry.

The early missionary Macminn in his manuscript dictionary translated the word "Lesa" as "God" but then penciled in the addition "quite new meaning?" (Macminn n.d., "d"). The anthropologist Audrey Richards (1939, 189, 377) made only 2 or 3 passing references to Lesa in her monumental belief in practice. In fact she identified the Bemba high god as Kampinda (Idem, 65). In her book Chisungu, she devoted ten introductory pages to the traditional religion with no mention of Lesa or a high god of any kind (Richards 1956). It is significant that none of the many prayers recorded in the early White Father literature or in Richards' books and articles referred to an intermediary role of spirits subordinate to Lesa.[5] In the tradition, spirits are all "chiefs" *Bashamfumu* in their own right, and like living chiefs, act independently on their own royal authority (Chanda IV).

To the dismay of Christian interpreters, the oral tradition has no articulated hierarchical structure grading spirits from subordination to supremacy. The Bemba scholar Garvey (1974, 35) states unequivocally that the Bemba did not develop a taxonomy of spiritual powers and did not attribute to Lesa any control over other spirits. Even the dedicated christianizer Ragoen (1935, 479) admits that Lesa does not seem to have complete control over spirits. He also points out that the frequent invocation and worship of spirits gives the spirits a functional priority and power over Lesa, who is "pratiquement impuisant contre les esprits." So supremacy is suspect.

Lesa: all good? No veneration was paid to Lesa in the tradition. The missionaries declared that the "goodness" of Lesa accounted for that. It was argued that people did not fear Lesa, who was absolutely good, and thus paid attention only to the other spirits. As causes of the obvious evil in the world, these latter were in need of appeasement. As a matter of fact, the tradition does conceive of a Lesa, who is fearful and capable of evil: *Lesa akupangukile* "May Lesa strike you down!" or *Lesa andye* "May Lesa swallow me up" (Labrecque n.d., 2-3). Lesa is even called the "fierce one who will kill you" *Lesa mukali akaku-kanda* (Labrecque n.d., 4).

Lesa: a pure spirit? The early protestant missionary, Macminn, wondered about the validity of translating Bemba notions

into Christian conceptions: "Whether the idea *Lesa Mupashi*
(Lesa is a spirit) was part of Bemba thought before the arrival
of Christianity is a question concerning which there may perhaps
be difference of opinion" (Macminn n.d., "d", 11). The evidence
is that there is no Bemba notion of a pure spirit. All Bemba
spirits exhibit human traits, with spouses, children, and various
emotions (See above, chap. 1, 20ff). The idea of pure spirits
with no previous human life is completely foreign to Bemba
mythology (Oger 1972, 10). So foreign, in fact, is the Christian
notion of spirit, when applied to God, that the first
missionaries imported the Swahili word "Roo" to designate the
Holy Spirit (Cf Dupont 1900). There are stories that describe
Lesa anthropomorphically, with a spouse and children, a
"beautiful face" *Uwayemba* , a "corpulent body" *no mubili ukulu,*
with eyes, ears and tongue (Tanguy 1954, 177). Lesa's spiritual
distance is like that of the *Ngulu* , Chishimba or Kabwe, whose
lineage has simply been forgotten. Lesa's uniqueness, too, is
like theirs--a proper name and a special function. Chief Mumena
declares, "There is only one Lesa, just as there is only one
Chishimba and one Mulenga" (Mumena III).

   Lesa: creator? The idea of Lesa as creator in Bemba
tradition is difficult to separate from Christian accretions.
Although Garrec (1916) and other early observers record creation
stories involving Lesa, he notes that other Bemba traditions do
not involve the intervention of a high god in creation.[6] In
fact, the story he records answers more to the origin of death
and evil than to the origin of humans and the world. It
concludes with the words: "Lesa s'en alla, ils ne le virent meme
pas; ils l'entendivent seulement parler" (Garrec 1916, 2).
Lesa's existence, like that of all the spirits, is predicated for
the oral Bemba not on visibility but on audibility. Whatever is
heard of Lesa is what Lesa is. Lesa, far from being creator, is
rather like all the spirits, who depend in the tradition on
repeated stories and cultic practice for their own survival.

   Lesa, however, is characterized as a master of life and
death, a tradition confirmed by the popular saying: *Mfwa Lesa* "a
Lesa-death," applied to death in old age (Etienne 1948, 58). At
any rate, the ambiguity in the tradition does not warrant
Etienne's (1948) declaration "L'idee de la creation est tres
precis." Tanguy's (1954, 178) *Ifya panonse Lesa apela imilungu
amaka ya kuficita* "Lesa gave the spirits the powers to make
everything on earth," at least recognizes the conflict, even if
he does record what reads suspiciously like a Christian
resolution. Whenever a traditional account of creation is
requested in these days, the enquirer is either entertained with
a garbled "Adam, Eve and Jesus" story, as at Shimwalule
(Shimwalule VII) or told there is none (Katewa XII). It is
significant that the charter myth, where the traditions are so
agreeably convergent on origins, makes no mention of Lesa.
Unless one wants to argue for Liulu, any sort of creator-god is
absent (Cf Chanda Mukulu IX).

Lesa: a high (heavenly) spirit? There are strong traditions that argue for Lesa as a high spirit. Lesa is called "the great one." Even so the paramount chief is called Chiti **Mukulu** and the titular mother of chiefs is called Chanda **Mukulu**. Sometimes a great chief is even spoken of as Lesa Mukulu (White Fathers 1954, 323; Mporokoso District Notebook, 241). But then so is the hunting spirit, Mushili, meaning "earth," also called _Mukulu_ (Garrec 1916, 9).

Lesa's position as a high spirit is enhanced by association with the sky. Lightning is called _Mamba ya Lesa_ "flakes of Lesa," and of thunder it is said _Lesa abulukuta_ , "Lesa is rumbling." In curses one hears _Lesa ampandaule_ "May Lesa (lightning) smite me to pieces." A powerful medicine is called _Mupandwa Lesa_ "tree splinters from a lightning strike" (Labrecque n.d., 22).

But there is another tradition, no less valid and no less original, about Lesa as a telluric spirit, which is nowhere preserved in the written sources. It is still in remnant form within the oral tenor. A routine question is asked about the "whereabouts of Lesa" _Kwa Lesa ni kwi?_ or the "direction" _Ntunga_ in which the spirit resides. The expected answer is _Ku mulu_ . This response is conditioned **both** by Christian prayers--_Malumbo kuli Lesa mu mulu_ "Glory to Lesa in the sky"--**and** by the political sloganning of the ruling party U.N.I.P. of Zambia-- _Ku mulu Lesa, panshi Kaunda_ "Lesa rules in heven, President Kaunda governs on earth." But, the Komakoma brothers at Cikunga reply unexpectedly, emphatically pointing to the ground: _Kwa Lesa, panshi_ "The residence of Lesa is down in the earth" (Komakoma XI).

So surprising and refreshing is this response, in contrast to the usual _Lesa ku mulu,_ that it leads to a knowledge of a previously muted voice within the multifarious tradition: _Lesa-panshi_ "the mother-earth spirit." This is the maternal and terrestrial conception of divinity, which Ong anticipates from an oral religion. Ong argues that Mother (earth) and Father (sky) are related to each other as tactile (proximate) and visual (distant). Since hearing is closely allied to the sense of touch, it develops in a person's contact with mother and grounds the experience of all later intersubjectivity. Ong therefore conjectures that the paramountcy in an oral pantheon of spirits will be accorded to a mother-earth spirit (Ong 1967, 206-07; 1977, 143). The next section will give detailed evidence that this, in fact, happens to be the Bemba case.

Lesa-panshi the mother-earth spirit. Missionaries and subsequent Bemba simply allege that Lesa is a father-in-heaven god, like unto the Judeo-Christian God. They then proceed to ignore or censor the feminine imagery used of the traditional Lesa. In the proverbs, for example, Lesa is variously referred to in women's roles, "as provident as a thrifty housewife"

Alabansa, as "a cook" *Aleteba,* "who does not burn food"
Talungusha, as one "who winnows" *Lupe .* In the *Cisungu* ceremony,
a mime represents the act of birth. A song encourages the
initiates to nourish the life they will engender. Both
explicitly refer to Lesa in a mothering role: "Following the
ways of Lesa, we imitate our mothers" *Kucilingana Lesa, tupashana
mayo* (Richards 1956, 88-9, 196). It must be remembered, too,
that the first Bemba contact with divinity was with the woman
Mumbi Mukasa. She descended to the "earth" *Panshi ,* as related
in the charter myth. Matriliny was enshrined as the Bemba link
to divinity.

The mother-earth spirit Lesa is associated with the mastery
of life and death. "The earth" *Mushili* is traditionally
considered a fertile wife, which the chief plows and sows. She
gives birth to crops as a mother brings forth children. *Mushili,*
the earth, is also the place of burial. In her corpses are
"arranged in a fetal position" *Kuonga* and laid "in the womb"
Munda, a term used figuratively of sleep and the sleep of death
in the tomb (White Fathers 1954, 528).

The first proverb that pops into anyone's mind, when asked
about Lesa, is *Kuimba kati Kusansha na Lesa* "To dig down (into
the red earth) for a little medicinal root is to mingle it with
(or involve) Lesa" (Chiboo IV). Throughout most of Bembaland,
when the top soil is removed, as it is when digging a grave,
there is a red-laterite underneath. The red soil is a sign of
death, and all red objects become associate signs of danger of
death and shedding of blood. The "red wood powder" *Nkula* is
used for anointing warriors, hunters, and anyone else requiring
courage to pass through the blood-shedding dangers of death
(Mutemba XII). A red flag flies over the *Musumba* "palace" and
all the *Kabilo* "councillors" wear red clothes to indicate the
death of the cief (Chisangaponde VII). The red earth evokes the
whole Bemba context of attributing good health and sometimes
death to Lesa's power. The ejaculation *Lesa ulenyensho mutende*
"May Lesa preserve me in health" is another example. *Bamucapi*
"witch cleansers" appeal to *Lesa wa Panshi,* as they administer
their medicines (Tanguy 1935).

But digging into the red earth for the health that Lesa
gives is also connected with digging the grave for the death that
Lesa will receive. So the phrase *Mfwa Lesa* (Labrecque
n.d., 2-3) applies not just to peaceful death in old age, but
signifies that all the dead belong to Lesa in the red earth.
When the Bemba swear a solemn oath, for example, they dip their
forefingers in the red earth and draw a line across their necks,
saying *Kwa Lesa ku matanda* "By the place of Lesa at the mats."
This refers to the red earth where corpses wrapped in mats are
buried, and means "May I die and be buried, if this is not true."
This oath is sometimes phrased explicitly *Ku mushili wakashika*
"to the red soil" (Komakoma XI). Similar sayings are used as
death-curses. *Nobe ukashimona ishamwene musholomwe* "You will

see what the red edible mushroom saw" (when it was deep in the red soiled earth) (White Fathers 1954, 493) or, *Lesa akulye* "May Lesa swallow you in (in the mouth of the grave)."

When the Bemba wax philosphical about death, they say *Tuli kwa Lesa kumbo uko Tushipilibuka* "We are from the place of Lesa, at the graveyard, where we are turned back into it." A person who dies is said to go "to great Lesa's place" *kwa Lesa Mukulu* . If a person thought to be dead, turns up unexpectedly, people say the person "has returned from Lesa's place" *Abwela fye kwa Lesa* . The solemn oath "At the cemetery in the red earth where Lesa dwells" brings all these themes together (Labrecque n.d., 2-3). If a person who is killed as a traditional "sacrifice" *Lipaki* to accompany a dead chief, survives the lethal blow, the Bemba say *Lesa (Mfumu) amufwita (amuluka)* "Lesa (the chief) has refused the gift (or vomited it back up from the grave)" (Etienne 1948, 96).

Both the spirits Mushili and Lesa are called *Mukulu* "great" and *Mufumu* "chief". They both seem to be related to the underworld as well. *Mushili-nshi* is the spirit of the dead (Garrec 1916, 3), and the Bemba say *Batwalo muntu kwa mushili mfumu* "They carried the person to Chief Mushili's place" referring to a burial. In one of the tales of death's origin, the name of the first person is Mushili (Tanguy 1954, 106). The Komakoma brothers even speak of their recently departed brother, *Kabilo* Cikunga, as Mushili, meaning that he is now there with all the rest of the *Mipashi* gathered together inMushili (Komakoma XI). Sometimes this burial spirit is called Mwanda nshi, another name for the earth. In the death oaths *Kwa mwanda-Lesa* "By the place of Earth-Lesa" and *Nalya mwanda-Lesa* "I have eaten the Earth-Lesa," the spirits are combined (Kacuka 1977, 30-1).

The name *Mwanda* may be derived from the word *Kuânda* "to spread out as roots or tendrils in the ground." In which case we are brought full circle to the life-giving connotations of Lesa's power. Garrec (1916, 9-11) applies the name *Mushili mukulu mfumu* to Lesa as spirit of good hunting and provider of nourishment. The spreading-forest is Lesa's residence *Impanga ni mwanda-Lesa, tabomanina* "The forest is *Mwanda-Lesa,* people do not argue over its produce" (Kacuka 1977, 30-1). A similar proverb *Imiti ingala sha kwa Lesa tashikomenwa* "Trees are the plumes on the head of Lesa; they are not to be quarreled over" (Richards 1939, 272) uses the image of trees as the royal headdress of Earth-Lesa. Again, *Lesa Mufimbwa na mpukutu* "Lesa covered with dry leaves" uses an image, which associates Lesa with the forest-floor and the earth.

So, too, is Lesa called *Lesa Kalunga mwine nkuni namenshi* "Lesa the hunter, owner of the woods and the water" and *Mwine wa Mushili* "owner of the earth." These are praise titles reserved for the chiefs (Kacuka 1977, 31). Just as the chief is identified with his land *Mfumu e calo*, and its vitality and fertility are dependent on his health-- *Calo nacikama* "The land is dried up" when the chief is sick--so, too, is the power of Lesa - panshi or Lesa - mushili operative in the earth's productivity. In 1949, near Lwena, an old man spoke of Lesa panshi as the one who gives life to the soil from within, so that tobacco and groundnuts grow. He hesitated to be baptized as a Christian, if, as a result, he would go *Ku mulu* "to heaven." He would rather go *Kwa Lesa ku mushili wa kashika* "to Lesa's place in the red soil," where he would be assured of an abundant supply of his favorite groundnuts and tobacco (Kapompole IV).

Thus, the tradition of *Lesa panshi* as mother-earth spirit, makes sense to a people as deeply attached to the soil as the Bemba are. There is strength, stability and vitality in the earth. Rocky outcrops, caves, mountains, springs from the earth, the forest itself, are all venerated. Cultivated lands are holy as well as inhabited places. Even "abandoned villages" *Cibolya* revert again to sacred forest. "The earth is the place of the ancestors" *Fikolwe ne calo*, and "The land is the chieftaincy" *Mfumu e calo* . Lesa is, without a doubt, in one strand of the tradition, a chthonic power with nascent and ever renewed life, springing up from the grave and from the fertile earth.

Lesa in Proverbs

The missionaries derive much of their precise definition of Lesa's nature from the large number of proverbs they have catalogued concerning this spirit.[7] Thus *Lesa ni Shimwelenganya* "The source of imaginings" is made to refer to the Christian God's incomprehensibility or unimaginableness (Ragoen 1935, 477). *Apatebeta Lesa tapafuka cushi* "Where Lesa cooks there is no smoke" is rendered as the Christian God's spiritual nature (Tanguy 1954, 177). *Lesa talaba iciminine* "Lesa forgets nothing that stands up," and *Lesa tona cakwe* "Lesa does not destroy belongings" are both taken to refer to the innate goodness of God. *Lesa shiwatutaula* "Lesa (lightning) breaks down hard wood trees" refers to the Christian God's omnipotence (Labrecque n.d., 2-3). *Lesa talombwa inama* "Lesa is not asked for meat" parallels the omniscient providence of the Christian God who knows human needs ahead of time (Labrecque n.d., 2-3). *Lesa te wa kubikila bunga mu muti* "Lesa is not one for whom you put flour at a tree" becomes the Christian God's absolute independence (Labrecque n.d., 2-3). It is clear that for Father Labrecque (Cf also, Tanguy 1954, 176ff; Garrec 1916, 3-11), these are vestiges of a primal revelation of the true God. A fairly accurate composite portrait of the Christian God can be contrived from the various features presented in the proverbs.

All manner of theological abstractions are squeezed from a host of proverbs, in which Lesa is the subject matter, without due regard to the diversity of their place and time of origin and their speech-setting. Ragoen (1935, 479) acknowledges the polymorphic content of the proverbs, but concludes that "le negre est en contradiction flagrante avec l'affirmation formelle . . . dans les proverbes . . . ." He then proceeds to make literate amends to the oral heritage.

The sheer volume of proverbs concerning Lesa (Labrecque 1931-1947; Hoch 1968, 68-70) would seem to testify to the central importance and widespread knowledge of Lesa in the traditions. More likely, exclusive documentation of these traditions is witness to how assiduously the missionaries collected favorable material to bolster Lesa's role as the Christian God. This may even have necessitated a discrete censoring of certain Lesa legends, which, though traditional, were unsuitable. For example, the story about Lesa's marriage with the moon, the Mukalesa "wife of Lesa," and Lesa's children (Chomba VIII) has all but disappeared from the oral repertoire.

A similar volume of songs, prayers and praises could probably have been collected for Chishimba, Mulenga and many other spirits. The White Father's Bemba-English Dictionary (1954) lists over a half-dozen proverbs relating to the *Mipashi* (s.v.) in their provident and ritual capacities. In addition, some of the proverbs, which the missionaries associate with Lesa, are also recited in the tradition with other spirit names. For example, Labrecque records *Lesa mukulu Kampamba mwatule ulu* "Great Lesa, Kampamba, you pierce the sky as lightning." Tanguy (1954, 176) runs the same proverb just in Kampamba's name. Other proverbs are traditionally applied to the chief, such as *Ku mfumu ni Kwifwe takubulila fintu* "The Chief's place is like a fountain which never runs dry" and *Uli mfumu taulombwa nama* "As chief, you are never asked for meat" (Hoch 1966, 60). These are blatantly commandeered for the christianization of Lesa (Labrecque n.d., 2-3). Such occurrences make one wonder whether some are not stacking the evidence in Lesa's favor.

Proverbs _and_ _orality_. At first glance there is much to recommend such a methodological study of the proverbs. They are, after all, another of the oral culture's devices for encapsulating the sententious wisdom of the ages: "A proverb," said Cervantes, "is a short sentence based on long experience." The Bemba pass on their knowledge in stylized authoritative sentences out of necessity (Cf Labrecque 1931, 211; Hoch 1968). Not only does an oral society preserve its thoughts in formulas, it does its thinking in such forms. "Formulaic expressions . . . are not added to thought or expression but are the substance of thought . . . . Oral cultures think _in_ formulas and communicate _in_ them" (Ong 1977, 103-30).

The oral convention is to realize traditional thought, to remember "in a curiously public way" (Ong 1980, 7). Little heed is paid by the oral community to an individual's original ideas. As the Bemba proverb has it *Amano uli weka tayashingauka ikoshi*

"Your own brains alone do not even stretch around your neck."
Thus creative thinkers never claim an idea as their own but
cleverly cast it into proverbial form (Kashoki n.d.), disowning
any authorship and enlisting instead the authority of the
ancestors (Milimo 1976, 46). A personal observation can be
inflated into a universal truth. Through the formula of the
pithy maxim, tradition becomes dynamic and open. The living can
enrich their communal heritage and pass an acquired wisdom and
experience into the tribal treasury of proverbs.

The traditional content and form of proverbs create a sense
of such obvious truth that listeners are less apt to differ with
and resist the rest of the message. Quoting a proverb is the
oral equivalent of quoting an authority. It shows how what one
says and thinks is socially acceptable and sanctioned. Nobody
argues with the ancestors. In this tradition, the living feel
the wills and prescriptions of their ancestors (Zahan 1970;
Milimo 1976). The proverb, in effect, is another of those means
by which the *Mipashi* "spirits of the dead" communicate with the
living and exert a continuing influence on their lives. Prayers
to the ancestors sometimes make explicit reference to the
following of tradition as the touchstone of the petitioners'
ritual worthiness: *Twaliponena amashiwi yenu* "We have clung to
your words" (Richards 1969, 363).

But the literate scholars' enthusiasm for extracting a
proverb out of the speech forum and tabulating it alongside other
similar sayings radically alters its oral character and readjusts
its semantic function. Making a list of proverbs is itself a
literate transmutation of the oral mindset. The oral person does
not even conceive of such a concatenation or compile lists of
anything (Goody 1977; Ong 1982). In its graphic setting, a
proverb can be cross-checked for contradictory and comparative
possibilities and for its universal truth value. Dismembered
from the body of oral discourse, its components are reassembled
into consciously contrived patterns and coordinated within a
collection of previously distinct oral units. In this setting
the proverb's meaning has been transformed beyond its original
intentionality, where its truth was judged by its appropriate
applicability. Like metaphors, proverbs are validly interpreted,
not by a substitution theory, but only in an interaction theory
(See above, chap. 1, 25). Devocalized and alienated from the
living colloquy of speaker and audience, proverbs can be made to
address questions of greater generality and provide answers of
greater abstraction, than the particular, concrete circumstances
of the oral discussion.

The oral life world is fraught with polemics (Ong 1967, 195-
209) and proverbs share in that constant tryst. A written
collection of proverbs, with their essentially disputatious tone,
is too peaceful a setting. The proverb serves more often to end
discussions than to encourage further thought. With a proverb, a
speaker aggressively attempts to impose traditional ideas and the

ancestral will on the audience (Abrahams 1968, 152). The literate theologian's reflective analysis exorcizes this partisan spirit, and, by calm exegesis, a proverb can be made to mean even what its antagonist intended. Thus organized and replayed into a manifold of other contexts foreign to the oral world, proverbs have a totally different cognitive potential (Goody 1977, 126-26).

The missionary distillation of the proverbs into Christian theological categories clearly violates oral abilities and purposes. The proverbs do not give a series of definitions or properties of Lesa. They describe expected behavior patterns in concrete instances, sharing in the tendency of orally preserved speech to eschew the universal (Cf Havelock 1978, 182). Monotheism, omnipotence, omniscience, omnipresence all fall outside the Bemba speaker's frame of reference (Cf Goody 1962, 38), no matter how satisfying these are to literate expectations.

The overliterate mind looks for a subtle and complex theological investment in the proverbs in order to reveal the essence of Lesa. But a proverb does not contemplate the nature of Lesa philosophically, so much as bring Lesa alive imaginatively. There is not some complicated conceptualization of Lesa's character, which underlies and dictates the content of the proverb. Each proverb shapes the character of Lesa for each instance. All proverbs are not to be understood together as their literate compilation suggests. Each is an oral whole, a discrete unit of communication, not supplementing or complementing others. Each is discursively unaware of the others. In a written list, proverbs lose their oral autonomy and are made to conform to a larger project. A Bemba person, applying a proverb in discourse, is absorbed with its particular appropriation in the circumstances and not concerned with the logical effect or the congruent consistency of the whole body of proverbs available in the tradition about Lesa.

Listing the proverbs in a text forecloses on this oral polyvalence (Havelock 1978, 335ff). Propositional categories certainly capture some of the meaning present in the proverbs and thus are verifiable. But, while they do not exhaust the range of oral possibilities, they actualize a single motif and effect a closure within the total repertoire. [8] Nearly a century of literate interpretations of the proverbs in a catechetical reprogramming of Lesa has eliminated oral inconsistencies. The incestuous genealogy of subsequent texts has produced its own patterns of verification. As a result of literate listing, the oral aptness of proverbs has been distorted and deformed. (See above, 70, for an example of literate mismanagement of oral narratives).

The quest for the "original tradition." So, which is the original version of the tradition on the relationship between Lesa and the spirits? Is Lesa unique, or one of many superior spirits? Is the tradition monotheistic or polytheistic? Is Lesa a high paternal god or a telluric maternal divinity? Does Lesa have a lost human lineage or is Lesa a pure spirit? Who is the power in charge, Lesa or other spirits? Is Lesa a *primus inter pares* or the absolute, supreme God facilely identified with Christian revelation?

It is vain to search for an "original form" of Bemba traditional religion. In the first place, that is a patently literate process which seeks to "look it up" and make comparisons of chronologically ordered texts (Ong 1967 and 1982). For obvious reasons related to oral storage techniques and homeostatic tendencies (Cf next section), discovering the original form is an impossible task. In the second place, the original form never existed. Each oral performance is a unique creation. In the oral tradition there is only a multiplicity of speech acts, relating a plurality of beliefs and rites, and answering to varying social needs. Oral speech forms are characterized by heterogeneity and cannot produce a single, composite, uniform, homogeneous tradition. Oral life escapes the control of any single authority. In the speaking forum, an agreement will be momentarily effected between the speaker and audience, but the oral repetition of many such discussions, with all their random ideas and disparate practices, results in a multiform and polyvalent tradition (Cf Havelock 1978, 336ff). The oral tendency is to pile up particular, even conflicting reports, or to recite a single account, subscribing to multiple truths or selecting one instance of truth. But a literate management of knowledge critically seeks to reduce oral pluralism to logical arrangements. It "looks" for proper subordination of ideas and systematic resolution of polarities.

Lesa and all spirits are inextricably bound to oral formulations in narrative form. The narratives, like the proverbs which cannot be systematized without violating their diverse origins and applications, are episodic. They are not recited together, *ever*, as an integral plot or system. The characters of Lesa, legendary heroes, other spirits, even historical chiefs, are typecast in order to be memorable and transmissible. They are figures of extraordinarily inflated human dimensions, and thus are almost anonymous and interchangeable (Cf Propp 1958). If they are to conform to the oral requirements, the characters must be typical and popular enough to ensure their survival in fickle human memories. But any full scale theological dossier, drawn up on the character and person of Lesa simply is not justified by the vagaries and variables available in the oral repertoire for Lesa (or spirits') traditions. [9]

The oral tradition redacted by homeostasis. There are innumerable changes in any living culture over time, but an oral culture does not have the technology for the intellect to understand them as mutations. There is an oral tendency towards cultural homeostasis (Cf Ong 1982, 46-9). This process is impelled by the social function of memory, which stores only what is socially relevant and conveniently forgets all else in a "structural amnesia" (Goody 1977, 14; 1968, 307-09). New constituents of the cultural heritage are adapted to the old, as the people strive after meaning by harkening after their normative past. The result is that the oral Bemba have little perception of the past except in terms of the present (Richards 1960, 179). They lack writing as a mechanism, by which they could build up a body of chronologically ordered statements to compare with their present views (See above, 85ff). Any present adjustments to the tradition will be gradually introduced as having always been so conceived, convincing the people that the new is in fact part of the true, venerable version of the tradition. Oral transmission, as a performance, then, is not a mechanized memorization but an imaginative process of continuous creativity (Ong 1982, 57-68). It reconstitutes and transfers elements within the latitude of the tradition (Goody 1977, 116-17). An oral tradition is never "an inert acceptance of a fossilized corpus of themes and conventions," but represents an "organic habit of recreating what has been received and handed on" (Lord 1964, xiii). Tradition is actually more of a process (traditio) than a product (tradita). Thus, even the successful debut of the Christian rendition of Lesa could be construed as due to this oral propensity to conceive of contemporary developments as "having always been so" in the tradition.

From this point of view, although the Christian notions have fixed a remarkable orthodox Lesa in the tradition by literate means, they cannot really be dismissed as a violation or deliberate falsification of the content of the tradition. Their acceptability to the Bemba must be recognized as a homeostatic readjustment of the tradition under the rules of its own oral-aural dynamic, which unobtrusively adapts early tradition to present needs. Homeostatis could then be understood as the oral equivalent of the new hermeneutical circle; just as the meaning of a text does not depend on the author's own intention, so too, the meaning of tradition does not depend on the intentions of the original oral performer.

Father Justin Chomba (1978) analyzes the relationship between Lesa and the spirits, in terms of a very tightly organized political hierarchy and precise functional subordination. Just as the chief governs by divine right through his "prime minister" *Mushika,* using "messengers" *Kapaso ,* so "God" Lesa has a such a prime minister *Makumba,* who uses the "spirits" *bashamfumu* as intercessor-saints, etc. This is a classic example of a literate's interference with an orally rendered tradition. Its oral character has been textualized beyond recognition and altered to suit the literary medium and the ideological demands of a developing African Christianity. (Chomba's stated purpose is to facilitate the adaptation of a Roman Catholic ritual better suited to Bemba religious needs). It makes Christian sense of

Bemba tradition for contemporary Bemba Christians anxious to justify their tradition with theological orthodoxy. It is a legitimate exercise in itself as an advance on or redaction of the tradition, (Cf Henige 1982), but there should be no illusions about the "tradition" that Chomba propounds as authentic. It is, in fact, a literate artifice. It was necessary to change the medium, to mute the plurality of oral voices in order to deliver a uniformly contrived message. But once one has "established" that the Bemba have always believed in an omnipotent, omniscient God, has one, in fact, discovered a fundamental dimension of Bemba religiosity or has one merely centralized a peripheral, perhaps local aspect of the tradition?

No matter how well one fabricates a Lesa to measure up to Christian standards, Lesa is certainly not central to Bemba traditional religion in the sense of forming the most frequent focus of religious activities.

In conclusion, it can be said that the oral evidence on the capitular position assigned by literates to Lesa is at least ambiguous enough that much of what passes for Bemba tradition in Christian writings is merely tendentious. They represent as facts of religious monotheism and supremely orthodox divinity what is actually the wishful thinking of the authors. The fact is that the notion of the whole, spontaneously operative in Bemba traditional religion, finds more evident expression in symbols apportioning transcendence among plural spirits than in any integrated conception of divinity. The tradition gives evidence that the Bemba notion of divinity seems to have sprung up from the soil (Lesa) and descended from the sky (Mumbi Mukasa) simultaneously. But it is also true that, nowadays, monotheism and its symbols seem to be a more adequate, certainly a more widely accepted, limit language for expressing the changed Bemba notion of the whole.

A Concluding Reflection

According to traditional religion, extraordinary experience in sacred time and space is the archetype of the really real. The fact that the traditional stories and the sounding environment no longer command serious religious attention alienates sacrality from space and time and abstracts a profane homogeneity. Spirits are alienated from their privileged places and times, which the oral religion recognizes as paradigmatic disclosures of central Bemba truths and values. But the literate alienation of the sacred from the extraordinary, which is a definite debit for traditional religion, becomes a capital asset for Christian incarnational theology and sacramental practice. In the Christian economy, the ordinary, the concrete, the everyday—once really lived, embraced and loved—manifest themselves as the extraordinary and become the major locus of the manifestation-event of the whole. According to Christian doctrine, the ordinary not the extraordinary is the central clue to the reality of the whole: "In the authentic spirit of manifestation, ultimately all reality discloses the all-pervasive power of the grace disclosed by that event [of the incarnation-as-self-manifestation of God in Jesus Christ]" (Tracy 1982, 376-86). To authentically and adequately represent that event, the Christian missionaries select one of the Bemba spirits' own peers, Lesa, as a symbol newly alienated by script from the oral pantheon, endowed with abstract omnipotence and omniscience, and elevated above maternal earthiness.

CHAPTER THREE FOOTNOTES

[1]Guillerme, _Dictionaire Francais-Chibemba_, Malines, 1920. The literate expatriates immediately began to compile dictionaries of the Bemba language (Cf Robertson, _Introductory Handbook to the Bemba_, L.M.S., 1904). As useful as these tools are for other literates, the dictionaries narrowed the oral field of meanings to the select connotations available in the limited experience of the compilers (Cf E. Havelock, _The Greek Concept of Justice_, Cambridge, Harvard University Press, 1978, 231). The dictionary extracts a particular meaning, regardless of its acoustic fit in other living contexts and assumes a despotic control over the polymorphic oral language, giving the excised meaning an illusory rigidity (Walter Ong, _The Presence of the Word_, Cambridge, Harvard University Press, 1967, 32, 65, 106 and _Orality and Literacy_, New York, Methuen, 1982, 106-8, 130).

[2]The following sources were especially useful in preparing this section: N. Garrec, "Croyances et coutumes religieuses des Babemba," Chilonga, 1916, 12-20; E. Labrecque, "Croyances et pratiques religieuses des Bemba . . . Notes sur la Religion des Babemba," Ilondola n.d., 4-9; Idem, "Les Ngulu, Les Mipashi," Rome, Typescript; L. Etienne, "A Study of the Babemba and the Neighboring Tribes," Kasama, 1948, 93-98; F. Tanguy, "The Bemba of Zambia," Ilondola, 1954, 4-9.
Interviews with these "traditional priests" _Shimapepo_ : Kalonga XII, Cingkalonga XI, Shimulamba IX, Namasala IX, Mutoba VII, Shimwalule VII.

[3]Mulenga, for instance, along with his wife Nakonkela, is thought by some to wander towards the East without a proper habitat (E. Labrecque, "Notes sur la Religion des Babemba," Ilondola, N.D., 2). Others think of him as a white man with albino children (C. Gouldsbury & H. Sheane, _The Great Plateau of Northern Rhodesia_, London, 1911, 126). Still others consider him as a "forest-spirit" Wa mpanga, announcing, with the very loud report of his gun, his evil deeds like the 1894 rinderpest, the 1909 dysentery epidemic and the 1924 small-pox outbreak (Cf L. Molinier, "Croyances superstitieuses chez les Babemba," _Journal of the African Society_, 3, 9, October 1093, 82). Yet some report a benevolent Mulenga, who teaches people how to domesticate animals (L. Oger, "The Bemba of Zambia . . . " Ilondola, 1972, 13) and leaves slain game in the forest as chiefs' booty (A. Richards, _Land, Labour and Diet_, London, Oxford University Press, 1939, 254.

[4]The following sources were especially useful in preparing this section: N. Garrec, "Croyances et coutumes . . ." 1-12; Labrecque, "Notes sur la Religion," 1-4; Etienne, "The Babemba," 91-93; and Tanguy, "The Bemba," 1976ff.

[5]The notion of subordinate intercession is a definite Christian gloss ; saintly intercession, at first competitive with

ancestral veneration, eventually gives room for symbolic and ideological borrowing. Many modern Bemba prayers ask that the spirit intercede with *Lesa--Mwe mipashi yandi . . . Mukunkwileko kuli Lesa mukulu* "You my spirits . . . cast yourselves down at the feet of the great Lesa . . ." (Kapwepwe VIII) but they are obviously influenced by Christian liturgical formulae.

[6] J.E. Lane, in his dissertation "Politics and the Image of Man" (Ph.D. dissertation, UCLA, 1977), opens chapter four with a paraphrase of what he calls the Bemba "cosmogonic myth," followed by an elaborate exegesis of this myth, in which he demonstrates its supposed central importance to Bemba social and symbolic worlds (75ff). An appendix to Lane's dissertation contains an English version of this myth, translated from the Dutch article "Het ontstaan der dingen in de Folklore der Bantu's" by P.A. Janssens (**Anthropos**, 21 (1926) 546-65). Janssens' source, in turn, is a series of articles, entitled "In Oeroealand," by a White Father missionary, Van Acker, published in his society's bulletin **Missien der Witte Pater's** from 1902-05 and, in 1924, re-edited as the book **Bij de Baloeba's in Congo**. But, both Lane and his source, Janssens, are mistaken in ascribing this creation story to the Bemba, for several internal and external reasons: (1) The "creator god" is identified as **Kabezya**, a name and a nominal form, which have no precedent nor foundation in the Bemba language. (2) The cosmography in the story centers on the two sides of Lake Tanganyika, which is a geographical feature unrelated to the Bemba territory. (3) The primary source of the cosmogonic myth is P. Van Acker, who, according to records in the White Fathers' Generalate in Rome--Fathers like Lane himself, never visited the Bembaland and certainly did not know the Bemba language. (4) P. Van Acker, himself, entitles his articles as "In the land of the Baluba" (Oeroealand), clearly indicating that the story originated among the Luba people. Van Acker, perhaps heard the story in his travels among the **Hemba** people of Upper Congo in the village called **Mbemba** near the **Nyemba** river. The confusion of the Bemba sounding names could then account for the later error of ascribing this cogmogonic myth to the Bemba people of North eastern Zambia. (5) All of the above is confirmed by P. Colle in his two volume work **Les Baluba (Congo Belge)**, Bruxelles, Institute International de Bibliographie, 1913, where he identifies **Kabezya Mpungu** as one of the created superior spirits of the Luba-Hemba people (Vol. 2, 419 and 495); his source is P. Vandermeiren, a companion of Van Acker. In the final analysis, we agree with the Bemba folklore expert, M. Frost, that there is no proper Bemba cosmogonic myth involving a creator god. Nevertheless, some of the elements in the Luba story--such as the two packets, one beautiful container of death, the other ugly receptacle of benefits, between which the male and the female are to choose--from which Lane makes his symbolic applications, are present in Bemba folklore, perhaps as residual parts of their original Luba heritage or due to later commercial contacts.

[7]Here are a few of the catalogues of proverbs: E. Labrecque "Amapinda," Ilondola, 1931-1947; P. Mushindo, _Amapinda mu Lyashi,_ London, University Press, 1958; J. Girard, "A Few Bemba Proverbs," Fort Rosebery, Mission Mimeograph, 1965; S. Mpashi, _Icibemba Cesu na Mano Yaciko,_ London, Oxford University Press, 1965; E. Hoch, "1111 Bemba Proverbs," Ilondola, Language School Mimeograph, 1966.

[8]M. Frost has amply documented the variable potentialities of the Bemba oral performaces. A single story registers marked variants according to the locality in which it is performed, according to the occasion of the performance, and according to the performer's choice in exploiting the potentials within the tradition, as she or he sets up a vibrant relation between what is spoken and the living reaction of the audience (Mary Frost, "Inshimi and Imilumbe: structural expectations in Bemba oral imaginative performances," Ph.D. thesis, University of Wisconsin, 1977).

[9]Stephen Mpashi, and Bemba poet-laureate, forecloses on single oral contingencies amidst the living oral options in order to carry out his own literary purposes in a saga of _Lesa_. The new literary creation which results, subsumes a plurality of vignettes about the spirits clustered in the oral tradition, where they have only nominal links to one another, and sets them under the control of a contrived plot about Lesa (Cf S. Mpashi, _Pano Calo,_ Nairobi, Oxford University Press, 1956). But it is clear to those familiar with the stories that oral voices and values have atrophied, while the literary mode came to wonderful life (K.S. Lutato, "The influence of oral narrative traditions on the novels of Stephen A. Mpashi," Ph.D. thesis, University of Wisconsin, 1980, 2-3). As a former catholic seminarian, Mpashi wants to understand the worship of the spirits as a surrogate quest for God.

The people forget that they ate Lesa in time of famine and confusion: _Balaba nefyo Lesa acilamoneka pa cinso, balaba na kuntu ele. Bamo balasonta ku lupili. Bambi balatontonkanya abati ali kumumana. Bambi abati ni ku culu, bambi ku mutengo ku cimuti icikalamba. Pa kufwayo kwibukisha bwino, bambi balepunamina mu mulu._ "They forgot how Lesa looked to the eye, and where he had gone . . . Some pointed to the mountain. Others thought he was at the river or at the anthill. Still others said he was in the forest at the big tree. In trying to remember, some looked up into the sky" (Mpashi, _Pano Calo,_ 39). The assumption that Lesa is really a transcendental hidden presence in the tradition is an admirable christian redaction. But Mpashi is more attune with the actual oral tradition in accounting for Lesa's disappearance from the Bemba consciousness in terms of social amnesia: to forget is the great social evil in an oral culture, which lives by what it recalls. Lesa is remembered when his character can be construed as socially relevant. In the meantime, other spirits have cultic ascendance.

CHAPTER FOUR

ORALITY AND AUTHORITY

The first part of this chapter considers the special nature and operation of oral authority, concentrating on its religious dimensions. The Bemba "paramount chieftainship" *Citimukulu* is selected for detailed analysis, because all other Bemba authorities derive their power from the paramountcy. They participate in the central religious character--the spontaneously operative notion of the whole--found in the preeminently successful limit-symbols attached to Citimukulu. The wane of chiefly power will be seen to be concurrent with the decline of oral religion. They were both provoked by the change from an oral to a literate agency and by the dwindling adequacy of traditional limit-language. The second half of the chapter will investigate the remarkable resilience of traditionally peripheral religious authorities, despite and, perhaps, because of the decay of, central religious tenets and cultural absolutes. This paradoxical phenomenon will be accounted for in terms of an obstreperous residual orality.

Central Speaking Authority and the Power of Knowledge

The oral medium is an essential factor in defining the nature and function of Bemba authority: *Bufumu e busosa* "The chieftainship is constituted by speech."[1] The most compelling symbols of Bemba chieftainship-- *cipuna* "the royal stool," and *mupunga* "fly whisk"--are applied to the oral authority's right to speak in relation to the duty of others to listen (Corbeil IV).

The kinship structure forms the framework of the Bemba political system. Authority is based on descent in the family, the village and the tribe. Power and prerogative are concentrated in the 'lineages' *Ng'anda* of a single matrilineal "clan" *Mukowa* or in families favored by them (Richards 1940, 85-95). There exists a vast network of family ties within the Bemba polity, which is essentially constituted and functionally characterized by the oral media of communication of authority. At every level of juridical, administrative, ritual, economic, and military power, relatives of chiefs and sub-chiefs serve as village heads, priests, advisors, messengers, et al. These are basically spokespersons and listeners--encouraging and criticizing one another, hearing and pleading cases, transmitting orders and commanding people, winning and bestowing favor, advising and discussing social affairs. The most powerful sanctions of authorities are their popularity and the sentiments of loyalty and cohesion. These in turn are fostered by the intimate knowledge and face-to-face encounters in the exercise of their power. One grows up into the fullness of authority by forging personal ties and demonstrating political success. In 1934 after two years of reign, Citimukulu declared, *Ninkula, tukekala ku mushi nomba. Bakamfunda fyonse fya kale* "I have grown up. We will stay in the village now. They will teach me everything according to the tradition" (Richards 1939, 362n).

The "they," who would teach him, were the *Bakabilo* "royal councillors," who represented the traditional charters and commonweal of the tribe. Their memories of the traditions and their control of the rituals, uniting ancestral spirits with contemporary Bemba chiefs, make them a force to be reckoned-with. This group of councillors are those who represent the chiefly confluence of "community and tradition" (Cf Booth, 1978). They are the living oral voices speaking out of the "storehouses of the wisdom of ancestors, who lived and suffered in times gone by" (Vansina 1965, xi).

That ancestral knowledge, which is Bemba communal property, is also a source of power within the community for its specialized wielders (Cf Ong 1968, 8-16). These are the individuals or select groups, to whom is entrusted the responsibility for keeping tradition alive and handing it on. These persons acquire authority and exercise discipline in matters with which their knowledge deals. The specialized knowledge of the *Cisungu* rite for example, places power over gynecological affairs in the hands of the *Nacimbusa* "initiator" (Richards 1956, 166-67). In addition, Bemba society is very conscious of seniority, and its tradition is heavy with the privilege and prerogative owed to rank and authority, called *Mucinshi* (Mpashi 1947). This proper hierarchy of respect opens the appropriate channels of communication to which that respect entitles one. The trappings of high status and power are not material possessions, but knowledge. Knowledge is the key to power, and access to knowledge depends on the power and privilege a person is expected to wield in the community. The distribution of knowledge is an allocation of power. Richards (1960, 186) records the case of *Kabilo*, "councillor", who even refused to share the specialized knowledge of his office with his legitimate successor, lest they become equals while the senior still lived. Frost (1977, chap. 5) records a story, in which the tortoise-- usually the only animal to outsmart the rabbit--gives away the knowledge which made him a clever trickster, and is thus rendered impotent.

Possession of special knowledge signals a certain transcendence over one's milieu and society. It frees the person from ordinary limits. For example, the chief's knowledge gives him the transcendence which poetically associates him with the uncanny: "Sampa had an axe cooked up for a royal meal and Bwembya excreted feathers" (Milimo, 1978, 152). The royal wisdom frees him from the communal rules of decorum: *Cikala camfumu tacitinwa* "the nakedness of the chief is not to be feared"

(Milimo 1979, 97-9). It also sets royal conduct above laws of social propriety: *Bashamfumu tababa ne nsoni* "chiefs have no shame" (Tanguy 1954, 17).

If knowledge is power, then knowledge within socially sanctioned order is politically powerful, conferring special speaking and listening rights on the authority. But inordinate knowledge is powerful witchcraft. An ordinary individual person with extraordinary knowledge is suspected of being a witch (Richards 1939, 202), who will use that knowledge to further selfish, private ends and not the common good (See below, 121ff).

Authorities and all powerful persons, therefore, are the ones who control the oral process of managing traditional knowledge and the channels of its communication.

Sound and Authority

The intricate and intimate political system of the Bemba is coordinated not simply through the information passing along the oral channels of officialdom. But a sense of the active power and personal presence of the office-holder accompanies the communication (See above, chap. 1, 1-3). Recognition of this attitude toward oral words is an anthropological cliché, but the conjunction of this attitude with the very nature of sound is seldom considered (Ong 1967, 112-13). There is a vital movement of an agent at source, an active use of power in its production, and an intimation of personal presence in its repercussions. As the phenomenologist, Ihde, observes: "The languages, which relate hearing to the invading features of sound, often consider the auditory presence as a type of 'command'" (Ihde 1976, 81). Whether the authorities themselves are actually speaking or their words are simply being repeated by their vicars, there is a sense of their active, powerful personal presence, eliciting the loyalties of their subjects and demanding commitment and obedience (from the Latin obaudire "to listen from below") (Cf Jaynes 1977, 97-99).

Chapter 3 already discussed the *Musumba* as a royal place of uproar. The centre of attention there is the chief who is borne on a wave of sound. The *Malumbo* "set praises" cheer the chief, and the noise of "clapping and ululating" *Kuomba amakuku* greet him. The *mishikakulo* --the sort of Luban glossalalia with their responding chorus of *Njobo* and *Upama* --accompany him everywhere, creating a hubbub of intensely loud activity with which everyone wants to be associated (Shimwalule VII). The royal poet likens chief Mporokoso to a drummer: "I am the son of the great drum-beater. The drums with which I built the village, are charging across the river with great authority" (Milimo 1978, 59). The uproar around the chief is an audible symbol of his power to attract the loyalty and obedience of his people and the ancestral sanction of his spiritual divinity.

Sacred Bemba Chieftainship

Technically, according to Richards (1968), it is the chieftainship itself, and not the currently enthroned chief, which qualifies as divinely sacred. The "paramountcy" *Citimukulu* is permanent, exempt from death, and living on by "ritual reincarnation" *Kupyanika* . The first paramount Citimukulu was conceived in the hierogamy of his father and heavenly mother, Mumbi Mukasa. Moreover, each succeeding Citimukulu becomes, by virtue of the matrilineal spirits reincarnate in him, a sacred being, an emanation of maternal divinity (Labrecque 1929). "Divinity accumulates with the length of the line" (Richards 1968, 26). The chieftainship grows heavy with many spirits and the living chief of this semi-divine line condescends to live among humans until at death he returns to his real status (Foulon 1907, vol. II). His waking call associates him with the spirit world *Mulungu mwine nkuni na menshi* "Spirit divinity, owner of the woods and waters" (Etienne 1948, 95). Because "the paramount chief is the source of all blessings through his ancestral connections" *Kwa Citimukulu kuli babenye e kufumo bupalo* , he is primarily a worshipping chief, whose worship is of his own ancestry (Richards 1956, 168).

The chief has an uncanny ontological power over his whole territory. He controls the land by his sex life and ritual leadership, "making it good, and setting it in order with his blessings" *Kuwamya, Kufunga mate no kulungame calo* (Richards 1939, 248). "The chief's life cycle affects the cosmic commonweal" *Ico calo nayandatila eka* (Milimo 1979, 219). "His sickness disturbs the world" *Ububwele bwa mfumu Litensha calo* (Idem, 36). "His death destroys the political order" *Mfwa ya mfumu lipenuna nsonshi* (Idem), and "a period of chaotic lawlessness" *Miconga* intervenes (Chomba 1979, 5), signalling "the earth's death" *Calo cawa*. This virtuality of the chief persuades the Bemba of their community's cosmic integration with the permanence of rhythmic nature.

The tradition dictates that, as the paramount enters his death agony, his powers and spirits must be prevented from escaping the land in his final breath. They are to be bottled up within him by "smothering him" *Kufumbulula* (Etienne 1948, 95) and his body is to be dessicated for immortality (Brelsford 1942). As a symbolic guarantee that the dead chief did not take away the life of the land, he is not buried until "the royal sorghum" *Masaka* planted at his death is harvested a year or so later (Shimwalule VII).

Clearly, then, if one were trying to locate the Bemba religious "center of the world" the **axis mundi**--the "cosmic umbilicus" with all of its Eliadean (1959) connotations of ritual renewal by a return to origins--it would be the Citimukulu. From his "royal city" *Musumba* , "the sun dawns" *Epo bubalili kuca,* from there "all roads lead" *Nga abulalekelesha mu mbali monse*

(Mushindo 1958, 5). The chief is the sacred center, <u>resounding</u> with spiritual authority characteristic of all sacred, acoustic space. At his death, with the center destroyed, the social order is disrupted and ritual chaos and rioting prevail (Roberts 1976, 81, 165).

Finally, if one were trying to identify, in Bemba religious life, the paradigmatic human manifestation of "the whole" with all the connotations Tracy (1981) assigns to it, the paramountcy qualifies. Upon the Citimukulu, as on a center, converge all the cosmic, spiritual and human powers. He exercises control over them, because he derives his uncanny power from his matrilineal contact with their source. United with all that is, he unifies and enlivens the tribe. Citimukulu is united with the spirits by royal ancestry and united with the earth by proprietary control of its productive fertility. He is united with the sky by matrilineal descent from the heavenly queen, herself the permanent pivot between the sky and the earth. The paramount's blood, his sex, and his fire, preeminently symbolize the Bemba religious contact points to "the whole." Standing at the "limits of" Bemba experience, he represents the "limits to" all contingent existence. His subject people, who prostrate themselves with fear and awe at his powers, respond to him with trust and dependence. In heeding his powerful words and acclaiming him with tumultuous rituals, they themselves participate in "the whole." Meaning and value accrue to their lives by obedient contact with this chief, who is the metaphoric presence of those uncanny qualities of ultimacy and transcendence associated with the notion of the whole. In the final analysis, Citimukulu is the priestly, almost sacramental mediator of whatever "of the whole" vicariously adheres in the Bemba community and tradition.

The Crisis of Oral Authority at the Center

How could this glorious "divine being" or "divine chieftainship," parcelled out among so many "demi-god" chiefs (Richards 1968, 26), be dethroned? How is it that such a religiously lofty person could be brought to such a political low in the colonial era? The demise of the chiefs has been amply accounted for in terms of the imposition of the Company Rule, which supplanted their secular hegemony. It has also been noted that the chiefs lost their own peoples' confidence as they succumbed to the seductions of Indirect Rule and, as hirelings, cooperated with their colonial masters (Meebelo 1971). The rise of a new elite who challenged their leadership and the usurpation of spiritual authority by Christian missionaries also contributed to the corrosion of the chiefs' command. Colonial annual reports repeat with monotonous regularity that the power of the chiefs was declining for such reasons (Cf Davis 1933, 250).

Another major contributing factor was the change of medium from an oral-aural management of society to a literate structure for the maintenance and deployment of political authority. A change of media is usually concomitant to a crisis of authority (Cf Nielsen 1954), which involves not just the literately alienated subjects but the oral rulers themselves. The latter, of course, are not easily persuaded that writing is as trustworthy and efficient a medium of authority as orality (Clanchy 1979). Let us now trace the demise of traditional chiefly authority--also the erosion of the traditional religious center--as a consequence of the change from orality to literacy.

The advent of British rule at the beginning of the twentieth century introduced new authorities, a new economy of money, wage-labor and commerce, and new government functions. These all meant new allegiances and new sanctions. In themselves, they would be enough to alter the chief's powers and subvert the personal relationship between the chiefs and their subjects (Cf Garvey 1977). But, coupled with major changes in the communication media of English and literacy, the colonial dominance over the Bemba population was doubly decisive. For example, all along the British made documentary agreements with Bemba chiefs, based upon the trappings of English law contracts. The oral authorities, of course, did not understand that by their marks on paper, they were ceding territorial rights and resources for the pittance of manufactured goods they were given. They certainly could not have intended to disinherit their tribes and to deprive tribal posterity of land rights. The chiefs, in fact, were not so much proprietors as custodians of tribal land, which belonged to the ancestral spirits, the real "owners of the land" *bene calo* . To the literate colonial authorities, it was a simple **quid pro quo** commercial transaction documenting a transfer of real estate (Meebelo 1971, 29-31).

The English language of government machinery was not one to which the traditional rulers had access. It was the young Bemba who learned to use this basic tool of the colonial powers. English was, of course, not at all wedded to the oral structure of Bemba authority; the vernacular was (Ong 1967, 240). The chirographically controlled English language alienated the ruled from their traditional rulers. It gave the youth a psychological distance from the Bemba life-world with its passionate practical concerns. It reduced to a minimum the connections with sound on which traditional knowledge and authority depended. English freed them from intimate involvement with the psychosocial roots of their culture (Ong 1977, 34-8; 1982, 103-08).

The first step in the detribalisation of the new generation of Bemba was taken. Now they had a common meeting ground with their new overlords and with other tribespersons, from which the traditional rulers were excluded. The chiefs and ruling classes had used an archaic Luba to exclude commoners from the decision-making processes of the tribe (Richards 1940, 111). Now they were shunted over as the outsiders by a new linguistic inside. Their powers were usurped by a wider government, whose literacy and English medium gave it greater ability to control larger secondary group relationships. Only primary groups of kin and clan are amenable to the intimate controls of oral management (Goody 1977, 15). In oral politics, there prevailed the seemingly more arbitrary demands of personal authority. The literate world sponsors the relatively fixed and individually manageable medium of the printed law (Ong 1967, 54).

The crisis of authority was a crisis of the word and produced psychological and sociological trauma as the culture shifted from oral to literate. Literacy was the real media-villain in the demise of the chiefs. Writing and reading break down the highly socialized and authoritarian structures of culture--and lead to the rise of individual consciousness. Reading is a private activity that forces isolated individuals out of tribal precincts "into the privacy of their own study", off by themselves and into themselves (Ong 1967, 270ff; 1982, 101-03). There they begin to scrutinize meanings and to subject knowledge to inspection and criticism. Their opinions become self-generated and self-verified. In writing, persons become reflectively aware of themselves as creative, original thinkers. They are not responsible to an immediately present audience, censoring their thoughts according to what tradition says (Ong 1967, 134). Instead, they are liberated from public tribunals, where problems are solved in the unquestionable and pressured terms of what others say and do. Both readers and writers are dissociated from the sounding world of speakers and listeners (Ong 1982, 170-71). The oral word itself is muted by textualization, and, without its sound and the socializing effects of physical encounter, interpersonal communication and participation are minimized (Ong 1967, 72, 283).

As the oral word loses its power, the holders of knowledge produced by the oral word lose their power as well. The collapse of oral noetics undermines the credibility and feasibility of oral politics. Oral authorities, who are the transmitters and guarantors of official inspired tradition, are dislodged. At the same time, the social procedures authenticating their succession and legitimating their government are dismantled. Already in 1899 the British rulers presided over the selection and installation of senior chief Mwamba; the other major party to the dispute was the literate catholic missionaries (Roberts 1973, 283-84). By 1916 official lists of chiefs published by the British South Africa Company were the legitimating medium. In 1925 British government officials short-circuited the lengthy, disputatious, orally complicated deliberations about rival candidates' rights and fitness for the Citimukulu, which had been traditionally carried on by the *Bakabilo* "councillors". They imposed a written, fixed system for the paramount succession (Richards 1940, 100-01). Recognition by the British governor was the final criterion for chieftainship. The oral authorities, who were the chief spokespersons for the tradition before which there was no appeal, became the puppets of literacy or were dethroned. Their word, which formerly was the oral law, was now classified into rigid texts. These prescriptions purported to represent customary law but were modelled on British codified law (Gouldsbury 1915-16). Thus the effects, resulting from the deterioration of oral structures, were extended and intensified by colonial politics.

The psychological structures supporting the corporate sense of tribal Bemba were weakened by literacy. For the ear, which was the chief organ for a sensorium organized to store and repeat, gave way to the eye (Ong 1982, 117-23). This shift freed the mind from its memory tasks and released energies for scanning, pondering, criticizing and composing knowledge from a variety of sources stored in books. The oral paradigm of Bemba understanding was *Kuumfwa* "to hear and to obey" (See above, chap. 1, 11 and chap. 3, 75). The literate model was to see and to inspect. The words of oral rulers were no longer accepted just because they were repeated; rather, they were written down for reflection to be weighed against other written words. Even the authority of the orally delivered Bemba charter myth was measured against the composite version frozen in White Father vernacular readers. Older oral authorities, like the Shimwalule, have been influenced by the humiliating "corrections" offered by impertinent literate youngsters to their traditional renditions (Cf Roberts 1973, 31, 31).

When the auditory approach to reality is altered by literacy, a new consciousness is introduced by the highly visual mode of perception. So the demise of chiefly power is, in part, also a revolt of minds, informed by the new laws of literacy governing psycho-mental mechanisms over against oral dominance. What is entailed here is not so much a struggle between the members of Bemba society separated by a generation gap. It is more a stress within individual psyches split by the media gaps (Ong 1967, 283). The chief from whom the young Bemba literates free themselves is, for the most part, their tribal selves.

At the same time, the socio-cultural mechanisms change from a loud, orally structured world to a silent, literate system. The means of communication and execution of law are no longer the personal, charismatic and familiar messengers. They had been armed with the forceful words of oral authorities, whose presence they actively conjured up by proclaiming in their name. In the new order, faceless, nameless bureaucrats, shuffling reams of papers and written codes, dispense justice according to objective issues, impose taxes according to numbered cottages, and lay down the law with impersonal indifference (Cf Weber 1947, 330-32; Bendix 1960, 419-20). The new officials do not seem to know or care to know one's family ties and village customs.

Literate changes in the sensorium change younger Bembas' feelings for their life-world. Personalist loyalties and tribal feelings and responses become less important and decisive in orienting oneself. Valuable oral relationships are cancelled, when the learning process moves from the village to the mission school. The oral teaching and mimesis of extended family elders, village authorities, religious specialists, and territorial chiefs, are less influential than the written words of the Christian missionary and the *Boma bwana* "government big-wig" (Snelson 1974, 19 and 272). All, who owe their authority to the fallible oral control of knowledge and the selective oral management of power, are distrusted. They are unsuccessful in the complex and exciting culture created by literate technology. The authoritative elites of tribe and tradition, of aristocratic blood and heritage, governing by arbitrary demands, are supplanted by the more abstract and uniform democratic citizenship of individual effort (Ong 1967, 54). The majestic proportions of the heroic chiefs and their powerful words, once so eminently credible, can no longer rally and hold the minds of the young. The new generation is alienated by their reading and writing skills from their oral heritage. As the young literates acquire the alien knowledge oral authorities lacked, they also acquire its attendant power to challenge oral hegemony.

Here it must be recalled that in the oral economy, knowledge is jealously guarded and carefully parcelled out. Customary political power depends on its responsible distribution. But, the profligate and promiscuous literate dissemination of new ideas in schools nurtured alien knowledge and power. These, too, posed a threat to the traditional authorities (Snelson 1970, 1-23). Also there were competent and authoritative Europeans, who despised the traditional mores, displayed contempt for the spirit-world which so powerfully sanctioned the traditional cultural patterns, and demonstrated superior control of the natural and human milieux through Western technology. These teachers did their share to shake loose the young Bemba from their roots.

Although the skills of literacy by the 1920's had only been acquired by a small minority of Bemba, they were the forces of the future (See above, Preface). The new media had already induced a manifest skepticism of traditional rulers and oral ways. Amidst the confusion, anxiety and hostility which abounded in this critical period of media-transition, the British sought to re-establish a semblance of the traditional prestige and power for oral authorities. They introduced, in a misdirected effort, the Ordinance of Indirect Rule in 1929. Under the rule of the crocodile clan, the Bemba traditions of *Mulasa* and *Mutulo* "tribute labor and tax" were orally negotiated in the tribe, based on personal loyalties and mutual responsibilities of chief and subject. During Indirect Rule, these royal rights were codified in British law analogous to taxation, and became unenforceable fossilized caricatures of the living customs

(Meebelo 1971, 211-20). As the tumult surrounding the chief diminishes, so, too, does his voice fall silent. Written demands for tribute and tax fall on deaf ears.

Coincidentally, but responding to the same critical circumstances, there were a few efforts by the deputies of the oral culture to regain ascendancy over the threatening new order. Traditional religious means were employed to play to oral proclivities. "Witchcraft accusations" *Buloshi* increased the levels of fear amidst an already polarized community. "Spirit-possession phenomena" *Ngulu* reinvigorated ancestral oracles. "Spirit consultors" *Ng'anga* pledged resumed communication with the spirits. And "witch-cleansing movements" *Mcapi* promised the purification of the old culture. But colonial efforts and traditional attempts to restore the oral medium were vainly peripheral and doomed by the central forces of literacy. Even the Zambian independent government's experiment with a resurgent oral authority in a House of Chiefs was short lived. The heyday of the chiefs is over. The literate medium is ascendant.

Resurgent Orality on the Periphery

Until now we have focused on **positive** religious factors in the tradition. These were identified in Chapter One as operative in the Bemba limit-experience and expression of the notion of the whole. Chapter Two examined the threshold experience of new life for a joyful tribe originating in the charter myth and celebrated in the puberty rite. In Chapter Three the limit-language narrating the ecstasy of spirit-encounters was analyzed. So far, Chapter Four has discussed the symbolic embodiment of holistic disclosure in the paramountcy eliciting reverential loyalty to tribal authority.

Limit-language and Negative Religion

We will now turn our attention to the **negative** crises of life, which also disclose "a limit"--"a religious" dimension or horizon. Instead of an occasion for revelation of and ecstatic at-one-ment with "the whole," there occurs concealment and estrangement. These frontier-experiences and the limit-language of their expression make people intensely conscious of the readily forgotten fragility of life and the radical need for revival. They are uncanny reminders that ultimately people are at the mercy of persons and events over which there is no infallible control. For self-protection, they must be constantly and anxiously vigilant, guarding against disturbing exposures of concealed iniquity. There is a limit-language, which the Bemba traditionally use to express their experiences and feelings of finite contingency and alienating shame for transgressing against social propriety. It is the language of witchcraft, divination and demonic possession. In the tradition, the marginal persons

who exercise authority in these negative affairs are held in
check by the positive, central authority of chiefs. The
potentially disruptive consequences of their adverse
presuppositions are counterbalanced by the assuring remedial
action of limit-symbols re-presenting "the whole." Recently,
these peripheral authorities have moved front and center in the
declining religious tradition. They now exercise virtually
unfettered and unlicensed sway over the symbolic practices for
convicting and exorcising the Bemba community of its iniquity.

Orality and Evil

As their oral religion is anthropocentric (See above, chap.
1, 20ff), the Bemba do not look beyond human agency for a cause
of evil. But neither do they leave anything to chance. Every
evil happening, besides having its obvious physical explanation,
is attributed to human beings who are believed capable of
wielding some form of mystical causation. Their covert activity
sets in motion the overt causes. This does not mean, however,
that when the Bemba enquire about evil, they interpret the term
primarily in terms of personal moral evil, as do literate people.
Evil for the Bemba is not a private or interior concern. It is
communal and affects the public weal (See above, chap. 2, 59ff).
Evil is personal only in the sense that the oral person is
programmed to grapple with environmental predicaments using
personalistic models (See above, chap. 3, 73ff). It is
individual only in the sense that anything is evil which stands
apart from the ordinary, and anyone, who does not conform to
social expectations, verges by his or her peculiarity on evil.
The singular is abnormal, and the unique draws a good deal of
negative attention. Any attempt to better oneself, to rise above
the mediocre, is a high risk procedure.

In the highly socialized structures of the oral Bemba,
anyone may be reputed as evil who possesses more personal
property than others, who knows more than personal status
warrants, who is healthier or more successful in enterprises than
other villagers (Richards 1939, 215). Anyone is suspected of
evil motives who takes bold initiatives, introduces novel
practices or promotes original ideas. In short, anyone, who
singularizes self or sets self above the village mean or apart
from others, is abnormal and quite probably evil-intentioned.
Self-assertiveness, so prized by literates, is despised by oral
societies. Originality and creativity threaten disaster to the
storage and management of knowledge, which orality must contrive
to serve in relatively rigid and unchanging formulae (Ong 1974;
1982, 38-42).

The popular presumption is that inordinate knowledge or
extraordinary accumulations for an ordinary person must have been
acquired by nefarious means. It is a well known fact that
"witches" *Baloshi* are those, who have more food than others and

who have a carefully calculated knowledge of how much others possess. Surplus food is better shared than amassed, and children are exhorted never to appear snooping around granaries (Richards 1939, 202 & 207). In brief, in the oral community, all prosper and all suffer together. Overweening success, or burdensome suffering, is an anti-social threat, and smacks of evil.

When a singular event occurs, then, the Bemba attend to it, seeking explanation. For example, that a person dies because lightning strikes or a snake bites, is rationally inescapable. Those are the laws of nature. But there is no law to account for this particular occurrence of a lightning bolt or this special coincidence of snake and human in the forest (Stuart 1972). The Bemba are not so much guilty of a lack of rationality as an over-rationality that seeks to explain the inexplicable. Even to a scientist, the "empirical residue" of a particular time and a particular place is irrelevant, nay impervious, to scientific explanation; the singularity of an occurrence is simply a matter of fact (Tracy 1970, 107-09). The Bemba account for specific occurrences of otherwise naturally regulated events by positing the voluntary interventions of personal agents: "Who sent the lightning to strike my brother-in-law, leaving your niece unscathed?"

This mystical causation of evil, lurking behind the natural coincidence, is what the Bemba name "witchcraft" *Buloshi* . The religious process of divulging the evil is called "divination" *Lubuko* and its "the diviner" is termed *Ng'anga* . A "permanent witch" is called *Muloshi* and one in whom a "possessing spirit" activates temporary mystical power is called *Ngulu* . The religious process of "eradicating a witch" is called *Mwafi,* and of "cleansing witchcraft" is called *Mcapi* . These terms are metaphors of evil, the limit-language, which the Bemba employ to symbolize those negative crises of their ordinary experience. Their religious usage exemplifies the Bemba anthropocentric tendency to equate all grave misfortune with moral misdemeanor. If adversity seems to emanate from the victim's own misconduct, then punitive action ensues from the ancestral spirits, as guardians of tribal morality. The results are some form of "violent possession" *Ngulu* and the need for placation and/or consultation by *Ng'anga* . If woes seem to befall from the wickedness of others, then the malevolence of witches is suspected. They must be identified by the prophecy of a "benevolent possession" *Ngulu* or "cleansed" by *Mcapi* (Cf V. Turner 1957, 142).

Reality and Evil

These limit-symbols of evil derive their reality and power basically from four circumstantial referents in Bemba life.

(1) A precarious life-situation.   As a forest people,   the Bemba   live   in a world of very high mortality,   where   they   are poignantly   vulnerable   to   malnutrition,   endemic   malaria   and bilharzia, as well as to frequent mishaps with snake bites, fires and beasts.   They   are prey to a host of other misfortunes   (Cf Roberts 1976, 146ff).

(2) An elementary "science" and a   rudimentary technology. In   a Bemba   village,   there is little mastery of   the   physical environment,   and the agricultural economy is one of   subsistence and   scarcity.   Where medicinal and hygenic knowledge is limited and   where unexpected death is frequent,   plausable   explanations for evil are devised in accordance with the fertile   imaginations of mythic minded villagers.   For the oral community, there is no mental   technology to develop a systematic and verified knowledge of objective causation.   Reports on the natural environment   and remarks   on the human community rely mostly on   "hearsay"--"oral-aural" myths and rumors.   The Bemba material technology provides them   with   very   few genuine health aids and   with   little   else beyond   subsistence-level farming,   so dependent on   capriciously seasonal rains.   They   are   left almost at the   mercy   of   their environment (See (4) below).

(3) A close-knit community life.   Bemba   village life clusters   kins-people and clans-people of sometimes   incompatible temperaments   into   irremediably   close   and   exhausting   daily contact.   The   publicity   and   communality,   which   characterize virtually   every aspect of their oral lifestyle,   contribute to a high level of negative feelings. Grudges, jealousies, arrogance, anger   and hatred pile up rampantly,   until they are released   in passionate   displays   of   malevolent   intentions.   These   are considered, and thus empowered, to have lethal consequences.

(4) An oral-aural conception of a   hostile   universe.   The Introduction (Above,   chap.   1,   24ff)   illustrated how the Bemba share   an   oral   world-view   that conceives of the   cosmos   as   a holistic   continuity   of   overlapping   personal   forces.   This personalized   cosmos is as full of overt hostility and   potential violence   even   as   the Bemba human community is   full   of   moral disorder (Cf   Ong 1967,   131,   195,   261).   Theirs is a   rather polemically   textured culture.   This is true not so much in   the frequency of actual fighting,   as in the way persons   experience, conceive   and   express themselves as participants in their   human and natural environments (Ong 1982,   43-5).   Bemba life seems to be a constant struggle (Cf Ong 1974,   2).   The parcelling out of disease   and   disaster is too capricious to be predicated of   an impersonal   fate,   and   too arbitrary to be due to   natural   law. Personal   decisions   are   being   made.   The   occurrence   of   any untoward   event   seems   the   work of   a   foe,   and   a   series   of afflictions   unmasks   an evident conspiracy of malevolent   wills. Such   a   conception of the universe as a naked   struggle   between personal forces of good and evil results in the high incidence of states   of   confused   excitement   and   disorganizing   anxiety   and

hostility. (Cf Ong 1967, 194-206). The Bemba traditionally display this temperament through belief in spirit-possession, spirit-consultation and witchcraft.

In the final analysis, the constant repetition of rumors, the oral proliferation of exaggerated tales, and the cantankerous profusion of accusations, all accredit the extravagant actuality with which these limit-symbols are endowed by Bemba believers.

Revisionist Responses to Evil

It would be unfair to characterize Bemba traditional religion as being primarily concerned with, or revolving around, the problem of evil. Most of Bemba religious belief and practice is preoccupied with good and value. Veneration of spirits under chiefly authority is motivated out of gratitude for, or sheer joy in, the good things of life. A bountiful harvest is a more likely occasion for ritual than any fear of impending disaster.

But, at the very time in which the central authorities and religion seem to be in decline, it is remarkable that there is an upsurging belief in outlandish practitioners who deal authoritatively with evil.

This section will argue that the increased preoccupation of the Bemba people with formerly marginal elements of religious tradition can be attributed in part to the intensified eruption of disorder into Bemba culture. It results from the clash with Christianity and colonialism.

The major part of our argument, however, will be that the negative aspects of the religious tradition have gained an unwonted ascendancy and centrality in modern times. One good reason is that, concommitant to the apparent rise in the level of evil confronting the people, there has been a gradual muffling of the oral integrity of the culture. In a last ditch stand against the usurpation by literacy of the authoritative position traditionally occupied by orality, spokespersons arise who seek to re-present the oral world. Their chief means are to proclaim words and perform deeds associated with ancestral spirits. [2]

Although they have always been operative on the periphery of traditional religion, witchcraft practices, spirit-possession and spirit-consultation phenomena all surge into Bemba-land with a ferocious intensity in this twentieth century. They follow in the wake of the bewildering complex of rapid change and misfortune, which accompanied colonialism and Christianity. Even the normally difficult circumstances of Bemba life have been greatly aggravated by cultural attenuation in the rural areas and by the competitiveness and anonymity of urban life.

In the city, foreign neighbors speak unknown languages and seem eccentric with their own customs. Advancement in employment is not based on traditional seniority, but on proficiency or educational advantages. Seniors jealously resent juniors' promotion. Juniors, suspected of using witchcraft for advancement, leave their jobs as too dangerous or become inefficient, since energetic initiative is punished by elder co-workers (Kapferer 1969, and Mitchell 1965). Women compete for husbands, luxuries and necessities amidst shortages (Schuster 1979). Sanctions of personal and tribal networks are not effective in the multi-tribal towns. Elders, resentful of the lack of attention and respect, become victims of witchcraft accusation in their isolated bitterness. Parents compete with urban attractions for control of their children. Students compete to pass exams and for peer acceptance. The sum total of the pressures of a literate Western cultural apparatus--the anxieties of a cash economy, the jealousies of success, the instability of families, the scarcity of commodities and decent accommodations, the development of a class society--all is grossly amplified by the density and heterogeneity of urban population.

Bemba society had no traditional answers or controls for these alien intrusions of white civilization. Some Bemba tried to make sense of the disturbances by applying their newly acquired skills of literacy in political organizations like Native Welfare Associations, labor unions and independence movements (Cf Meebelo 1971). Other Bemba sought refuge in syncretic religious movements, like the Lumpa-Church of Alice Lenshina (Cf Garvey 1974, 329-50). Some others joined Christian Sects, which emphasize millenarianism, for example, the Watch Tower Movement (Meebelo 1971, 133-85). Still others coped with the harsh realities by heightened involvement in mainstream Christian Churches, for example, Protestant Bible Study and Catholic Action groups (Garvey 1974, 302-19).

But, many Bemba people turned to traditional realms of the supernatural in order to cope with all the foreignness and disaster. Colonial administrators actually aggravated this option in 1901 by outlawing witch-accusation and eradication. The prohibition greatly inhibited the public oral release of pentup anxieties and served to increase the fear of uncontrolled malice. At the same time, missionaries mocked or denied the reality of witchcraft and spirits, and so precluded any genuine Christian aids.

Into the void left by the colonialists, Christian missionaries, and fading primary oral authorities, there rushed a virtual invasion of "witch-cleansers" *Bamucapi* around 1933. Increased activity of "spirit-mediums" *Ngulu,* and intensified importance of "healers" *Ng'anga* were also evident. All three answer perennial Bemba religious needs and are rooted in the traditional means for dealing with evil (Cf Ranger 1972).

Ng'anga, Mcapi and *Ngulu,* as spokespersons for a resurgent oral tradition, give at least a short term feeling of well being to Bemba community. In the long term, the circumstances of the community worsened with the onslaught of two European wars, the depression, the struggle for independence, the economic and political woes of the new Zambia and the violent uncertainties of the Zimbabwean war. The Bemba also remained much confused by the twofold dynamic of acculturation to European values and the renascence of Africanity.

The *Ng'anga* "healers" conjure up ancestral spirits to speak out of the cosmos to disturbed persons. The *Ngulu* "possessed persons" reproduce benevolent *Mipashi* to prophetically bring ancestral judgment down on cultural chaos. The re-establishment of the malevolent *Fiwa* in renewed "witchcraft" *Buloshi* generates its own counter-force in the "witch-cleansing movement" *Mcapi* . Such attempts play to and conform to fundamental principles of oral hermeneutics and oral efficacity. They voice their appeal at the very moment when there is a crisis of confidence and credibility of official oral authorities, as structures for facilitating and legitimating their rule are being overruled by the written medium. So freed from the constraints of the religious and political consortium which govern through oral apparatus, spirit-possession, spirit-consultation phenomena and witchcraft practices assume untraditional and fearful proportions. They become, in fact, superstitions. By Harold Turner's definition, superstitions are actually only the debris of a once living tradition. Although they still carry some voltage, they are no longer integrated and relativized by the total context of other religious factors (Turner X). Theirs is a pathetic effort to remystify life for Bemba votaries amidst the spiritual aridity of much of modern life. It is a pitiful disintegration. In the original context of oral religion, they contributed to its sense of wholeness.

The persons, who control these religiously conceived activities, have survived the onslaught of literacy and constant Christian condemnation with remarkable resilience. This is partially due to the fact that they are traditionally concerned with the restoration of order within a disrupted society. The distinction, which V. Turner (1975) makes, between revelational and divinatory processes may clarify their anomalous endurance.

Divinatory vs. Revelatory Processes

In Bemba ceremonies, revelational processes conceive in symbolic form what otherwise resists conceptualization in available linguistic terms. Revelation requires liturgical actions and communal caucusing. Tribal ethics, for instance, are revealed in the *Cisungu* ceremony. Tribal history is re-enacted at the installment of a chief. Religious ideology is dramatized in the cult of ancestors. Social economics are reenforced by rites associated with agricultural cycles (Richards 1939, passim). Political structures are reaffirmed in religiously elaborate rituals of burial and succession, etc. Each institution and each ritual serve as mnemonic devices, synthesizing and re-asserting the culture's basic truths. They create a sacred time and place, where the Bemba can reflect on vital meanings and deliberate on healthy values, which inform and motivate their community and the world around it. Duly constituted and officially sanctioned authorities preside over these revelatory processes. Under their auspices, the community is conducted on a "return to origins." They also rally the tribal energies and talents around the traditional ideals in pursuit of a common goal. During the revelational rites, limit-symbols generally are re-presentative of _positive_ "peak experiences" which restore a sense of the basic meaningfulness and worthwhileness of life, empowered by a notion of the whole.

On the other hand, divinatory processes seek to disclose concealed causes of sickness, death, misfortune, personal and agricultural infertility. Through the operation of mechanisms of redress for affliction, public and private maliciousness thought to be infecting the community is uncovered and exorcized. Divination employs mantic techniques; through a kind of psychosocial analysis, it exposes dark demons of secret personal malignity festering in and fracturing the social body. Its limit-symbols arouse those **negative** existential crises, where the very meaning and value of life are called into question by an apparent absence of the whole.

In modern times, literacy, amidst other forces, is undermining the orally constituted order of those authorities who control revelational processes. Under these intensely chaotic conditions, the arcane specialists, who direct divinatory processes, thrive. The circumstances of upheaval confronting the Bemba are conducive to the allurements of _Ngulu, Ng'anga_ and _Mucapi_ . As oracles of the old order, they provide the requisite leadership to an occult craft, which bears resemblances to "revitalization cults."3 They fight the apostasy and agnosticism of former adherents of the oral religion. Their strategy is to regain control of the cult of spirits and blame the uncertainties of the present period on the discontinuity with the past.

For the most part, _Ngulu, Ng'anga_ and _Mucapi_ conduct "rites of affliction." During these, each outstanding case of personal misfortune becomes "the occasion, in which the moral norms and values shared by all . . . are prominently displayed" (V. Turner 1957, 292-301). Thus, under pretext of settling a local conflict between kith and kin, wider politico-social linkages are kept alive and reaffirmed; an appeal to common interests is eloquently expressed in symbols representing the pivotal aspects of oral culture (Cf V. Turner 1957, 302). Whenever disturbance threatens in a specific situation, the unity of all is stressed by ritual restatement of ancestral wisdom and social propriety. In the end, the conflict between the oral culture and literate incursions is ultimately irresoluble, since it springs from contradictory means of structuring society. The divinatory processes provide only a temporary respite, producing the illusion of harmony and stability amidst the harsh reality of the radical disintegration of orality.

These peripherally located religious specialists are private practitioners, who now exercise a very pervasive and unofficial influence on the spiritual lives of the Bemba. But they are not particularly popular figures, as they deal with the seamy side of social life. The total range of their skills involves malignancies that plague their communities (Cf V. Turner 1975, 216). Many of them have a refined sense for discerning deception and secret malice. This is partially due to the fact that many of them are also persons of moral turpitude, who seduce the young and exploit the old. In many cases, this does not impugn, but seems to enhance their credentials. As perverse themselves, they polarize evil and are all the more effective for being an integral part of the evil routed (Cf Zahan 1970, chap. 7). In the public consciousness, they are unsavory characters who skulk at the shadowy limits of society. These venal persons appropriate private vice to combat social evil in the name of public virtue. Of course, many accusations of charlatanism are levelled at them. The real measure of their divinatory success, however, lies in their capacity as negative limit symbols. Branded by bizarre behavior and excessive bursts of pent up energy, these marginal figures effectively expose the chaotic powers, which lurk on the edges of culture threatening devastation and dissolution.

The divinatory activities of each adept are outlined below, emphasizing the oral-aural elements.

"Traditional healers" *Ng'anga* .[4] *Ng'anga* is usually translated as "witchdoctor." While that emotional connotation can be correctly associated with the person, *Ng'anga's* role ranges diversely in Bemba society, from that of witchfinder to medical and psychic healer. *Ng'anga* are duly respected for their intelligence and sensitivity to personal and social dynamics. They cleverly draw upon the fundamental cultural belief in the centrality of human control over the cosmic continuum (Cf Burton 1961, 81).

Such healers derive their powers from their specialized knowledge in deciphering the cosmic code and even in eliciting messages from the sounding universe and the vocal spirits. They have a remarkable knowledge of the intrinsic therapeutic properties of various herbs as well as the powerful, metaphorical meanings conventionally assigned to certain materials and events by tradition (Cf Moore 1940, 41; Kapompole n.d.). But healers do not simply read a cultural map; they creatively and ingeniously employ traditional principles for navigating around the sorry circumstances confronting their clients (Cf Frake 1977, 6-7). Of course, the supposed answers from the cosmos and spirit world are not decisive. The discernment depends on the special information supplied by clients and the general knowledge of community affairs painstakingly acquired by healers over the years. They are really central organs with prodigious memories for filing and processing all personal and social data available in the area from casual gossip, private informants, public discussions and surreptitious investigation (Etienne 1948, 18-19, 101-02).

All this intimate information is delivered with suggested uncanny clairvoyance to enchant the clients during the "consultation" *Kusanshilisha* . Since all evil is communally conceived, the family or clan must be present at all stages of the healing to provide a supportive social network. It symbolically represents the whole, into which clients are to be reintegrated.

The healers sport feathered headdresses to show how far above ordinary mortals they soar with their special abilities to tap spiritual resources for their knowledge and power. They may affect a sort of Bantu glossolalia, voiced by ventriloquist techniques associated with the movement of objects and attributed to the language and voices of familiar spirits who possess them (Ng'andu IV). Their residences are often on the out-skirting limits of the village in an area hidden by overgrown bush and tall trees. They can be reached only by a narrow and barely perceptible labyrinthine path (Ng'andu IV; Mwela VII). Thus clients are forced to seek out healers by a sort of pilgrimage. Its itinerary reflects the sinuousities of thought and mystery, which comprise *Ng'anga* knowledge and power (Cf Zahan 1970, ch. 7).

Their paraphernalia, generally called *Bwanga* "medicinal apparatus," are mostly "horns, amulets and talismans" *Nsengo, Mpimpi, Mikano.* These are crafted into metaphoprical harnesses of the transferrable natural dynamism of organic and inorganic objects (Tanguy 1954, 242-56). They operate on the apotropoeic principle *Similia similibus* , or associative thinking. Characteristics are sometimes communicated by contact, as when diarrhea is cured by tying an acorn around the waist to deliver a hard, sealing quality. Oftentimes a similarity of sounds is a sufficient cause, as when the tail of *Nsonto* "a little rat" is added to direct medicine toward an illness, since the verb *Kusontoka* means "to come straight on" (Etienne 1948, 111).

The specialized divinatory processes over which healers preside are those of *Lubuko* , "a discernment of private malice through augury and seance."

The indigenous reason for *Lubuko* is *Pakuti balelamika balelungika mukosose milandu* "in order that they may be appeased and set in order by speaking on affairs" (Garrec 1916, 23). (The "they" refers to the powers-that-be, whether of spirits or other forces, in the universe.) The Bemba themselves want to discern why they feel temporarily at variance with the whole network of powers and spiritual influences. Then they can make any necessary adjustments in their alignment:

> *Lubuko* implies a world-view in which all things are bound to each other in a "web of relationship," so that a condition existing anywhere in the cosmos may be reflected elsewhere. A rupture in the fabric of human relationship may be expected to produce its identifiable counterpart in the material world (Booth 1977, 47).

Lubuko (Cf Labrecque n.d., 15-16; Ng'andu 1923; Etienne 1948, 98-102; Ng'andu IV) is basically a limit-language affair. As a colloquy between living humans and ancestors, it is a form of logotherapy, which uses verbalization and paralinguistic conventions to ease personal hostilities and tensions (Cf Ong 1967, 202). In a culture where word and event are largely indistinguishable, words and their symbolic surrogates become physical instruments which cause things to happen. Events, objects and persons are all pulled into the orbit of healers' control by their oral words. While they are incanting spirits and "consulting clients" *Kusanshilisha*, healers manipulate special objects whose structure and properties give semantic possibilities to their interpretation. Through a variety of metaphors, they construct a special logic between things and humans. The ruse depends on the chattering of consultation coordinated with the clattering of mystic devices. Healers exorcise wild and wayward forces by calling them up by name and then banishing them in this ritual. Their verdicts are ratified by an appeal to ancestral spirits.

One very common form of *Lubuko* is the *Lwa lusuku* "the fruit seed," which is set on a duiker skin and covered with an inverted pot. In turn the pot is rubbed back and forth from East to West with the seed "rattling" *Kolokota kolokoto* against its sides while spirits are invoked. Any similar combination of elements of the spiritual (invocation), animal (duiker-skin), vegetable (fruit seed), human (pot), cosmic (East and West) will do (Garrec 1916, 23-9), since the configuration is derived from the spontaneously operative notion of the whole.

The healers then follow a general pattern from *Lubuko*. It begins with an "incantation" *Kuuma ntembo* such as *Ce co canga candi, Kali kapunda kapita Bacimbwi bansofu ukuselebenda* "This is my big charm, it is a little hole, through which easily pass hyennas, and elephants, as through an open space." The message is that, through the divinatory process, terrible and momentous affairs will be uncovered. The alliterative sounds of the chant, repeated over and over and counterpunctuated with the rattle of devices, are the harmonizing media within which all elements speak. Amidst them, healers outline the case under study and insert agreed upon "rules of the divination" *Kuuma ntembo,* such as, "If so and so is at fault, then the device will react thus and such."

Next, concerned spirits are "named" *Kulumbula* . These are either suspected of being the causes or may indicate human suspects in their clan. When the name of the right suspect spirit or human is uttered, then *Cafika kebo* "the little word is reached," and the device suddenly stops its noisy activity. Finally, a "remedial action" *Kulapuluka* is prescribed giving the client a way out of the "difficulty" *Bwimikilo* . This may entail destruction of a *Ciwa* "evil spirit," a ritual offering to spirits, or application of some medicine. The healers will skillfully adapt their eisegesis of given circumstances to indicate judgment that somehow readjusts the balance of rival social forces, relieving malevolent tensions and restoring a sense of unity.

There are as many techniques as the fertile imaginations of *Ng'anga* can develop. The general repertoire varies from region to region and from specialist to specialist. New devices are added, such as discarded radio sets, even sculpted models of them, or a crank-handled telephone plugged into a tree. Anything will suffice, which suggests communication with spirits and the cosmos. The basic religious principle, symbolized in all forms of *Lubuko* , of course, is that the notion of the whole is spontaneously operative in all such limit-linguistic devices.

<u>"Spirit possessed"</u> *Ngulu* .[5] This section will attend to spirit-possession, (a) relating its oral features and (b) reporting its historical development. It is not our purpose here to analyze various interpretations ascribed to spirit-possession phenomena. It is enough to note that the incidence of these phenomena increases as deep changes within society generate frustrations and insecurities. The possessed are ill-prepared to cope with such situations, and hence seek compensation through cults of affliction. There seems to be a valid correlation between those who are oppressed in society and society's sanctioning of an acceptable medium, through which grievances can be conventionally expressed. Unrestrained behavior will be tolerated temporarily to promote some <u>conceptual</u> or <u>social</u> adjustment (Firth 1968).

<u>Conceptually</u>, spirit possession reproduces dramatic evidence for the religious reality of the spirit world and allows fantasy free play in the flexible belief system. When chaos looms, the resident and possessing spirits remind the negligent Bemba of their duty to reorder their lives according to ancestral

tradition. Socially, for oppressed women (and for some men who feel socially inadequate), spirit-possession phenomena constitute a very vocal group. It provides otherwise voiceless persons a say in society's affairs. Women in general are the most oppressed individuals in Bemba society and the most neglected persons in the educational revolution (Cf Schuster 1979). But, since they are also natural vehicles of ancestral spirits' rebirth in the community, women are the most frequent residences of familiar spirits seeking a medium. Many symptoms seem to be associated with menstrual, parturient, and menopausal difficulties. This is probably due as much to symbolism pregnant with spirit gestation as to actual gynecological functions (Oger 1972, 2-5; Kapompole n.d.).

(a) In addition to physiological symptoms, there are many others related to the communicative intent of the patient. After "being struck" *Kupamwa*, or "fallen upon" *Kuwilwa*, or unexpectedly "gusted into like a wind" *Kufumfuma no mwela*, the victim begins "to belch" *Kubiya*, "to yawn" *Kuala mwau*, "to mumble" *Kung'winta*, "to sing" *Kuimba*, "to utter oracles" *Kusabaila* and "to roar like a lion" *Kung'onta* (Labrecque n.d., 10-11). Many symptoms and functions are not susceptible to visualist expressions, for they are interior. Some symptoms are related to inner ear functions; others are audible events. The *Ngulu* is conceived as functioning oracularly (Labrecque n.d., 9-10), ululating and reverberating in the rhythm of the song and drum that accompanies her.

Recall that it is sound which makes oral people think of spirits. *Mipashi* are a sounding-event: they make known their "anger in thunder and rattling rain" *Yafulwa yalenga imfula yalapanta*, or in the "clatter of a hailstorm" *Imfula ya chitalowe*, or in the "roaring of lions" *Inkalamo shaisa mu kulila* (Macminn n.d., "g" and "l"). So, too, *Ngulu* are marginalized persons, who become auditory events resonating with the life of possessing spirits that live and speak from within. Evidence from psychiatric research into the bicameral brain by Julian Jaynes (1977) corroborates our understanding of Bemba spirits in oral terms. Uncontrollable voices avowedly welling up from the unconscious depths of the brain's right hemisphere will be processed into actual speech attributed to spirits by the left hemisphere. Ong (1982, 29-30) suspects that the bicameral psyche and the oral mind are roughly equivalent.

Accordingly, with all their chthonic powers, ancestral spirits, who are the *Bene calo* "owners of the land," reassert themselves and find their voices by talking noisy-possession of people: *Umuntu atendeka ukuku tumanta kuta alabuluma* "The person begins to be preoccupied and to roar like a lion" (Macminn, n.d., "g" and "h").

Mapoma (1980, 57) describes spirit-possession as an event of sound, which is conceptualized in terms of the songs and drums:

Shalile ngoma "the drums have sounded," and *Shacilila lelo* "there was singing last night." It seems that possessed people need music to induce the trance, which establishes contact with the appropriate spirit. The continuing possession is expressed with dizzying dances. Though the grievances that motivate *Ngulu* are socially generated, they are __interiorly__ and __personally__ felt. Music is also the conventional medium for expressing such private and deeply personal matters.[6] In music, dance and song, the inhibitions of the injured party are greatly reduced (Mapoma 1980, 42). Likewise, the harsh, antisocial message of *Ngulu* is more apt to receive a fair hearing, while the audience is being entertained through a medium conventionally accepted as the reliable channel of truth (See above, chap. 1, 3ff).

The people will greet the possessed person with drums and ululations, paying royal attentions to her with gifts and services. She responds to the title *Mfumu* "chief," or *Mfumu ya Mipashi* "spirit-chief" or *Muka mfumu* "spirit-spouse," and is dressed in royal ivory, leopard skins and plumed headdress (Tanguy 1954, 218). Like the excesses and licenses excused in a chief's behavior, the *Ngulu* can break social conventions and be excused because of the royal privileges *Ni ngulu ni mfumu* "It is a spirit; it's a chief" (Oger 1972, 6). The *Ngulu* is then a mobile *Musumba*, a noisy tumult around a royal, sacred residence. The uncanny power of the whole is disclosed in this limit-situation.

(b) In the nineteenth century, *Ngulu* perhaps provided a dramatic means of acting out and commenting on the stereotype of aliens encountered in trade or war. Maybe it developed, as Werner (1971) suggests, as a political protest against the Bemba, who imposed the cult of their royal ancestors on conquered peoples; through indigenous *Ngulu* cult, a resentful non-Bemba people would have a religious alternative. It may also have been a way for migrating and raiding Bemba to carry their spirits with them to maintain tribal ties in the alien and dangerous world outside their homeland.

A great upsurge of *Ngulu* prophetic protest occurred around 1907, when the *Mitanda* "traditional deep-bush temporary farms" and *Citemene* "traditional slash and burn farming" were forbidden by company officials. So many protesting *Ngulu* were operating in the late 1940's in the wake of world war and in the political unrest prior to the Federation, that district officials feared that a secret society of *Ngulu* was threatening European control (Abercorn District Notebook 1950, vol. II). Again around 1960, the revival of vatic spirit possession was symptomatic of Bemba uncertainties and hostilities, as the struggle for political independence heated up (Oger 1972, 1). Contemporary increased phenomena are related to hard economic times and an anxious sense that modernity will not deliver on its promises.[7] They also compensate displaced and landless Bemba urbanites for their powerlessness and uprootedness by immediate contact with venerable and comfortable ancestors (Cf A. Turner 1972, 1-16).

Both prophetic protest in the name of tradition and an existential need for secure roots seem to be factors in the frequency of spirit-possession incidence.

"Witch-cleansers" *Mucapi* . Our discussion turns now to witchcraft and the means used to combat it. The focus will be on their relation to an oral-aural theory of culture and the demonic forms that the notion of the whole may take.

Some of the evil corrupting a community is thought to be the result of a *Ciwa* [8]"evil spirit" (See above, chap. 3, 79ff) possessing a witch. *Alibuka ciwa cilya bantu* "An evil spirit has arisen and is devouring the community" (Etienne 1948, 20). In the oral context of Bemba witchcraft, the type of person likely to be accused of possessing a *Ciwa* is anyone, who is on the periphery, isolated, secretive, asocial or eccentric. In short, the abject is anyone who deviates from the social norm by uncouth manners or strange appearance. Such a person represents the invasion of the individual and the singular into the substantially social (Cf Douglas 1963, 141; V. Turner 1967, 114). It may be a quarrelsome person, who does not respect communal tranquillity (Richards 1939, 271-74). Either a meticulous person, who sets strictly precise boundaries to a garden, or a cantankerous old person, may be suspected of witchcraft (Richards 1939, 73). Meanness, criminality, impiety, spitefulness, maliciousness, and jealousy, are all understood as evil powers emanating from a habitually or occasionally perverse individual (Paliani 1971, 18). It is enough that these vices be given voice for their desired or threatened effects to take place. The oral words in a "curse" *Kutipwila* or "insult" *Kutuka nsele* , which abound in the language, are thought capable of, and so actually do personal injury to their victims (See above, chap. 1, 2). For example, *Uli nkulungu, walya mwako uno* "You are dust and will eat it this year," *Shimpa minwe panshi, umone nga nailingana* "Set your fingers in the ground (the sign of mourning) and see if you are equal to it;" *Mu mulemfwe tawakaendemo* "You will not walk again in fresh green grass" (Labrecque n.d., 24). Such serious "promises of calamity" *Kukonkomwena filai* can strike a fatal inevitability into their hearer's heart (Idem). There is nothing really mystical about it. Evil comes into operative being in the spokenness of a curse.[9] By word or by actual deed, the *Muloshi* "witch" is said "to throw its craft to kill a person" *Kuposa buloshi bwa kukolo munto* (Oger n.d.).

Just as the witches' special knowledge is thought to be tortuously sown with contradictions and antinomies, so is their power occult and uncannily active in their devices. Witchcraft paraphernalia are usually deformed and bizarre figurations of what they intend to represent. For example, a witch's necklace may be made of lion's claws and a few human bones, alternating with a python's vertebrae and glass beads strung along a jackal's nerve. Witches also may use incongruous collages of familiar objects, like a drinking gourd upholstered with a civet's skin and stuffed with dead weeds and feathers (Corbeil IV). These unnatural combinations connote lethal powers and symbolize physical and moral flaws, which the wielder turns against victims. As negative limit symbols of anxiety, they gainsay the basic meaningfulness and worthwhileness, promised by the whole, and they re-present the deranged threat of disquieting chaos with their muddled juxtaposition of miscellaneous elements (See above, chap. 1, 23ff).

Prior to the Witchcraft Ordinance of 1901, which prohibited the practice of witchcraft and the execution of witches, the Bemba publicly administered "the poison ordeal" *Mwafi* to suspected witches (Garrec 1916, 41-6). When in the severely troubled early 1930's the *Mcapi* "witch-cleansing" movement originating in Southern Malawi burst upon the Bemba scene, its methods and messages were not totally novel to the Bemba. They resonated with indigneous religious problems and solutions concerning witchcraft (Cf Vansina 1971). The novel elements of *Mcapi* "witch-cleansing" (from the *Chinyanja* verb *Kucapa* "to wash") were homeostatically integrated in the tradition with the more drastic (and lethal!) *Mwafi* "witch-eradication."[10]

The following brief outline of their theatrically elaborate ritual will highlight the oral dynamics and exemplify the limit-symbology.

The divinatory paraphernalia of the *Bamucapi* [11] are: a horn of "the cleansing medicine," an *Ikalashi* "a glass mirror" for spotting the witchcraft, and a *Mupunga* "fly whisk," which is a traditional speaker's symbol of social cohesive power (Tanguy 1935). Their speaking rights are based on their pretense to an esoteric knowledge of the causes of evil and its attendant power to purge the community of the agents of evil through their medicine.

With their troupe of frenzied singers and dancers, the *Bamucapi* make a noisy entrance into a village troubled by witchcraft. They set up at the village "foundation pole" *Chishipa* , where the powerful medicine of purification and reconciliation, called *Coni* , rests in the religious center. Here a white chicken is sacrificed in honor of the ancestors and its blood sprinkled on the pole and "spirit-shrine" *Lufuba* . The people and the *Bamucapi* pile up all private hoards of medicinal horns. Then *Bamucapi* address the assembled people in the alien *Cinyanja* language. Their speech is full of apocalyptic discourse: *Capwililila fye* "it is all over with." Their rhetoric rings with millenial promises: *Tamwakalowekwe* "no one will ever be bewitched again" and *Kuwamyako calo* "the whole earth will be purified." They hold "aloft" *Pa mulu* a bottle of *Mcapi wabuta* "white colored *Mcapi* " as a sign of "life for people" *Bumi ku bantu* . This they distinguish from a bottle of *Mcapi wakashika* "red *Mcapi*" placed "on the ground"

Panshi as a sign of "death to people" *Mfwa ku bantu* . *Bamucapi*
then divide their captive audience into lanes of men and women.
Using the mirror, the cleansers single out suspected witches
(already known by discrete inquiry or rumor); these are subjected
to mockery, insults and blows administered by their neighbors.
All the villagers and their horns are then profusely doused with
Mcapi -medicine to neutralize the witchcraft potential. The
cleansing ceremony closes with hilarious singing, and dancing and
feasting, celebrating the restored "innocence" *Kaele* of the
community.

Finally, the *Mcapi* rite dramatically evidences the oral
contentiousness of fliting (Ong 1967, 207-22; above, chap. 1
13ff). The benevolent *Bamucapi* set themselves up as
adversaries of their pathological doubles, the witches. *Mucapi*
represents the forces of good, and *Muloshi* is evil personified.
The witches and their horns are separated from the community,
which then releases its polarized personal tensions in the
concerted exchange of abuse and verbal combat. Each act of the
rite is monotonously repeated by each participant to bring home
the ethical lesson. The horns are piled up, the *Mcapi* is
sprinkled and then consumed by each villager in turn. The songs
and dances set the lessons to rhythmic reinforcement. The
polarization and personalization of otherwise abstract concepts
of good and evil and the repetition and mimetic action all follow
acoustic laws of learning (Havelock 1978, 155; Ong 1982, 57-68).

Enter Modernity and Literacy

An earlier section (See above, 127ff) suggested that *Ng'anga,
Ngulu* and *Mucapi* are involved in divinatory, as opposed to
revelatory, processes. This fact provides a clue to their
extraordinary continuity amidst so much discontinuity elsewhere
in the oral world. The very function of the "diviners" is to
thrive in adversity, as they seek to disclose the obscure forces
of decline and to restore the dynamics of social vitality. But
they will enjoy only a temporary reprieve from irrelevance and
ineffectiveness. For, literacy, which delivers them this final
heyday of disturbance, has also released forces for a terminal
dissolution of divinatory authority. As this chapter has already
noted, reading and writing are fostering an individualism,
creating isolated thinkers. These can privately augment their
knowledge of and control over their environment, independent of
tribal consciousness and traditional social concourse (See above,
121ff, also Ong 1967, 53-60). As new literates silently turn
inward on themselves and develop an immanently determined
direction of their consciousness, they will interiorize those
hostilities and emotions once freely released in the public forum
(Carothers 1959, 311). Thus introverted, they can fall victim to
depressive, compulsive and anxious aberrations of the
psychoneurotic type, not accessible to extroverted divinatory
therapy. Their withdrawal into self, sponsored by literacy,

moves them from a shame to a guilt culture, in which categories
of the paranoidal type are more pronounced (Idem).

The unaccustomed frequency of spirit-possession incidents,
the proliferate recourse to spirit-consultation, and the
untraditional intensity of witchcraft related activities, all can
be advantageously conceived as an anchronistic attempt on the
part of advocates of traditional orality to inspire renewed,
though imperiled, vitality to their world. *Ngulu, Ng'anga* and
Mcapi movements have historically represented the conservative
and peripheral forces of the oral tradition confronting malignant
cultural intrusion. In order to account for evil in the Bemba
world, they seek to discern the ill-natured motivations of
others. This reenforces the oral view of fellow human beings as
frequently inhumane, and of the remaining cosmos as persistently
inhospitable. In every crisis, divinatory processes provide "a
coherent, if illustory, system which translates into cultural
terms the mental structures of paranoia . . .," and suggest "a
kind of resolution of the social relationships disturbed or
broken by the crisis;" this is "achieved only at the cost of a
running total of hate" (V. Turner 1975, 25).

Witchcraft, spirit-possession and spirit-consultation have
an oral matrix. Their continued vitality is related to their
reassertion of the massive oral residue in Bemba culture.
Divinatory practitioners are controversial and ambiguous persons.
They are what people believe and declare them to be. They are
orally defined public figures. They take for granted the
praeternatural beings and forces alive in oral culture and do not
seek to go behind them to the psychic or social or cosmic forces
they represent (V. Turner 1975, v. 231). They depend on the
voracious capacity for rumor and the preposterous credulity of
clients, which oral structures inflate. The orally conditioned
people desperately want to hear again the stark re-presentative
words of the spirits and to feel anew the uncanny disclosive
power of the limit-symbols. It used to be that these were quite
effective in making them while. But the limit language of the
past is becoming increasingly inadequate and inappropriate for
several reasons.

(a) Today, the *Ngulu* continue their oral protest,
agitating for a renascence of traditional African values and
symbols in a society and religion predominantly oriented to
Western culture and Christianity. The *Ngulu* in the oral
culture speak out spirits' words, and by these effect their
incarnate presence. The words of ancestors and their
authoritative presence are inseparable. They are concrete
evidence, in a last ditch stnd, that the spirits of ancestors
are not dead, as Christianity would have them. They are still
powerfully active and deserve, even demand, traditional
veneration. But literacy's inexorable powers of interiorization
will make the Bemba more susceptible to personal obsessions and
less bedeviled with spirit possession.

(b) The *Ng'anga*, applying their techniques with traditional finesse, reassure their oral adherents that all the various forces of the cosmos are essentially continuous with personal reality. They then reassert human control of the communication and coordination of those benign powers to combat evil. But now *Ng'anga's* former clientele will have to turn increasingly to psychiatrists. These doctors may be less directive in their approach, in order to allow their patients the freedom they need to individually clarify the psychoses and neuroses they have interiorized (Cf Carothers 1959).

(c) So, too, *Bamucapi* witch-cleansers, in a futile effort, are dramatic oral witnesses to the incapacity of the tradition. They can no longer adequately identify nor effectively cope with the problems generated by the new order. The terms (witchcraft) and techniques (cleansing or eradicating medicines) available to the old order, will have no currency in a literate economy.

Although their disestablished campaign is highly suspect in the eyes of the new elite, *Ng'anga*, *Ngulu* and *Bamucapi* still have a wide audience. It consists of those who have been pushed to the margins of the new society. They are culturally disenfranchised, and remain formally orate in an increasingly literate society, utterly penniless in the coin of the new culture. Orality is not legal tender in the market of literate modernity. The people, who continue to consult the *Ng'anga*, to be moved by the *Mucapi's* ministry, and to be involved in *Ngulu* spirit-possession phenomena, are not just disposed by tradition to give the message a hearing. They are those who are dispossessed of tradition, who are caught as marginals in cultural transition, or who have failed in the effort to break into modernity. Elder Bemba bereft of oral authority, middle-aged Bemba confused by cultural conflict and disillusioned by unfulfilled hopes of Independence, young Bemba drop-outs frustrated by lack of opportunity for a fair share in the elites' prosperity, and women of all ages and classes in the moneyed economy, are equally liable to be moved by the millenial message (See Jules-Rosette 1981, for a study of traditional symbols adapted to the novel conditions of urban life). The vagrant *Mcapi*, the eccentric *Ng'anga*, the outcast *Ngulu*, move along the fringes of society, with vain promises to reintegrate the rootless into an orally reconstructed traditional society, which actually no longer is solid ground.

These specialists in divinatory craft launch a direct attack on the hostilities and anxieties of their participants, whose special personality structures are orally organized and are likely to be psychologically faced outward (Ong 1967, 131-34). Words and human behavior are closely connected and controlled by an oral society. Contrary words and actions are suspicious and received with hostility. But although intellectual freedom is hampered by the need to conform and ethical freedom is inhibited by social propriety, temperamental freedom is encouraged. Emotions are freely extroverted in spirit-consultation, spirit-possession and witchcraft incidents, where expressed hostilities can be purged in an oral catharsis (Carothers 1959 and Opier 1956).

But now the oral values of propriety and compliance are on the wane. Success in the new literate order is measured by personal aggrandizement and individual responsibility. It is not inherited, but achieved through self-assertion and exertive competition. The Bemba oral world considers these literate virtues not only as not worthwhile, but as anti-social, even malicious motivations. In the oral world, literacy is a profoundly alienating medium (Cf Schneidau 1976, 1-50). The oral world and its captive population are becoming irrelevant, even deviant.

The villagers, who are still bound by the oral structures of the Bemba cultural setting, have a predictable, however multiple, set of interpretive possibilities open to divinatory craft (Turner, A., 1972, 1-16; Zahan 1970, chap. 6). But even village-practitioners have to deal with retiring urbanites or returning urban drop-outs. The worldly-wise have broken loose from the homogeneous cultural network which, in the oral tradition, determined their destinies. They have acquired unknown relationships by the alien condition of urban life and literacy. The wider contacts have altered them and made them inscrutable and intractable to divinatory techniques. The modern practitioner at work in the suburbs is far less effective. There is less intimate knowledge of the personal lives of patients, more heterogeneity in the melange of tribal traditions and a mounting literacy which operates on clients.

Consequently, there are growing numbers of literate Bemba who call the *Ng'anga* "a charlatan" *Wa bucenjeshi* , the *Mucapi* "a mercernary" *Wa bunonshi* , and the *Ngulu* "a lunatic" *Wa bulwele*. The days of the incontrovertible power of divinatory processes and of the effectual religious authority of these divines, like those of the chiefs and those who control revelatory processes, are numbered. Ironically, mass-media dissemination of witchcraft and spirit stories, which fill Zambian radio broadcasts and newspaper columns,[12] give a short-term but intensified lease on life to these phenomena, just as the invention of the printing press did in Medieval Europe (Cf Eisenstein 1980, 43ff and Russell 1972, 234). But, in the long run even this reprieve by "secondary orality" (Ong 1977, 298-99) can be only temporary. The erosion of the oral world, which began at the center, will overtake the periphery, too. The oral revitalizers cannot recapture the past. The praises they sing of orality are really its threnody.

A Concluding Reflection

The authority and sacrality of the paramount chief are the closest Bemba analogues of the power and transcendence emanating from the notion of the whole. Both are symbolized by the vicarious presence of spirits, who are believed to reside in and constitute the speaking-authority of the chief. But the abstractive power of literacy will codify the law previously promulgated by the paramount's will. Similarly, the alienating power of literacy will liberate his subjects from that despotic rule with the democratization of knowledge, which school-learning entails. The notion of the whole is traditionally exteriorized in clamorous pronouncements of orality's quasi-divine authoritarianism. It will become more and more interiorized as the cognitional and volitional processes of the individual self are respectfully appropriated in literate society.

During the intervening crisis of authority, _Ng'anga_ plays for time with his divining game and seeks traditional solutions to intractably new problems; meanwhile, an objective universe is being abstracted from the cosmic continuum and his clientele is being alienated from that belief system. Spirits reassert themselves in possession-phenomena, and witch-cleansers revive the oral efforts to exorcize the tradition of its alienating demons. All three, by exploiting the cultural confusion, try to repristinate the Bemba and to stem the inexorable tide of the new literacy. They can restore only peripheral features of the oral religion, which, though alienated from the total belief system, retain a certain valence. Meanwhile, Bemba society, residually oral and emergently literate, must suffer the pathetic consequences of continuing to take its oral symbols of evil literally. When Bemba society at large has more deeply interiorized the effects of writing (Ong 1982, chap. 4 and 7), its more educated members will submit its limit-symbols to the serious reflection, which literate distanciation would prescribe (Tracy 1982, 208).

CHAPTER FOUR FOOTNOTES

[1] For this section, these sources were particularly helpful: Audrey I. Richards, "The political system of the Bemba tribe--north-eastern Rhodesia," in _African Political Systems_, ed. M. Fortes and E.E. Evans-Pritchard, 1940, 83-120. Idem, "Keeping the King Divine," Henry Myers Lecture 1968, Proceedings of the Royal Anthropological Institute, 23-25; W. Vernon Brelsford, _The succession of Bemba chiefs: a guide for District Officers_, Lusaka, Government Printer, 1944; Brian Garvey, "Bemba chiefs and Catholic missions, 1898-1935," _Journal of African History_, XVIII, 3, 1977, 411-26.

Interviews with these Bemba "chiefs" _Mfumu_ : Chewe Ng'andu XII, Chandamukulu IV, Mumena III, Shimwalule VII, Nkula VII, Nkolemfumu IX, Mporokoso IV, Nkweto VIII, and Shibwalya Kapila IV.

[2] These ideas are directly derived from the oral model of early Christian prophets developed by Werner Kelber, who kindly permitted a pre-publication reading of his manuscript, _The Oral and the Written Gospel: The Hermeneutics of Speaking and Writing in the Synoptic Tradition, Mark, Paul, and Q._ Philadelphia: Fortress Press (1983).

[3] For example, see Anthony F.C. Wallace, _Culture and Personality_, New York, Random House, 1961, Chapter 4, where it is shown that it is possible for severely stressed individuals in a community seriously disrupted by change to marshall their energies and spontaneously restore the equilibrium of their cultural system. Wallace names the process "cultural revitalization."

[4] For this section, these sources were especially useful: E. Labrecque, " . . . Notes sur la Religion des Babemba," Ilondola, n.d., 15-17; L. Etienne, "The Babemba," Kasama, 1948, 98-102; F. Tanguy, "The Bemba," Ilondola, 1954, 256ff.

Interviews with these _Ng'anga_ "healers": Ng'andu IV, Mwela VII, Kapompole IV.

[5] For this section, these sources were especially helpful. N. Garrec, "Croyances et coutumes," Chilanga, 1916, 20-23; E. Labrecque, "Notes sur la Religion," Ilondola, n.d., 9-11; L. Etienne, "The Babemba," Kasama, 1948, 105-08; White Fathers, "Enquete," Rome, 1958, 550-55; L. Oger "Spirit Possession among the Bemba," Lusaka, 1972; R. Macminn, " _Ukwisa Kwa Ndalu_," and _"Ukuwilwa kwa Ngulu,"_ Lubwa, n.d.

[6] In other circumstances, old people (another marginalized minority), complain, solicit help, seek justice in communal affairs, and proffer advice and criticism through a collection of songs called _Mfunkutu_ . These are sung mostly at beer parties (another uninhibiting factor) and, though the repertoire is

traditionally old, they can be addressed to new social conditions (I.M. Mapoma, "The determinants of style in the music of Ing'omba," Ph.D. thesis, University of California, 1980, 42).

[7] *Ngulu* are so prevalent in the urban centers that the Roman Catholic Archbishop of Lusaka, Emmanual Milingo, braves the official criticism of his christian community and devotes a major portion of his pastoral energies to healing the possessed and exorcising the spirits in a syncretic ritual drawing heavily on African tradition blessed with Christian theology (E. Milingo, "The Church of the Spirits. Is it to Blame?" Lusaka, Archdiocesan Mimeograph, 1978). In April 1982, Milingo was recalled to Rome for a reeducation in Christian doctrine.

[8] For a full description of Bemba witchcraft see the following: N. Garrec, "Croyances et coutumes," Chilanga, 1916, 41-46; E. Labrecque, "Notes sur la Religion," Ilondola, n.d., 20-26; Idem, "La Sorcellerie chez Les Babemba," Anthropos 33, 1938; L. Etienne, "The Babemba," Kasama, 1948, 203-05; J. Sambeek, "La Sorcellerie au Bangweolo," Kasama, Manuscript, 1925; F. Tanguy, "The Bemba," Ilondola, 1954, 261-68ff.

[9] Cases of "voodoo death" by word alone are well documented. There appears to be certain changes, stimulated by one's psychological state of extreme helplessness, in the mechanisms of the central and parasympathetic nervous system; these send a massive discharge down the vagus nerve, which results in a sudden inhibition of the cardiovascular system and, potentially, in death (Cf E. Fuller Torrey, The Mind Game, New York, Emerson Hall, 1972, 48 and note 15).

[10] In the early nineteenth century a certain Fipa tribesperson, Mwine Nsano, was given a Bemba village to rule by chief Nondo, as a reward for his success in wiping out witchcraft with *Mwafi* (A. Roberts, A History of the Bemba, Madison, University of Wisconsin Press, 1973, 100). The Bemba today describe Nsano's advent as *Musango wa bamucapi* "in the manner of a witch cleanser;" his successor in the line of village heads still functions as a famous *Mcapi* minister (Kayambi Diary 4/5/55).

[11] These sources were especially helpful for this section: F. Tanguy, "Mucapi's Business," Ilondola, Bemba Manuscript, 1935; A. Richards, "A modern movement of witch-finders," Africa, 8, 4, October 1935, 448-61; S. Paliani, 1930 Kunadza Mcape, Lilongwe, Likuni Press, 1971; T.O. Ranger, "Mchape and the Study of Witchcraft Eradication," Lusaka Conference, August 31-Sept. 8, 1972.
Interviews with an ex-Mucapi in Chiboo IV and with G. Stuer V.

[12] The broadcast of radio news and the printed word of newspapers amplify the oral abilities to circulate rumors and the

oral capacities to believe the most preposterous of tales.
Witchcraft and spirit-possession feed on and are reenforced by
front page reports in mid-1979 Zambian newspapers. For example:
a meeting of Kitwe city council to discuss witchcraft threats
against the mayor (Times, May 22); a popular Ng'anga who
identifies a puff-adder as the incarnate spirit of a vengeful
mother terrorizing her family (Daily Mail, May 28); a wooden
witchcraft statue, which exhumes corpses, eats their flesh and
kills people, and a photo showing two witchfinders with the
statue in custody, after they caught it eating chickens (Daily
Mail, July 12); a magistrate's ruling that three people had a
case to answer to conspiracy with the black ghost of King Solomon
to defraud a prominent business of about $25,000 (Daily Mail,
Aug. 14); an editorial calling for action by local Ng'anga and
state-hospital psychiatrists to rid a haunted school of evil
spirits harassing pupils (Daily Mail, Aug. 15).

CONCLUSION

For those studying cultural interaction,
developments in the technology of the
intellect must always be crucial. After
language, the next most important advance in
this field lay in the reduction of speech to
graphic forms, in the development of writing .
. . . Communication by eye creates a
different cognitive potentiality for human
beings than communication by word of mouth
(Goody 1977, 10 and 128).

. . . It is the present writer's view
that it is the lack of the written word that
is the factor of transcendent cultural
importance for mental development that
distinguishes the African from the European
mode (Carothers 1972, 121-22)

"Myth and Ritual, Divinity and Authority in Bemba Tradition:
an Analysis of their Oral Features and of their Hermeneutical
Transformation by Literacy." This was the original title for our
book. It presented a twofold task: to explore the medium in which
Bemba religion is traditionally conceived and communicated, and
to explicate the conversion to new meaning which its interaction
with a new medium entails. So far the study has been pursued
more in terms of orality than of literacy. But its conclusion
lies in the wider context of the hermeneutics of orality and
literacy. The transformed hermeneutics of Bemba religion raises
the question of its survivability in a literate dispensation and
the mode of that endurance. Obviously, the hermeneutical
problems raised by the encounter of orality and literacy cannot
be solved in this conclusion, but the path towards a solution can
be indicated. The integrity of the treatise requires that these
closing considerations prove to be congruent with both Ong's
oralist and Tracy's religious perspectives which have thus far
impelled the argument. [1]

Refocused Review

The prefatory remarks on orality made the observation that
the differentiation of the "self" and the evolution of cultures
occur as functions of the media available for controlling
knowledge. Each chapter has proffered evidence from Bemba
religion, which converges on traditional notions of the whole,
the self and the world, as they are presented in the limit-
symbols available to the oral culture. Each chapter ended with a
special conclusion remarking on the traumatic transition from an
oral to a literate medium. In order to sustain wider hermeneutic
reflections on the data, this general conclusion needs first to

refocus the chapters briefly onto the Bemba self and to review the inescapably relentless oral process of socialization.

Chapter One introduces the limit-language of traditional symbolism. It makes the point that, for the Bemba, there is a sacred relationship between human culture, nature and the transcendent world of spirits which a network of root metaphors proclaims. Because there is no real separation of entities, the notion of the whole, as a distinct, transcendent ground of everything else, tends to degenerate into the sum of interrelated parts. This oral synthesis is so complete that the interiority of subjects is projected onto the exterior world of objects. In this way, the Bemba are caught up and integrated into a homogeneously personified and socialized world of intercommunicating forces.

Chapter Two argues that the prime referent of the myths, rituals and symbols is the Bemba way of being-in-the-world as a religious participation in the manifest power of the whole. The charter myth narrates the divinely activated foundational experiences of tribal unity. Rituals, like *Cisungu* , dramatically intensity this tribal consciousness, sanctioning a communal knowledge of ancestral traditions and an ethics of social propriety. As a result, each Bemba person is so totally and thoroughly socialized that there is virtually no individual self-consciousness. Criteria of truth and value are socially, not internally, generated and applied; responsibility is communal, not conscientious, and public shame, not a guilty self, is the penalty for moral contravention.

Chapter Three discusses the limit-language of Bemba spirits. The notion of the whole is not focused onto a single spirit, but functions in a plurality of spatio-temporal symbols, ideally representing the divinely/ancestrally sanctioned territorial and cultural unity of traditional Bemba polity. It also involves the probability of a mother earth spirit. Just as the idea of the divine is not individuated, neither is any Bemba tribesperson considered as an individual self. The Bemba limit-language presents each tribal member as a community of a proper spirit plus at least one other matrilineal reincarnation of an ancestral spirit.

Chapter Four presents the oral authority of the chief as the unifying symbol of the diverse positive representations of the notion of the whole; the chief exercises a central revelatory power to rally the tribe for rededication to its traditional truths and values. Peripheral authorities, deriving their powers from the preeminent prerogatives of the chief, divine and exorcise the negative forces, insinuating their evil divisions into the Bemba community. Both these limit-symbols heighten the Bemba sense of an external locus of control for whatever good and bad are effected in their society. Tribespersons are conditioned to obey the powerful words of authorities, not to weigh them according to personal knowledge and individual rights. The cultural evolution toward personal reflection and deliberation, fostered by literacy, is matched by a countervalent reaction of irregular diviners, seeking to reimpose, by traditional intimidation, the external oral dominance, and, in effect, to retribalize persons in society.

These reformulated conclusions, propaedeutic to a critique of oral hermeneutics, are essentially conversant with the phenomenological assessment that "sound is profoundly socializing" (Ihde 1976). The deepest repercussions of this phenomenon can be stated in three hermeneutical presuppositions.

1) The Bemba notion of self is that of a thoroughly socialized tribesperson.

2) That notion of sociality totally embraces all reality into a context of mutual implication.

3) That notion is constituted by the Bemba people's instinctual confidence in their capacity to detect the order of the world and to live in harmony with it.

From the evidence presented in the body of our treatise we have discerned that these assumptions are operative in the orally conditioned sensibility and tradition of the Bemba. The Bemba mental logic rewards dogged rote learning, but not the kind of daring involved in making creative and unorthodox intellectual connections. Their civic logic is social propriety, mutual obligation, hierarchy and the overriding primacy of the group. We will now enforce the argument we have been making all along, namely, that the modern Bemba espousal of literacy inevitably forges a transformation of their hermeneutical apparatus. With respect to the three principles at hand, literacy effects a distanciation between self and society and between objects and subjects in the world. It also enables a linguistic distanciation that can differentiate between the Bemba efforts to symbolically comprehend their world and a precise explication of the mental operations necessary to verify meanings. This literate distanciation of a self, an object world and a technical language, is the keystone for a hermeneutics and the subject of the next two sections.

The Differentiaton of the Self and Objects

Tracy's position on the self and meaning is correlative to his concepts of "limit" and "the whole."[2] For, every symbol of "limit situation" and of "the whole" is at the same time a disclosure of the self, its world and the intrinsic relationship between them and the whole. The self operates within a basic horizon, wherein the self's fundamental trust in the world's meaning and worth includes at least implicitly operative the notion of the whole (Tracy 1970, 251ff; 1981, 51, see above, chap. 1, 15ff).

It follows that a fundamental hermeneutical control for developing and articulating ordered relationships to the whole of reality is the level of critical differentiation of the self (Tracy 1981, 430). But a mediated understanding and articulation of that self and its operations depend on the culture's ability to distinguish the personal world of the self from the objective world of other selves and other things. This critical level of meaning, in turn, varies as a function of the hermeneutical distance achieved by spoken and written expression respectively. And, while it is true, argues Tracy, that "all expression involves some distanciation" (Tracy 1981, 210), distanciation is far less detectable in an oral performance, wherein the agreement between the the reciter's intention and the audience's reception is negotiated in the actual speech-event (Idem 1975, 75; cf also Ong 1977, 255-58; see above, chap. 3, 70,77 and 103 for examples of literate distanciation in narratives, definitions and proverbs). The distanciation impelled by literate expression is a more pronounced and pervasive process variously manifest in the defamiliarizaton and alienation of the self from the meaning of the text and its referents (Tracy 1975, 50 and 75).[3]

In media perspectives congruent with Tracy's transcendental analysis, oralist scholars find that, the literate technology of mind promotes a reflective withdrawl into self consciousness apart from tribal consciousness (Cf Havelock 1967, chaps. 1, 2 and 11; Ong 1967, 30 and 1977, 17-22; Goody 1963, 337-40; Schneidau 1976, chaps. 1, a and 5; Tyler 1978, 73-87, 360-83). A writer works alone dissociating words from the total situation of their original dialogue. The writer analyzes elusive sounds into abstract spatial components, making processes of greater analysis possible (Ong 1982, 90 and 101; Havelock 1082, 77-88). Because of the reflective isolation demanded of a writer,

> writing . . . is essentially a consciousness-raising activity . . . . With its drive toward carefully itemized introspection and elaborately worked out analyses of inner states of soul and their inwardly structural sequential relationships . . . a greater internalization of conscience [is achieved] (Idem, 150-51).

The primary hermeneutical advantage of a differentiated self is that such a self-possessed and unified consciousness serves as the paradigm for systematic knowledge, open to and communicating with all other objective systems (Ong 1977, 336-41). Writers, absent from the reading of texts, generate original thoughts from within their own creative resources, and readers, absent from the writing of texts, independently weigh the worth and import of ideas (Ricoeur 1971, 136). These literates are freed from the constraints of the socially engineered learning process and alienated from tribal authority (Goody 1968). These liberated selves appeal to their common personal performing structures and products of experience, intelligence, rationality and responsibility (Tracy 1981, 57, 63, 70, 74). These are the grounds and conditions for internally generated criteria of truth and sanctions for behavior. Sociality in knowledge and propriety in behavior are no longer so valued or valid (Ong 1967, 178).

It follows that the emancipation of the self from the tribe is the first critical effect of literacy on religious practice. Oral religion, as manifestation, maintains a crucial emphasis upon the radical sense of participation in the whole, disclosed and elicited by the power of the whole. Under the impetus of literacy, religious expression is likely to include the dialectic of proclamation. This recognizes that the self's feeling of dependence on the whole, in which self participates, "implies the individuals's nonidentity with the whole and thereby the presence of a finite individual self" (Tracy 1981, 208). This self, saturated with the power of the whole, is also estranged from the whole. The process of distanciation of the self from the whole carries with it a sense of the whole as itself an individual, personal, transcendent "who." This 'totally other' totaliter aliter calls out to another responsible, conscientious finite person, and freely interacts in ordinary history and time (Idem). The religious encounter is irrevocably existential and irreducibly personal. The ultimate reality of the whole, a mysterium tremendum et fascinans invites and empowers a decision from a fragile yet obliging self (Idem 211).

But the experience of the detribalized self in a world of objects, which literacy sponsors, is not an incidental religious fact. It is an elemental advance in the power of the self to control meaning.

The Development of Technically Precise Language

The differentiation of the self and objects is the first critical and fundamental control for the development of culture effected by literacy. The next significant control for a culture's meaning is that process of deeper distanciation of the knower from the known, i.e., of selves from the objects of their understanding (Tracy 1975, 50). This is realized in the development of a technical language.

Any use of language, in successful communication, is a moment when meaning and understanding effectively coalesce. Understanding does not take place in some purely non-linguistic way and language is not simply a tool for expressing what is understood. Understanding occurs in a linguistic form (Cf Tyler 1978, passim). People retrieve and appropriate their inherited meanings through their language and culture by the interpretive mediation of their understanding (Tracy 1981, 103-06).

Tracy appreciates that everyday life is expressed in a pre-reflective, pre-conceptual, pre-thematic language (Tracy 1975, 47). It finds inchoate and undifferentiated expression in what Tracy calls "common sense terms" (Idem 66-68), which have only broad meanings and wide applications. Common sense language has grammatical controls over meaning, but registers only a fluid and subtle correspondence between saying and meaning.[4] It employs rhetorical formulations, artfully designed to persuade people to act (Ong 1971, 1-23). It describes things as they relate to peoples' perceptions of them.

Tracy also recognizes a further specification of reflective understanding which determines the exact logical status of the originating language of a tradition and generates an internally coherent system of more precise concepts (Idem, 69-70). The operations of precise conceptualizaton, controlling logic and methodic deduction, on this reflexive level, do not just enhance and extend the grammatical powers of meaning and expression. They transform them to generate a new horizon of meaning. They seek to explain things, not in descriptions relating them to persons, but in technical terms relating them to other thing.[5] In point of fact, meaning codified in a text is already distanced from the situation of persons in actual dialogue. As Tracy further observes, this distanciation makes such written meaning all the more subject to semantical and logical controls, independent of the social psychology operating between speaker's intention and listener's reception (Tracy 1975, 78; cf Tyler 1978, 378-79).

The media analysis, conducted by scholars like Goody, Tyler and Ong concurs with Tracy's transcendental analysis.[6] The distanciation effected by writing is intensified by the development of a technical language itself a consequence of writing, which "encourages special forms of linguistic activity associated with the developments in particular kinds of problem-raising and problem-solving" (Goody 1977, 162). Tyler, too, knows that oral discourse and written texts are capable of developing their own distinctive set of "commonplaces" (1978, 202-6, 232-48). The commonplaces of commonsense, enunciated in the oral world, are motivated by the practical purposes of getting things done and persuading people to do them; the commonplaces of science, constructed by texts, are directed toward universal truths and the formulation of theoretical knowledge (Tyler 1981, 19-20). While Tyler recognizes that writing can alienate meanings from their original concourse, he avoids extreme deconstructionism by celebrating

> . . . the world of commonsense, arguing that everyday life is far more rational and interesting than any scientific perversion of

it and that the commonplaces of everyday
experience are more fantastic than those extra
small and extra large worlds of modern science
(Tyler 1978, xi).

In other words, while appreciating the obvious gains of a
language precisely honed by texts, Tyler would agree with Tracy
who finds "fantastic the pretensions to pure objectivity" and
seeks to expose "the myth of a pure autonomy achieved solely
through a mastery of technical controls upon all allowable
meaning" (Tracy 1981, 106).

While maintaining some healthy respect for orality's
commonsense commonplaces, Ong, too, extols the merits of
literacy's technical commonplaces. According to Ong writing
things down frees the mind from its burden of remembering
everything and releases its energies for other conceptual
operations. It becomes possible to "abstract" knowledge from its
oral investiture of memorable narratives about special persons
active at particular times and places. It becomes possible to
"objectify" knowledge, detaching it from the dialogue of persons
and fixing it into general classifications, where it can be
inspected visually and manipulated spatially. It becomes
possible to develop a "technical language" of precisely defined
terms strung out into a cumulative, universally valid order of
causal connectives and logical sequences (Ong 1967 and 1977
passim).

Ong unpacks the process of distanciation in a way that is
also representative of the other oralists (Cf Tyler 1978; Goody
1977). When the tools of writing are sufficiently internalized
by literates, their natural thinking processes are artificially
restructured and technologically transformed. The different
contours of thought shaped and enhanced by writing are registered
in expression (Ong 1982, 105). Language becomes autonomous,
divorced from the control of an audience and from interaction
with non-verbal events (Idem, 160). At this distance, language
has to achieve a new precision. It is called upon to mean with
words alone, apart from the existential situation wherein oral
language is deeply encoded. The meaning of written language is
restricted to the linguistic code itself (Idem, 106). Written
language is forced to develop a richness of vocabulary in order
to compensate for the poverty of its content. Dictionaries are
composed to record and define the multiple meanings. Grammars
are devised to rule complications of linguistic structure and
usage (Idem, 106-8). Insulated from interference from the total
life-world, written language with its precisely honed techniques
prompts efforts at exact observation and complete description
(Idem, 134). Thus, writing serves both as mortician to the
hearsay evidence of the oral-aural world, and as midwife for the
birth of scientific language and method in the abstract world
(Idem, 114). In sum, says Ong:

> [Scientific expression] hedges words about
> with definitions and restrictions of all
> sorts, in order to prevent them, to a certain
> extent, from leading their own uninhibited
> life in the mysterious interior world of
> communications between persons, wherein they
> came into being (Ong 1962, 30).

Ong adds an important corollary. He recognizes the affinity between early modern science's need to hold at arm's length the human life-world and its use of "Learned Latin" which operates at a formalized distance from that world. The concepts, vocabulary and cognitive style of "Learned Latin" were very different from the common sense mode of the European vernaculars. The differences promoted the development of large scale abstractions, highly intellectual constructs and logical structures, which service the kind of non-involvement that modern science and technology demand (Ong 1977, chap. 1). Ong's corollary is significantly suggestive for the Bemba case. Their religion and culture are being transformed not merely by the distancing of writing but also by the emergence of "Learned English." Its use as the technical language of Zambia is distanced at another remove from the Bemba vernacular (Cf Idem, 41-2; see above, chap. 4, 117ff).

Clearly, the oralists' and intentionalist's consensual conclusion is that the evolution of culture and the differentiation of consciousness are greatly facilitated and accelerated by writing. As a technology of mind, writing intensifies the distanciation required for salient linguistic and cognitional advances.[7] Religious thought, too, evolves attendant to the quickening reflectivity of its practitioners. So, in addition to the paramount advance in the differentiation of the self "through intelligent and critical introspection" (Idem, 66), there must be concomitant development in religion of what Tracy calls an "explicitly conceptual language" (Idem, 70). Religion requires an "adequate technical articulation" (Idem, 188) for the ultimate or final horizon of meaning it discerns in nature and culture.

Bemba "Common Sense" vs. Christian Technical Vocabulary

Despite the fact that orate Bemba people are as intelligent and reasonable as literate peoples in the practical affairs of life's routines, there are important hermeneutical differences (Tracy 1970, 111ff).

There is a great deal of difference between being able to cope intelligently with one's environment, on the one hand, and, on the other, meeting the demands of a systematic, theoretical perspective. The reasonableness and religiosity of the ordinary Bemba need not imply that they are philosophers and theologians, any more than "the practitioner of traditional medicine" *Ng'anga* could operate effectively as a modern doctor in a university teaching hospital. Thresholds of meaning are crossed as one moves from popular common sense specializations of intelligence to systematic universes of discourse (Tracy 1970, 114-15).[8] The Bemba oral people speak more for that specialization of intelligence just named "common sense." Their language remains an oral prisoner, tied to the descriptive level relating things to persons.[9]

Recall this treatise's discussion of the relationship of "God" to "Lesa" (See above, chap. 3, 90ff). The Christian missionaries (and the African revisionists) assume, or pretend, that the Bemba and Christian understandings of divinity are somehow comparable, if not identical. Therefore, the names "Lesa" and "God" could be considered univocal. In fact, a review of the data has shown that the event of understanding, which traditional Bemba "common sense" attaches to the name "Lesa," is radically alien to the reflexive insights, which ground the logically controlled and systematically defined concept of "God" imported from Christian doctrine. The Christians, at first, implicitly recognized that what they meant by "God" could not adequately be formulated by the Bemba word "Lesa." So they used the supposed neutrality of the Swahili imports "Mulungu" to represent their understanding of God and "Roo" to designate their conception of God's purely spiritual nature. This signalled to the Bemba that a new event of understanding was required in their conversion to Christianity. Later, when the cognitive adjustments were thought to be progressing well, the indigenous name "Lesa" was safely reintroduced. In effect, then, the word "Lesa" is a neologism, a term carrying a new meaning, when it represents the Christian intent. Behind it remains, not the Bemba "common sense" notion of "spirit" but the Christian technical concept of "divinity."

For another example, sheer common sense tells the Bemba how to identify respectful behavior and how to distinguish respectable persons from their opposites. They also believe that, by throwing bones onto intersecting lines drawn East and West on banana leaves with white flour and red camwood powder, while invoking ancestral spirits, they can determine the secrets of deeds already done or the consequent course of deeds still in progress. But, if they were asked about this treatise's concepts of "social propriety" (See above, chap. 2, 59ff), "limit-symbols" or "the notion of the whole" (See above, chap. 1, 14ff), they would be tongue-tied. They are like people who know how to add and divide, but when asked to define addition and division, they can only state that what they just did is "adding," or repeat what they just did when they divided. They are adept in the use of "common sense" discourse and unschooled in the intricacies of technical language.

Any attempt to transform essentially "common sense" expressions into a technical problem for hermeneutics is a legitimate exercise in itself for arriving at something more sublimely significant. Nevertheless, it must be recognized that the oral tradition is little inclined and poorly equipped to create processes that actually cross several levels of language and meaning and arrive at concepts of an order different from its popular metaphors. As Tyler observes, there is all the difference in the world "between merely using a metaphor and using a metaphor with the intention of 'metaphorizing'" (Tyler 1978, 320). Interpreters have to respect substitution of later technical language for "common sense" expressions (Cf Tyler 1981, 26).

Symbolic Language: A Special Case for Hermeneutics

The religious language of a people with its limit-symbols and reference to the whole seems to have its own peculiar hermeneutical bearing. It is too sophisticated to be simply the result of "common sense" and too ambiguous to be an achievement of theoretic meaning. Symbolic expression somehow spans these categories (Cf Tracy 1970, 212-17).

Tracy's analysis suggests that it is the symbols' authentic limit-character, which rescues them from irrelevance and triviality. Symbols require that their religious dimensions be taken positively and seriously, as intending more or less adequate representations of basic beliefs. It is a categorical mistake to subject them to "literal" scrutiny and consequently judge them negatively, for reasons other than their artistic inadequacy or misapplication (Tracy 1981, 162):

> [Symbols, metaphors, rituals and] myths, insofar as they function as the first narrative representation of our experiences as selves holding certain basic beliefs, have fully positive meanings (Idem 1975, 162).

Tracy takes his cue from Ricoeur's thesis that "The symbol gives rise to thought; yet thought is reformed by and returns to symbol" (Ricoeur 1967, 347-58). Reflective thought is prompted by the symbol, whose sensible multivalance is never exhausted by rational exegesis. In symbol, understanding reaches its limits and, dialectically returning to the sensitive contents of the symbol, makes "a wager" (an act of faith, really) for its own renewal.

We agree with Tracy that the essence of religion and its symbols is to express the intentionality of the human spirit (mind and heart) as it develops its potentialities. But, symbolic language is a complex, flexible and developing network of images. With symbols, members of a linguistically constituted universe achieve conviction (believe), not by serious rational enquiry into grounds, premises and conclusions, but through the power of suitable rhetorical devices to evoke enthusiasm, loyalty and religious fervor (Tracy 1981, 99-107, 205-6).

For example, in Chapter Two we noticed the simultaneous and multiple meanings present in the symbols of *Cisungu* . The women initiators have positively and consciously mastered artistic controls for meaning. Their media demand an elaboration of carefully determined aesthetic forms in colors, pottery, songs and dances. These symbolic products are works of exceptional fertility and suggestiveness. They evidence a spirit of remarkable creativity and technical expertise. Clearly the initiators' art is an expression of the primordial pattern of meaning, present in the spontaneous and structured unfolding of human consciousness. But these symbolic expressions do not pretend to be dominated by the detached and disinterested desire to know characteristic of objectivity (Cf Tyler 1981, 17-20). *Mbusa* "initiation pots" are saturated with the affectivity and aggressiveness that subjectively relate the Bemba to their worlds of meaning within those conventional religious symbols. Therefore, it is important to distinguish between the authentic thrust toward self-transcendence and the particular embodiments it receives in space and time. The authentic thrust of a symbol is carried by its positive emotional power to reorient the basic mood and motivations of a community and thus "affect" a more desirable way of living in the world (Tracy 1975, 92 and 208; 1981, 205-6).

In Bemba religious symbolism, the expressions of both (a) the positive "peak moments" and (b) the negative anxious moments have authentic elements. Let us recall the examples from Chapters Three and Four.

Positive peak experiences. Following Tracy's line of thought and employing his terms in Chapter Three, we affirmed the reality of the religious dimensions of Bemba experience. We explored the existential significance and limit-character of the originating language of its religion, especially its limit-language of "spirits." Narratives about spirits and particular proverbs about Lesa, it was claimed, redescribe Bemba experience in such a manner that there is disclosed a limit at which and for which the Bemba can live. The chapter further remarked that this limit-language and experience of "spirits" made a cognitive claim. Their objective ground or referent is the basic Bemba belief that the whole of their world somehow makes sense and their way of being-in-the-world is worthwhile. This, in sum, is the religious dimension of Bemba life, which is manifest in their symbols and in their everyday language: in their communal experience, as Bemba tribespersons, there is a final dimension or horizon of ultimate meaning which is objectively referred to as "spirits." These "spirits" are the very ground of their being and the touchstone of all that is real, true and valuable in their lives. Functioning similarly to the oral contrivance of proverbs, spirit-talk preserves the voice and prolongs the authority of the tradition which originates with the ancestors "in the beginning."

Negative anxious moments. Again following Tracy's lead in Chapter Four, we affirmed the paramount chief as the authoritative embodiment of the notion of the whole. But we also acknowledged the inevitable fact of evil in the Bemba community as they deliberately deviate from, or simply feel themselves estranged from, that authoritative wholeness of their tradition. This leads them to search out the possibilities for their transformation and to tap their spiritual powers for implementing their resolve. The symbols, in which the Bemba express both the evil and the redescription of their lives for their possible rescue from evil, fix the blame on forces which lie beyond personal freedom. Hence, witches and evil spirits.

But, it is true that there are existential and experiential elements in the fact of evil, which seem impervious to human reason, because individuality and freedom are intrinsically inexplicable and mysterious. Evil really is more than just a matter of wrong choices by individuals. It does, in fact, also operate through subconscious psychological forces and through large-scale sociological conditions. So, evil has suprapersonal dimensions, which go beyond the practical control of individuals.

And it is also true that the human confidence in the final reality of life as trustworthy is in fact constantly threatened by absurdity and malignity from both nature and the human community. Reassurance is sorely needed.

Consequently, the Bemba idioms of spirit possession, divination and witchcraft practices can be finally understood as negative religious symbols. They are correlative to the experience of evil as a power transcending individual perpetrations and requiring communal compensations. The conclusion is not that those phenomena are simply symbols. They really exist as symbols of social stress. They are the cultural expressions of psycho-sociological experiences. Following a line of Weberian thought (Weber 1947), we can say these symbols come to live lives of their own with ideas and images feeding back effectively and indiscriminately into human behavior, sometimes tragically as with the witch-slaying of *Mwafi* , more often pathetically as with the *Mcapi* witch-accusation of often innocent old people, sometimes pathologically as with the *Ngulu* spirit-possession, and other times pretentiously as with the divinatory practices of *Ng'anga* .

A Prognosis and Remedy for Bemba Religion

Equipped now with the necessary hermeneutical apparatus, we can make an informed assessment of the mode of survival for Bemba

oral religion. Unless religion is to be simply shunted aside to
an area of comfortable irrelevancy, it must keep apace of the
evolving consciousness of its adherents. Oral systems of thought
are closed, protective against new alternatives to their
laboriously hoarded meagre supply of knowledge; they anxiously
regard new ideas and new ways of thinking as threats (Cf Horton
1967, 155). Writing opens thinkers and their systems to
previously inconceivable questions and new ways of searching for
responses (Cf Goody 1977, 41-51). Coupled with what Ong calls
the "ontogenetic growth" of individual consciousness, literacy
excites "phylogenetic growth" by a "massive exfoliation" of
knowledge (1977, 43-7).

Bemba traditional religion, however, remains tied to its
oral origins and closed to the raised consciousness of Bemba
literates. It might have developed along literate lines had not
literacy itself come to the Bemba world firmly allied to a new
religion. Christianity was already prosperously acclimated to
the modern world. It had negotiated an appropriate separation of
religion from the secular world. Bemba "common sense" no longer
seemed as effective as the science and technology of Christian
society. Christianity had adjusted itself to the rising
visualism sponsored by the written and printed word. Bemba
religion somewhat confused the realms of things and persons, but
Christianity separated objects from subjects. Where Bemba
religion totally subsumed the secular and concerned itself with
the personalized, denatured cosmos, Christianity concerned itself
more compartmentally with the spiritual life and let science deal
with a desacralized, depersonalized nature. Where oral religion
was subject to seemingly arbitrary control of magical and
communal encounters, Christianity depended on the individual
acceptance of precisely formulated creeds and laws. Where Bemba
religion tended to mystify cosmic origins and physical
occurrences, Christianity proclaimed that, the more people knew
about the cosmos as scientific fact, the more they knew about the
God who created it. In brief, while Christianity had already
made its peace with the literate sciences, oral religion, relying
solely on the resources of its symbol system, could not cope with
the rising new consciousness of Bemba literates.

In the previous section we took notice of the positive power
of religious symbolic discourse to capture imaginations, to whip
up emotions and to lead people to action. This strength is also
its potential weakness. For myths and rituals, with their
symbolic lure compelling affective commitment to traditional
answers to traditional questions, can place severe restrictions
on the range of inquiry and the emergence of insight. In this
way, symbols' hermeneutical value, which rests on their intention
of truth and their association with the proper development of
self knowledge, is subverted.

As a people becomes more reflective and introspective under
the impact of their literate skills, they begin to resent and

then to doubt any symbol system which inhibits their interior growth and their external quest for greater knowledge. Within the oral disposition, if they intend to take symbols seriously, they have no recourse other than to interpret them "literally". As a people of undifferentiated consciousness, they make no distinction between image and idea, and have no reflexive technique to liberate their insights and judgments from their luxuriant burdens of aggressivity and affectivity (See above, chap. 1, 3-4). One's personal responsibility for truth recedes as the basic dynamic of enquiry is submerged in communal consciousness--or in what Durkheim calls "collective representations" (Durkheim 1965). Corroborative or corrective events are disallowed in judgments, for the operative criterion of truth in the oral community is that the real is what is sensitively expressed and communally accepted.

The Bemba tribesperson, for example, is situated in a history and society of an ambiguous heritage of orally funded meanings. Merely imagined entities--like *Mipashi* -are described, domesticated and brought under the scope of communal meaning simply by being named; they are deeply embedded in the rituals, myths, symbols and authorities of the tradition. So certain and ingrained is this inherited oral wisdom that fundamental questions are not easily raised or struggled with, for the responses are too familiar and too well formulated (Cf Tracy 1981, 103).

As we have seen, the symbolic idiom of "spirits" [*Mipashi* and *Milungu*] effectively renders something of the fundamental drive of the human spirit to transcend itself. These limit-symbols enjoy a degree of religious authenticity insofar as they represent a **manifestation** of the whole. They can deliver over to the oral Bemba an intensified assurance that their world makes fundamental sense and their lives are ultimately worth living.

But it is not enough for a literate people to be convinced of this basic belief by some manifestation of the whole itself and to be committed to authentic living by the experienced power of religious symbols. The areas of experience indicated by symbols need to be taken seriously. For literate Bemba the danger increases that symbols become obscurant. For example, the symbols of evil in divination, witchcraft and possession, by so imaginatively exteriorizing evil, can evacuate that degree of responsibile control for human destiny which literates feel is rightfully personal and individual. A literate people sooner or later will demand that the **proclamation** of their religious reality be cognitively reconciled with their own heightened consciousness and their experience of the nature and finality of all other realities (Cf Tracy 1981, 43).

Thus, we conclude that, only through the introduction of the written medium, can Bemba religious culture be expected to move from an existentially meaningful realm, which everyday life and common sense language discloses, to the theoretic determination of the exact truth-status of its religious symbols, where its cognitive claims can be explicitly examined (Tracy 1975, 70). Literacy introduces new logical controls for precisely defining and correcting meanings according to deductive reasoning; these exceed syntactical rhetorical and grammatical controls, which pattern the meaning of Bemba speech. A written text can then rise to the explanatory level where technical language will relate one thing to other things, distancing a knowledge of them from the vagaries and discrepancies of personal perception.

This is a move from the particular concrete reality of a religion described by history and phenomenology, to its abstract, general, universal and necessary features, explained by fundamental theology (Tracy 1981, 162). Then the presuppositions of that existential faith in the final worth and truth of ordinary life and language can be represented as an express, thematic, and conceptually precise expression of full self-consciousness. Formulated in explicitly transcendental terms, this basic faith is "the condition of the possibility of our existing or understanding at all" (Tracy 1981, 153-54).

For Tracy, the attempt to thematically articulate that basic belief, implicitly present in ordinary experience and explicitly affirmed in the limit-symbols of religion, is best resolved in monotheistic terms. "Without the truth of theism, religion tends to become an existentially useful, but not cognitively serious question" (Tracy 1975, 163). Authentic, transcendental reflection on religious limit-experience and language will develop genuine limit-concepts with a theistic referent (Idem 155; cf also Tracy 1981, 160-64).

Now, as we saw in Chapter Three, Bemba oral religion could only be designated monotheistic by some poetic or anachronistic leap of the most benevolent Christian interpreter. But the truths it orally espouses and the unconscious psychic sway it wields with mother-tongue tenacity over English-speaking Bemba literates should not be ignored (Cf Ong 1982, 163). Traditional limit-symbols need to be appropriately and adequately integrated with the Christian symbol system already found resourceful by the standards of literacy (Cf Tracy 1975, chaps. 4-8). It is a double irony that the survival of certain oral features of Bemba religion depends on their redemption by Christianity and that the remedy is literacy.

Literate Death of Bemba Oral Religion

The visual culture in which Christianity shares is antithetical to the hermeneutics of the oral culture, which maintains Bemba religion (Ong 1967, 34). When they are brought into historical proximity, there seems to be a fight to the death. What Kelber calls the "oral ontology of language"

(1983, 203) makes oral words efficacious. To speak of spirits is to give them life. The transcription of the oral life world to the printed text preserves it from decay, only in the illusory manner of a collection of butterflies pinned down to their matting, captured but dead (Cf Ong 1977, chap. 9). *Mipashi* and *Ngulu* "spirits" whose very life depends on the oral performance of myths and rituals are entombed in silent texts, inspected and found not apprehendable by the new hermeneutical criterion of reality, visibility. The spirits die as surely as Nietzsche's God, when the harmonium, in which they live, grows silent (Ong 1967, 16). The myriad voices of the spirit-chorus in the oral world are deadened, when the Christian God, who lives in the visible splendor of the written word, depopulates their pantheon. God of the printed text is as individualized and isolated from the spirit-society as the Bemba literate is detribalized from oral culture. The world no longer speaks, but is observed. Like Buber's God (Ong 1967, 71) Bemba royal spirits, who represent the oral religious center, are silent. Those authorities, who spoke in their name, have lost their voices; those, who listened to them, now see with literate eyes. The net result is the mortification of Bemba traditional religion, which shares in the decline of the oral-aural culture. As the proverb says *Mweo wa muntu waba mu kutwi* : The very life of a person resides in the ear" (White Fathers 1954, 299).

Literate Resurrection of Bemba Christian Theology

But every dying makes room for new life. Bemba oral religion can live a new kind of life, first of all in its written form, secondly in its living readership, and thirdly in its creative incorporation of its beliefs and practices into the Christian literate economy.

Firstly, preserved in its written form, Bemba oral religion can enjoy what Ong calls the "limitless fecundity of texts:"

> The word reduced to an inscribed surface, silenced, then resurrected, has a potential, new fecundities, even regarding our relationship to the oral word, which are forever denied to the purely oral word. The word must die and be resurrected, if it is to come into its own (1977, 256-57).

Secondly, this "fecundity" is directly related to the cardinal cultural events of distanciation already discussed as the effects of literacy in this Conclusion: the evolution of conscious mental life and freedom of individuated readers and their consequent development of science, theology and the humanities (Cf Ong 1977, 256). But the cultural advantages of writing will not be exploited for the benefit of traditional religion, not even by literate Bemba. Over 72% of the tribal population has already converted to Christianity (Catholic Secretariat Statistics, 1981). It is clearly too late for a literate revision of oral religion as a whole. Its future belongs in alliance with the usurper. Christianity's own vitality among the Bemba, however, stands in need of a massive transfusion of the spirit of Bemba tradition.

Thirdly, just as literate Christianity has learned to live with the oral matrix and massive oral residue of its scriptures (Cf Kelber 1983), so too it must learn to live with the oral antecedents of its Bemba converts. The particular philosophical concepts and system used to translate Christian theology must be made commensurate with the special genius of Bemba oral religion (Cf Tracy 1975, 149; and 1979, 97-99). The Christian mission, in its incarnational interface and interaction with the Bemba, must become a thoroughly open system transforming and being transformed by a dynamic communication with oral religion. In Ong's view the relationship of literate Christianity with its own oral origins is a model of transformative interaction:

> Finally, to sum it all up, given that the resurrection of Jesus Christ is like nothing else in all creation, the insertion of any text into present discourse, the reentry of any text into the oral world is a kind of resurrection, is the Christian to think of the individual's and the community's here and now appropriation of the word in the Bible as a resurrection suggesting that of Jesus? Given that writing is not just the visual equivalent of speech and that there is a psychological progression from orality to a literate culture, how necessary was it that the Good News of the death, resurrection and ascension of the Lord itself die and be buried in a text in order to come to an later, resurrected life throughout history? (Ong 1977, 271).

How necessary is it that oral Bemba religion, with its myths and rituals, its spirit-divinities and sacred authorities, die itself and be buried in this and other texts in order to be transformed by a later, resurrected life in the Christian economy.

FOOTNOTES TO CONCLUSION

[1] This transition will be facilitated by the fact that the meanings behind our discussion's primary oral categories (borrowed from Walter Ong) and primary religious categories (taken from David Tracy) are radicated in the same hermeneutical tradition. On the one hand, while the oralist Ong is explicitly concerned with the phenomenology and history of religious culture, his methodology is implicitly informed by the Thomist philosophical tradition in which he is admittedly well schooled. On the other hand, the theologian Tracy, who deals directly with the hermeneutical problems presented by religion, has made his own Kantian "turn to the subject," as the foundation for hermeneutics, under the explicit influence of the transcendental methodology developed for contemporary Thomism by Bernard Lonergan (_Insight_, New York: Longmans, 1958 and _Method in Theology_, New York: Herder, 1972).

Tracy breaks with the Thomist tradition when, in searching for an adequate and appropriate expression for his metaphysics, he critically opts for the conceptual apparatus of process theology instead of Lonergan's revised Thomist categories (Cf Tracy, _Blessed Rage for Order_, New York: Seabury, 1975, 172ff).

[2] Tracy's methodic approach to the self is admittedly mediated by Lonergan's cognitional analysis, though Tracy adds his own distinctive reinterpretations (Cf Tracy, _Blessed Rage for Order_, New York: Seabury, 1975, 113, n. 26-114, n. 44).

[3] The new hermeneutics of textual criticism can distinguish between "sense" and "referent;" the former regards the internal structure and meaning of the text, and the latter registers, not the real intention of the author or the social-cultural situation "behind" the text, but the changed way of perceiving reality, which the text opens up "in front of" the reader (Cf Tracy, _Blessed Rage_, 50-52). Thus, the interpretation of Bemba oral tradition is not properly a task for the new hermeneutics; for, the relevance and meaning of Bemba traditional religion to present day peoples, except for an increasingly marginalized minority of the Bemba, is no longer an issue. It is only of scholarly interest to establish the semantics and historical dimensions of a vintage oral culture.

[4] The distinction between the grammatical and technical modes of expression is artificial and too simplified, since ordinary language expresses more than just grammatical structures. Nevertheless, it helps to clarify the general differences between grammatical and logical structures, and between ordinary and technical languages.

[5] Tracy's insistent distinction between common sense language and technical meanings is grounded in Lonergan's terms and thought (_Insight_, New York; Longman's 1958, esp. chap. 6).

[6]The *Preface* of this treatise agreed with Ong's relative view that, although a media analysis would certainly shed a great deal of light, orality could not be understood as the cause or explanation of everything in Bemba consciousness and culture (See above, xix). In a similar vein, this *Conclusion* agrees with Goody that literacy does not single-handedly invent these specialized operations of the human mind, which are demonstrably universal potentialities of language and knowing and are virtually present in their every function. But, literacy can be accurately said to crystallize in definitive form the implicit possibilities and exhaustive potentials of a relentlessly systematized mental operation (Goody, *Literacy in Traditional Societies*, Cambridge, 1968, 36ff and 105ff, and *The Domestication of the Savage Mind*, Cambridge, 1977 51).

To the function of writing, Goody ascribes the specific cognitional refinements, which Tracy demands for progressive stages of language and consciousness (Goody, *Domestication of the Savage Mind*, 1977): the development of logic, mathematical operations and syllogistic reasoning, in the sense of strict analytic procedures (pp. 11-12); greater abstraction, systematization, decontextualization and generalization of knowledge (pp. 13-14); enhanced reflection, criticism and the likelihood of skepticism (pp. 44-47); reorganized concepts, reclassified categories, and clearly distinct definitions (pp. 109-11); elaborate and explicit rules for stringent methods of experimenting and verifying knowledge (Chap. 7); viable alternative programs in the repertoire of dealing with data (p. 111). The tools for these increments in cognitional possibilities are the literate devices of drafting tables of comparative knowledge (Chap. 4), making lists of known items (Chap. 5), and drawing schemata to analyze knowledge (Chaps. 6 & 7).

[7]Tracy's theory of cognition and the oralist complementary theory on orality and literacy are both corroborated by the findings of the Soviet experimental psychologist, A.R. Luriia (*Cognitive Development*, Cambridge, Harvard, 1976). In a unique study of non-literate Russian peasants compared with subjects who had at least short-term school instruction, Luriia found that mental procedures, such as abstraction and categorical classification, definition of concepts and the use of generic terms (Idem, 48-99), and theoretical thinking implied in syllogistic deduction and inference (Idem, 100-16), were completely foreign to illiterate ways of thinking; the non-literates refused or failed to engage in any hypothetical problem-solving and discursive logical reasoning within formal conditions extraneous to their personal, practical and concrete experience (Idem, 117-33). In addition, the non-literates were either uninterested or incapable of self-analysis and self-awareness, representative of individual consciousness (Idem 144-60). Luriia's conclusions adhere to the Marxist theory on the socioeconomic dynamic operative at various phases of historical development: the radical transformation of modes of thought,

which illiterate peasants underwent, was induced by the social interaction, which education and collectivization entail (Idem 161-64).

But Luriia's evidence also converges on and corroborates the thesis that the acquision of the technology of literacy is at least partially responsible for the changes in cognitional operations. This interpertation, proffered throughout this treatise on the Bemba case, is justified by Luriia' own general conclusion:

> Our investigations . . . showed that, as the basic forms of activity change, as literacy is mastered, and as a new stage of social and historical practice is reached, major shifts occur in human mental activity . . . which radically affect the structure of cognitive processes [Luriia 1976, 161 (emphasis added)].

[8] As specializations of intelligence differ, so do hermeneutics differ. The more technical the acts of meaning-- that is, the less they are embodied in historically and culturally limited terms--the simpler is the task of interpretation. Consider how little hermeneutical apparatus is required for people of all times and cultures to agree on the meaning of Euclid's Principia, whose correct understanding is unique.

However, there is no basic, garden variety of "common sense." "Common sense" assertions, whose meanings may be quite obvious to members of a particular community, are not common to all persons of all times and all places, but only among people in successful communication with others in the same community. When "common sense" meanings are transposed to another time and place, where there are different experiences, interests, values, social apparatus and cultural horizons, then the problems of interpretation arise (Cf Lonergan, Method in Theology, New York, 1972).

[9] What is invariant in oral minds and literate minds is the intelligent spirit of inquiry, unfolding in a normative pattern of conscious intending, which Lonergan calls the dynamic and heuristic structure of knowing (Lonergan, Insight, New York, Longmans, 1958, passim). Literacy is a technology enabling a different mode of consciousness, to which all intelligent people have access. It goes without saying that literate Bemba persons are as competent and creative in handling the technical language and theory appropriate to their level of education and profession. In our discussion here we are concerned with formally oral Bemba tribespersons.

SOURCES CONSULTED

Oral

The citations in the text, which have only a name and a Roman numeral, refer to this list of principal interlocutors and the month between October 1978 and September 1979 when the interview took place. The table also includes the names of the other discursants present, their official status, and the location of the interview. The transcripts, referenced according to the principal name and Roman numeral, will be available in the Special Collections Library of the University of Zambia from October 1985. The asterisk* indicates that there is no transcript of the interview; there are only the personal notes of the author. (Grateful acknowledgment is here made to Mr. Chitika Mwambazi and to Mr. Andrew Kapambwe, both of whom assisted in transcribing and typing the taped interviews).

Informants	Status	Age	Location
*R. Mwansa X	Catholic Priest	35	Lusaka
*I. Bantungwa X	Catholic Priest	35	Lusaka
H. Turner X	Professor, Univ. of Aberdeen	55	Lusaka
E. Mwelwa XI	Farmer	55	Kabula's(Village)
M. Chileshe	*Kabilo*		
E. Chiboo	Farmer	55	
M. Chileshe XI	*Kabilo*	80	Ituta's Spring
A. Muselela XI	Villager	85	Malole
R. Mukolwe XI	*Mwinemushi*	80	Mutamba's
F. Tampulo XI	Farmer	65	Mutamba's
R. Musabandesu XI	Catechist (retired)	70	Fele's
J. Chalusa XI	Villager	70	Mulala's
T. Chimanga	*Mwinemushi*	70	
S. Sampa XI	*Nacimbusa*	80	Fele's
T. Kapolyo	Villager	80	
S. Komakoma XI	Farmer	60	Chikunga's
M. Komakoma	Local Court Judge	65	
F. Mwila XII	Villager	60	Chishika's
B. Mukuka	Villager	70	
J. Mutale	Villager	70	
F. Taulo	Villager	35	
E. Shinaka	Villager	70	
B. Kalonga XII	*Shimapepo*	80	Chishimba Falls
Mumena XII	*Mfumu*	70	Musumba
E. Ngoshe	*Kabilo*	60	
J. Musonda	Villager	65	
M. Mwango XII	*Mwinemushi/Kabilo*	80	Mulewa-Chinfwembe's
J. Lesa	Catechist	40	
G. Mpundu	Catholic Priest	35	

Informants	Status	Age	Location
Nsenshi XII	*Mwinemushi/Kabilo*	70	Nsenshi's
A. Katewa XII	Wood carver	55	Mulala's
Chewe-Ng'andu XII	*Mfumu*		
Kalubila		80	Musumba
Mutemba XII	*Mwinemushi/Kabilo*	65	Mutemba's
N. Chileshe	Villager	80	
*G. Mpundu III	Catholic Priest	35	Malole
*B. Kapompole III	Catholic Priest/		
	Ng'anga	65	Lwena
Chilubula III			
An interview with 25 senior catechists from all over Bembaland			
*J. Gamache III	Missionary	60	Chilubula
B. Ng'andu IV	*Ng'anga*	65	Kangwa's Spring
*T. Smeldt IV	Missionary	75	Chilubula
Chanda-Mukulu IV	*Namfumu*	80	Musumba
Banapenge IV	*Nacimbusa*	60	Cheleseni's
Ngalande IV	*Mwinemushi*	75	Ngalande's
*J.J. Corbeil IV	Museum curator/		
	Missionary	70	Moto-Moto
			Museum
L. Kabwe IV	Retired Catechist	65	Mporokoso
R. Katuna IV	*Mwinemushi*	55	Lumangwe Falls
N. Mukuka	Villager	55	
*J. Foret IV	Missionary	50	Mporokoso
*Mporokoso IV	*Mfumu*	60	Musumba
Shibwalya-Kapila IV	*Mfumu*	65	Musumba
R. Nseluka	*Kabilo*	70	
S. Mutandabala	*Kabilo*	70	
J. Chanda IV	Catholic Priest	35	Kapatu
L. Shikaputo IV	Villager	75	Akatobo's Tree
P. Kapembwa	Villager	70	
E. Chiboo IV	Farmer	55	Nkumbula's
C. Nkumbula	*Mwinemushi*	70	
M. Chileshe	Villager	80	
Machemba	*Mwinemushi*	70	
M. Mwamba	Retired	65	
*P. van der Linden V	Missionary	55	Kayambi
*L. Oger V	Missionary/		
	Bemba Expert	65	Ilondola
*A. Kucuka V	Catholic Priest	60	Mungwi
D. Katema	Museum Assistant	70	
C. Mwaba	Catholic Priest	60	
*G. Stuer V	Missionary	50	Mpulungu
M. Mulutula V	Catechist	55	Kaputa's
Mulilansolo V			Mulilansolo
A discussion with 25 Catholic prayer-leaders from all around Bembaland.			
L. Kamukwambwa V	Bemba Language Teacher	60	Ilondola
J. Muyeleka V	Villager	75	Nkula's

Informants	Status	Age	Location
D. Makombe	Villager	70	
Cingkalonga V	*Shimapepo*	75	Cembe's Monolyth
D. Nkandu V	Villager	65	Fulanshi's
Mutoba VII	*Shimapepo*	80	Chishimba Falls
P. Mwela VII	*Ng'anga*	60	Kalungu River
*Chisanga-Ponde VII	*Kabilo*	65	Chitimukulu's
Chitikafula	*Kabilo*	75	
Nkolemambwe	*Kabilo*	65	
Shimwalule VII	*Mfumu/Shimapepo*	75	Mwalule
Cibingo	*Kabilo/Mwinemushi*	70	
Cilangisho	*Kabilo/Mwinemushi*	70	
2 Bamukabenye	"Wives of the Relics"	70	
*S. Mpashi VII	Bemba Author	65	Lusaka
*Nkweto VII	*Mfumu*	70	Musumba
*Nkula VII	*Mfumu*	55	Musumba
Kapinka-Milandu	*Kabilo*	65	
A. Nkamba	*Shimapepo*	60	
*S. Kapwepwe VIII	Former Vice-President of Zambia	60	Chiyembwe
J. Chomba VIII	Catholic Priest	35	Lusaka
Shimulamba IX	*Shimapepo-Kabilo*	70	Canga's Cave
Namasala IX	*Shimapepo*	70	Canga's Cave
*Nkolemfumu IX	*Mfumu*	70	Musumba

"STATUS" terms translated:

Kabilo	=	Royal councillor
Mwinemushi	=	Village-head
Nacimbusa	=	Woman-initiator
Shimapepo	=	Traditional Priest
Mfumu	=	Chief
Namfumu	=	Titular mother of chiefs
Mukabenye	=	Guardian of royal relics
Ng'anga	=	Healer
Mucapi	=	Witch-cleanser
Musumba	=	Royal village

Archival

A. London, Archives of the Archdiocese of Westminster: "Bishop Hinsley's Apostolic Visitorship in East Africa 1928-38-- Report on the Vicariate of Bangweolo," Edouard Labrecque. TS. 39/3(b) 23B.

B. London, Archives of the Council for World Mission, University of London, School of Oriental and African Studies: London Missionary Society, Bemba Mission: Correspondences, Annual and Decennial Reports.

C. Great Britain, Public Record Office. Foreign Office files:
(a) British South Africa Company, Original Correspondences and Annual Reports for North-eastern Rhodesia.
(b) Colonial Office, Original Correspondences and Annual Reports for North-eastern Rhodesia.

D. Edinburgh, Scottish Foreign Mission Acrhives, Natural Library of Scotland:
(a) Scottish Missionary Society Manuscripts.
(b) Universities' Mission to Central Africa Correspondences and Annual Reports.

E. Roma, Archivista Generale, Padri Bianchi (White Fathers Archives):
Dupont, Joseph
  1895 "Letters to Mgr. Livinhac." MS Kayambi, December 26, WFA 106/016.

Etienne, Louis
  1949 "Dieu, les *Ngulu*, les *Mipashi*." TS. WFA 803.11.

Foulon, P.
  1907 "Les Babemba: moeurs et coutumes." MS. 3 vol. WFA 803.11.

Garrec, Nicholas
  1916 "Croyances et coutumes religieuses des Babemba." TS. Chilonga: WFA 803.11.

Guille, Raoul
  1896 "Letter to the Motherhouse." TS. Kayambi. December 2, WFA 108/323.

Kayati, Abbe
  1944 "Coutumes babemba." MS. Mpweto: WFA 803.113.

Labrecque, Edouard et Garrec, P.
  1931 "Quelques notes sur la religion des Babemba et tribus voisines." TS. WFA 803.11.

174

Oger, Louis
N.D.   "L'Art Bemba."   TS.   WFA 700/113.

White Fathers
N.D.   "Enquete sur les moeurs et coutumes des Babemba, Bamambwe et Babisa."   TS.   Vicariat Apostolique de Kasama, Northern Rhodesia.   WFA 40.

Mission Diaries for the early years (1891-1935):   Chibote, Chilonga, Chilubula, Kaputu, Kayambi and Mambwe.

F.   Lusaka, Zambia National Archives, District Notebooks:
Abercorn KTN/1/1/1:   " *Butwa* --An Immoral Festival," 1920, 71-71; " *Banyama* ," April 1944; " *Ngulu* ," May 1950; "*Mucapi*" June 1959.

Chinsali KTQ 2/1: Vol. I " *Awemba* Religious Beliefs," 229; " *Awemba* History as I have heard it," Robert "Bobo" Young, 1898, 231-239; " *Awemba* --Some Native Customs," 243; " *Awemba* Burial Customs of Commoners," 247; "On the Death of a Chief," 248; "Some Native Punishments-- *Awemba* ," 250. Vol. III "Notes on *Shimwalule* and *Nkweto* ," W.V. Brelsford, 1940, 67ff; "Installation of Chief *Nkula Chewe* ," August 16, 1937, 204-14; "Description of House-breaking Ceremony at Chief Nkula's Village," June 13, 1938, 215-26; "Chief Nkweto's Installation," 1942, 268-75.

Kasama KDH 1/1:
Vol. I "Changa Cave," August 12, 1955, 65; "Bemba History Notes," by P. Guilleme, 1902, 400-14; "Chiefs in Northern Rhodesia," by D.B. Hall, January 23, 1958.

Luwingu KS2 5/1.

Mporokoso KSU 3/1: "Mythology," 241.

G.   Ilondola, Language Centre Archives
Belin, Jean P.
1960   "Report on marriage."   TS.

Chomba, Justin
1979   "Bemba religion."   TS.   Minutes of the Central Deanery Meeting, Mulanga, July 6-7.

Corbeil,J.J.
N.D.   "The sacred emblems (Cisungu)."   TS.   Moto Moto Museum, Mbala.

N.D.   "Bush medicines."   TS.   Moto Moto Museum, Mbala.

Girard, J.A.
    1965 "A few Bemba proverbs translated and explained."
          TS. Fort Rosebery.

Hoch, E.
    1966 "One thousand, one hundred and eleven Bemba
          proverbs." TS. Ilondola: Language School.

    1963 "Know your home: a study of Northern Rhodesia
          and in particular of the Babemba country and
          their neighboring tribes." TS.   Ilondola:
          Language School.

Kapompole, Bonaventure
    N.D. "*Imiti ya Babemba*." TS.

          Various essays and notes on Bemba traditional
          religious practices and beliefs. TS and MS.

Lacrecque, Edouard
    N.D. "Croyances et pratiques religieuses des Bemba et
          des tribus avoisinantes: Notes sur la Religion
          des Babemba." TS. Ilondola: Language School.

    1931-37 "*Amapinda, ificoleko, malumbo*, etc." MS.

Ng'andu, S.A.
    1922-23 "*Misango ya Cisenshi iyo bacita;*" "*Ubulwele no
          Lubuko;*" "*Imiti;*" "*Imilandu ya Kulima;*" "*Kupyana
          no Lupupo.*" MS.
Oger, Louis
    1972 "The Bemba of Zambia: outline of their life-
          cycle and beliefs." TS.

    N.D. Various essays and class notes on Bemba
          traditional religious beliefs and practices.   MS
          and TS.

Tanguy, Francois
    1954 "The Bemba of Zambia." TS.

    1935 " *Mucapi's* business." Bemba TS.

White Fathers
    1962 "Notes on the Christian adaptation of Bemba
          religious practices." TS. Mbala.

H. Kasama, Archdiocesan Archives
    Etienne, Louis
        1948 "A study of the Babemba and the neighboring
              tribes." TS. Kasama.

    Gamache, Joseph
        N.D. "Notes on God in Bemba belief." TS. Chilubula.

Hering, Josef
    N.D. "Assorted papers." TS.

Sambeck, J.
    1925 "La sorcellerie au Bangweolo." MS.

White Fathers
    1970 "The spirit world of the Babemba." TS.
         Archdiocesan Commission for the Study of Bemba
         Customs.

    1970 "*Kukuna*--the practice of adapting the female body
         for the future marriage act." TS. Kasama.

I. Salisbury, Zimbabwe National Archives
    Doke Collection. The Papers of R.D. Macminn, PL8068 Mac:
        (a) "Native religious beliefs"
        (b) "*Amapinda*"
        (c) "Bemba customs"
        (d) "Bemba-English dictionary"
        (e) "*Ichisungu*"
        (f) "African history"
        (g) "*Ukwisa kwa Ndalu (Kasesema)*"
        (h) "*Ukuwilwa kwa Ngulu*"
        (i) "The validity of translating native texts into
            English"
        (j) "*Ukucolekana*"
        (k) "*Misango ya Cibemba*   " by Paul Mwendacabe
        Typescripts and Manuscripts from 1913-1954.

Bibliographic

Abel, Ernest L.
1971   "The psychology of memory and rumor transmission
        and their bearings on theories of oral transmission
        in early Christianity." The Journal of Religion
        51, 4, October, 270-81.

Allport, G.W. and L.J. Postman
1965a   "The basic psychology of rumor." In Basic Studies
        in Social Psychology (ed.) H. Proshansky and B.
        Seidenberg, New York.

1965b   The Psychology of Rumor. New York: H. Holt and
        Co.

Bascom, William
1969   Ifa Divination: Communication between Gods and Men
        in West Africa. Bloomington: Indiana University
        Press.

Beattie, J. and Middleton, J.
1969   Spirit-mediumship and Society in Africa. London:
        R.K.P.

1960   Max Weber: An Intellectual Portrait. New York:
        Doubleday.

Berger, Peter
1967   The Social Construction of Reality. New York:
        Doubleday.

Biesheuvel, S.
1943   African Intelligence. Johannesburg: South African
        Institute of Personnel Relations.

Booth, Newell S.
1978   "Tradition and community in African religion."
        Journal of Religion in Africa, 9/2, 81-94.

1977   African Religions: A Symposium. New York: NOK
        Publishers.

1975   "Time and change in African traditional thought."
        Journal of Religion in Africa, 7, 2, 81-91.

Brelsford, W. Vernon
1950   "Insanity among the Bemba of Northern Rhodesia."
        Africa, 20, 1, Jan., 46-54.

1944a   "The succession of Bemba chiefs: a guide for
        District Officers." Lusaka: Government Printer.

1944b   "Aspects of Bemba chieftainship."   Communications, 2. Lusaka: Rhodes-Livingstone Institute.

1942   "Shimwalule: a study of a Bemba chief and priest." Africa Studies, 1, 3, Sept., 207-23.

1937   "Some reflections on Bemba geometric decorative art." Bantu Studies, 11, 1, March, 37-45.

Burton, R.F.
1873   The Lands of Cazembe: Lacerda's Journey to Cazembe in 1798. London: Tylston and Edwards.

Burton, W.F.P.
1961   Luba Religion and Magic in Custom and Belief. Tervuren: Musee Royal de l'Afrique Centrale.

Calmettes, J.L.
1978   "The Lumpa Sect: rural reconstruction and conflict." Master's thesis, University of Aberystwyth, Wales.

Carothers, J.C.
1972   The Mind of Man in Africa. London: Tom Stacey.

1959   "Culture, psychiatry and the written word." Psychiatry. 22, 307-20.

Chanda, Vincent M.
1981   "On Bemba dynastic poetry." Ph.D. thesis, Hamburg: Deutches Institut fur Africa--Forschung.

Chele, Stanislaus
1979   "The role of Shimweshimwe in Bemba narratives." Seminar Paper, Department of Languages and Literature, University of Zambia.

Chikoti, S.B. and Bwalya, Theresa
1958   Inkulilo sha Babemba . Lusaka: Publishing Bureau.

Clanchy, M.T.
1979   From Memory to Written Record, England 1066-1307. Cambridge: Harvard University Press.

Colle, Pierre
1913   Les Baluba (Congo Belge). Bruxelles: Institut International de Bibliographie.

Colson, Elizabeth
1970   "Converts and tradition: the impact of Christianity on Valley Tonga religion." Southwestern Journal of Anthropology, 26, 2, Summer, 143-156.

1966 The Plateau _Tonga_ of Northern Rhodesia (Zambia): Social and Religious Studies. Manchester: University Press.

1964 "The alien diviner and local politics among the _Tonga_ of Zambia." Paper presented at the Annual Meeting of the American Anthropological Association, Detroit.

Cross, Sholto
1972 "The Watch-Tower, witch-cleansing, and secret societies in Central Africa." Paper presented at the Lusaka Conference on the History of Central African Religious Systems.

Cunnison, Ian G.
1959 The _Luapula_ Peoples of Northern Rhodesia. Manchester: University Press.

Davidson, S.
1949 "Psychiatric work among the Bemba." Human Problems 7, 75-86.

Davis, J.M., ed.
1933 Modern industry and the African: An Enquiry into the Effect of the Copper Mines of Central Africa upon Native Society and the Work of the Christian Missions Made Under the Auspices of the International Missionary Council. London: Macmillan.

Doke, Clement M.
1959 "The linguistic work and manuscripts of R.D. Macminn." Africa Studies 18, 4, 180-9.

1931 The _Lambas_ of Northern Rhodesia. London: Harrap.

Douglas, Mary
1970 Natural Symbols: Explorations in Cosmology. New York: Pantheon Books.

Dupont, Joseph
1900 Catechisme en Langue Kibemba. Saint-Cloud: Mission Press.

Durkheim, Emile
1965 The Elementary Forms of Religious Life. New York: The Free Press.

Eisenstein, Elizabeth L.
1980 The Printing Press as an Agent of Change: Communications and Cultural Transformations in

Early-Modern Europe. Cambridge: Cambridge University Press.

Eliade, Mircea
1963   _Patterns in Comparative Religion_. Cleveland: The World Publishing Co.

1959a   _The History of Religions: Essays in Methodology_, with Joseph Kitagawa. Chicago: University of Chicago Press.

1959b   _The Sacred and the Profane: The Nature of Religion_. New York: Harcourt, Brace & World.

1954   _The Myth of the Eternal Return: Cosmos and History_. Princeton: University Press.

Evans-Pritchard, E.E.
1965   _Theories of Primitive Religion_. Oxford: The Clarendon Press.

1951   _Nuer Religion_. London: Oxford University Press.

1937   _Witchcraft Oracles and Magic among the Azande_. London: Oxford University Press.

Fernandez, J.W.
1979   "Africanization, Europeanization, Christianization." _History of Religions_, 18, 3, 284-92.

1974   "The mission of metaphor in expressive culture." _Current Anthropology_ 15:119-45.

Finnegan, Ruth
1970   _Oral Literature in Africa_. Oxford: Clarendon Press.

Firth, Raymond
1969   "Foreword" to _Spirit Mediumship and Society in Africa_ by J. Beattie and J. Middleton. London: R.K.P.

Fortes, Meyer
1959   _Oedipus and Job in West African Religion_. Cambridge: University Press.

Fortes, M. and Dieterlen, G. (eds.)
1965   _African Systems of Thought_. London: Oxford University Press.

Fortune, George
1962   _Ideophones in Shona_. London: Oxford University Press.

Frake, Charles O.
    1977   "Plying frames can be dangerous: some reflections
            on methodology in cognitive anthropology." The
            Quarterly Newsletter of the Institute for
            Comparative Human Development. The Rockefeller
            University, 1, 3, June, 1-7.

Freud, Sigmund
    1963   Introductory Lectures on Psycho-Analysis. London:
            Hogarth Press.

Frost, Sister Mary
    1963   " Inshimi and imilumbe : structural expectations
            in Bemba oral imaginative performances." Ph.D.
            thesis, University of Wisconsin.

Gaba, Christian
    1973   Scriptures of an African People. New York: NOK
            Publishers.

Gamitto, A.C.P.
    1960   King Kazembe and the Marvae, Cheva, Bisa, Bemba,
            Lunda and Other Peoples of Southern Africa: Being
            a Diary of the Portuguese Expedition to That
            Potentate in the Years 1831-1832. 2 Vols.
            Translated by Ian Cunnison. Lisboa.

Garvey, Brian
    1977   "Bemba chiefs and catholic missions, 1898-1935."
            Journal of African History, 18/3, 411-26.

    1974   "The development of the White Fathers' mission
            among the Bemba-speaking peoples: 1891-1964."
            Ph.D. thesis, University of London.

Goode, William J.
    1956   Religion Among the Primitives. Glencoe: Free
            Press.

Goody, Jack
    1977   The Domestication of the Savage Mind. Cambridge:
            Cambridge University Press.

    1972   Myth of the Bagre. Oxford: Clarendon Press.

    1968   Literacy in Traditional Societies. Cambridge:
            Cambridge University Press.

Goody, Jack and Michael Cole and Sylvia Scribner
    1977   "Writing and formal operations: A case study among
            the Vai." Africa 47, 3, 289-304.

Goody, Jack and Ian Watt
1963   "The consequences of literacy." Comparative Studies in Society and History 5, 304-45.

Gouldsbury, Cullen
1915-1916   "Notes on the customary law of the Awemba and kindred tribes." Journal of the Africa Society, 14, 56, July, 366-85, Oct., 36-85; 58, Jan. 157-84.

Gouldsbury, Cullen and Sheane, Herbert
1911   The Great Plateau of Northern Rhodesia. London: Edward Arnold.

Guillerme, L.
1920   Dictionaire Francois-Chibemba. Mechelen: Mission Press.

Hall, Richard
1965   Zambia. New York: Praeger.

Harvey, John
1980   Personal letter to Kevin B. Maxwell on the local Bemba religious practices. TS. Shiwa Ng'andu. March 10.

Havelock, Eric A.
1982   The Literate Revolution in Greece and Its Cultural Consequences. Princeton: Princeton University Press.

1978   The Greek Concept of Justice: From its Shadow in Homer to Its Substance in Plato. Cambridge: Harvard University Press.

1963   Preface to Plato. Cambridge: Harvard University Press.

Henige, David
1973   "The Problem of feedback in oral traditions: four examples from the Fante coastlands," Journal of African History 14, 223-35.

1982   "Truths yet unborn? Oral tradition as a casualty of culture contact." Journal of African History 23, 295-412.

Heusch, Luc de
1973   Myths et Rites Bantou: Le Roi Ivre on L'Origine de l'Etat. Paris: Gallimard.

1958   Essais sur Le Symbolisme de L'inceste Royal en Afrique. Brussels: University Libre de Bruxelles.

Horton, Robin
1971   "African conversion." *Africa* 41, 2.

1967   "African traditional thought and western science."
          Africa 37, 1 and 2.

1964   "Ritual man in Africa." *Africa* 34, 2.

Hudson, W.
1960   "Pictorial depth perception in sub-cultural groups
          in Africa." *Journal of Social Psychology* 52:183-
          203.

Idowu, E. Bolaji
1973   *African Traditional Religion: A Definition*.
          London: SCM Press.

1962   *Olodumare: God in Yoruba Belief*. London:
          Longmans, Green & Co.

Ihde, Don
1976   *Listening and Voice: A Phenomenology of Sound*.
          Athens: Ohio University Press.

Jahn, Jahnheinz
1961   *Muntu: An Outline of Neo-African Culture*. London:
          Faber & Faber.

Janzen, John M.
1977   "The tradition of renewal in Kongo religion." In
          African Religions by Newell S. Booth, Jr. (ed.) New
          York: NOK, 69-116.

Jaynes, Julian
1976   *The Origin of Consciousness in the Breakdown of the
          Bicameral Mind*. Boston: Houghton Mifflin Co.

Jousse, Marcel
1975   *La Manducation de la Parole*. Paris: Gallimard.

Jules-Rosette, Bennetta
1981   *Symbols of Change: Urban Transition in a Zambian
          Community*. Norwood, N.J.: Ablex.

Jung, C.G.
1958   *Psyche and Symbol*. New York: Doubleday.

Kacuka, Albert
1977   *Lesa Wa Zambia* . Kasama: Mission Press.

Kapferer, Bruce
1969   "Norms and the manipulation of relationships in a
          work context." In *Social Networks in Urban*

184

Situations by J.C. Mitchell, Manchester: University Press.

Kapwepwe, S.M.
1962   *Utunyonga Ndimi* . Capetown: Oxford Univesity Press.

Kashoki, Mubanga
1975   "Migration and language change: the interaction of town and country." African Social Research, 19, June.

1972   "Town Bemba: a sketch of its main characteristics." Africa Social Research 43, June.

1967   "A phonetic analysis of *Icibemba* : a presentation of Bemba syllable structures, phonemic contrasts and their distribution." MA thesis, Michigan State University.

N.D.   "The sociocultural setting of verbal play: A description of some riddles among the Babemba." TS. UNZA Archives.

Kelber, Werner
1983   The Oral and the Written Gospel: The Hermeneutics of Speaking and Writing in the Synoptic Tradition, Mark, Paul and Q. Philadelphia: Fortress Press.

1979   "Mark and oral tradition." Semeia, 16, 7-55.

Labrecque, Edouard
1938   "La sorcellerie chez les Babemba.: Anthropos, 33.

1933-36 "La tribu des Babemba." Anthropos, 28, 5/6, Sept.-Dec. 633-48, 31, 5/6 Sept.-Dec. 910-21.

1931   "Le marriage chez les Babemba." Africa, 4, 2, 209-21.

Lane, James Eric
1977   "Politics and the image of man." Ph.D. thesis, University of California in Los Angeles.

Leach, Edmund
1966   "Ritualization in man in relation to conceptual and social development." Philosophical Transactions of the Royal Society of London, 251: 403-8.

Leiris, Michel
1958   La Possession et Ses Aspects Theatraux Chez Les Ethiopiens de Gondar. Paris: Plon.

Levi-Strauss, Claude
1966   The Savage Mind. Chicago: University of Chicago
         Press.

Lienhardt, Godfrey
1961   Divinity and Experience: The Religion of the
         Dinka, Oxford: University Press.

Livingstone, David
1875   The Last Journals. Edited by Horace Waller,
         Chicago: Jansen and McClurg.

Lonergan, Bernard J.F.
1972   Method in Theology. New York: Herder & Herder.

1958   Insight: A Study of Human Understanding. New
         York: Longmans.

Long, Norman
1968   Social Change and the Individual: A Study of the
         Social and Religious Responses to Innovation in a
         Zambian Rural Community. Manchester: University
         Press.

Lord, Albert
1960   The Singer of Tales. Cambridge: Harvard
         University Press.

Lumpp, Randolph F.
1976   "Culture, religion and the presence of the word: a
         study of the thought of Walter Jackson Ong." Ph.D.
         dissertation, University of Ottawa.

Luriia, A.R.
1976   Cognitive Development: Its Cultural and Social
         Foundations. Cambridge: Harvard University Press.

Lutato, Kalunga S.
1980   "The influence of oral narrative traditions on the
         novels of Stephen A. Mpashi." Ph.D. thesis,
         University of Wisconsin.

McLuhan, Marshall
1962   The Gutenberg Galaxy: The Making of Typographic
         Man. Toronto: University Press.

McVeigh, Malcolm J.
1974   God in Africa: Conceptions of God in African
         Traditional Religion and Christianity. Cape Cod:
         C. Stark.

Maier, Hans
1976   "Les arbres qui grandissent font la foret: aspects

symbolique de la vie Bemba." Memoire de Maitrise, Strassbourg.

Makungo, I.F.
1966   "Description of some traditional Bemba customs." Bulletin, 1, 53-58.

Malinowski, Bronislaw
1954   Magic, Science and Religion. New York: Doubleday.

Mapoma, I. Mwesa
1980   "The determinants of style in the music of Ing'omba." Ph.D. thesis, Univesrity of California.

Marwick, M.G.
1965   Sorcery in its Social Setting: A Study of the Northern Rhodesian Cewa. Manchester: University Press.

Maxwell, Kevin B.
1981a   "The transition from the oral medium to literacy exemplified in the demise of the Bemba chieftainship." Paper presented to the Humanities and Social Sciences Seminar Series, Institute for African Studies, University of Zambia, Lusaka, Zambia, July.

1981b   "An oral medium analysis of Cisungu, a girls' initiation ceremony among the Bemba of Zambia." Paper presented at the annual meeting of the Western Association of Africanists, Colorado Springs, Colorado, March 7.

Mbiti, John
1971   New Testament Eschatology in an African Background. London: Oxford University Press.

1962   African Religions and Philosophy. New York: Frederick A. Praeger.

Meebelo, Henry S.
1971   Reaction to Colonialism. A Prelude to the Politics of Independence in Northern Zambia, 1893-1939. Manchester: Manchester University Press.

Melland, Frank H.
1904-05 "Some ethnographical notes on the Awemba tribe of north-eastern Rhodesia." Journal of the Africa Society, 3, 11, Apr. 247-56, 4, 15, Apr. 337-45.

1903   "Extracts from letters by F.H.M., an official in the N.E. Rhodesian Service of the BSAC." Journal of the Africa Society, 8, July, 380-99.

Meyer, Leonard
1973   Music, the Arts and Ideas: Patterns and
          Predictions in Twentieth Century Culture. Chicago:
          University Press.

Milimo, John T.
1978   "Bemba royal poetry." D. Phil. thesis, Wolfson
          College, Oxford.

1976   "A study of the proverbial lore of the Plateau Tonga
          of Zambia." B. Litt. thesis, University of Oxford.
Milingo, Emmanuel
1978   "The Church of the Spirits. Is it to blame?" TS.
          Lusaka: Roman Catholic Archdiocese.

Mitchell, J. Clyde
1969   Social Networks in Urban Situations: Analyses of
          Personal Relationships in Central African Towns.
          Manchester: University Press.

1965   "The meaning of misfortune for urban Africans.' In
          M. Fortes and G. Dieterlen (eds.) African Systems
          of Thought. London.

Molinier, L.
1903   "Croyances superstitieuses chez les Babemba."
          Journal of the Africa Society, 3, 9, Oct. 74-83.

Moore, R.J.B.
1940-41   "Bwanga among the Bemba." Part 1, Africa, 13, 3,
          July, 211-34. Part 2 bantu Studies 15, 1, Mar.,
          37-44.

Mpashi, Stephen A.
1978   Uwauma Nafyala . Lusaka: NECZAM.

1965   Icibemba Cesu Na Mano Yaciko . London: Oxford
          University Press.

1956   Pano Calo . Nairobi: Oxford University Press.

1947   Umucinshi . Cape Town: Oxford University Press.

Mukuka, Jacob B.
1952   Imikalile ya ku Lubemba . Lusaka: Publishing
          Bureau.

Mushindo, Paul B.
1976   A Short History of the Bemba: as Narrated by a
          Bemba. Lusaka: NECZAM.

1958   Amapinda mu Lyashi . London: University of
          London Press.

Nadel, S.F.
1954   *Nupe* Religion. London: Roultedge & Kegan Paul.

Nielsen, Eduard
1954   Oral Tradition. A Modern Problem in Old Testament
         Introduction. London: SCM Press.

Nkandu, Gregory E.
1981   "The function of *Ciwa* as a literary symbol in
         some typical narratives of the ba Bisa-Lala of
         Serenje District, in Zambia's Central Province."

         Seminar Paper, Dept. of Literature and Languages,
         University of Zambia.

Nurnberger, Klaus
1975   "The Sotho notion of the supreme being and the
         impact of the Christian proclamation." Journal of
         Religion in Africa 7, 3, 174-200.

Obiechina, Emmanuel
1975   Culture, Tradition and Society in the West African
         Novel. Cambridge University Press.

Oger, Louis
1972   "Spirit possession among the Bemba--a linguistic
         approach." Paper presented at the Lusaka
         Conference on the History of Central African
         Religious Systems.

1962   "Le mouvement *Lenshina* en Rhodesie du Nord."
         Eglise Vivante, 14, 128-38.

Okot p'Bitek
1971   African Religions in Western Scholarship. Nairobi:
         East African Literature Bureau.

Oliver, Curtis F.
1979   "Some aspects of literacy in ancient India." The
         Quarterly Newsletter of the Laboratory of
         Comparative Human Cognition, University of
         California, San Diego. October, 1, 4, 57-62.

Ong, Walter J.
1982   Orality and Literacy. New York: Methuen Press.

1977   Interfaces of the Word. Studies in the Evolution
         of Consciousness and Culture. Ithaca: Cornell
         University Press.

1974   "Agonistic structures in academia: Past to
         present." Daedalus: Journal of the American
         Academy of Arts and Science. 103, Fall, 299-38.

1971   _Rhetoric, Romance and Technology: Studies in the Interaction of Expression and Culture_. Ithaca: Cornell University Press.

1969a   "Review of _The Theory of Avante Garde_ by Renato Poggioli." _American Literature_, 40, January, 589.

1969b   "Worship at the end of the age of literacy." _Worship_ 43, October, 478.

1968   _Knowledge and the Future of Man: An International Symposium_. New York: Holt, Rineholt & Winston.

1967a   _In the Human Grain_. New York: Macmillan.

1967b   _The Presence of the Word. Some Prolegomena for Cultural and Religious History_. Cambridge: Harvard University Press.

1962   _The Barbarian Within_. New York: Macmillan, 1962.

1948   "Finitude and frustration: Considerations on Brod's _Kafka_." _Modern Schoolman_, 25, March, 173.

Paliani, S.A.
1971   _1930 Kunadza Mcape_. Lilongwe: Likuni Press.

Parsons, Robert
1964   _Religion in an African Society_. Leiden: E.J. Brill.

Peabody, Berkeley
1975   _The Winged Word. A Study in the Technique of Ancient Greek Oral Composition as Seen Principally through Hesiod's 'Works and Days'_. Albany: University of New York Press.

Poortinga, Y.h.
1971   "Cross-cultural comparisons of maximum performance tests: some methodological aspects and some experiments with simple auditory and visual stimuli." _Psychologia Africana_. Monograph Supplement, 6.

Propp, Vladimar I.
1968   _Morphology of the Folktale_. Translated by L. Scott. Austin: University of Texas Press.

Radcliffe-Brown, A.R.
1952   _Structure and Function in Primitive Society_. London: Cohen and West.

Ragoen, J.
1935   "L'idee de Dieu d'apres les proverbes et les
          dictons des babemba." *Grands Lacs*, 54, juil, 477-
          9.

Ramsey, Ian
1957   *Religious Language*. London: SCM Press.

Ranger, Terrence O,
1972   "*Mchape* and the study of witchcraft eradication."
          Paper presented at the Lusaka Conference on the
          History of Central African Religious Systems.

Ranger, Terrence O. (ed.)
1975   *Themes in the Christian history of Central Africa*.
          Berkeley: University of California Press.

1972   *The Historical Study of African Religion with I.N.
          Kimambo*. Los Angeles: University of California
          Press.

1968   *Aspects of Central African History*. Evanston:
          Northwestern University Press.

Ray, Benjamin C.
1976   *African Religions: Symbol, Ritual and Community*.
          Englewood Cliffs: Prentice Hall.

Richards, Audrey I.
1971   "The councilior system of the Bemba of Northern
          Zambia." In *Councils in Action*, eds. A.I.
          Richards and Adam Kuper. Cambridge: Cambridge
          University Press.

1968   "Keeping the king divine." Henry Myers Lecture.
          Proceedings of the Royal Anthropological Institute,
          23-25.

1961   "African kings and their royal relatives." *Journal
          of the Royal Anthropological Institute*, 91, 2, 135-
          50.

1960   "Social mechanisms for the transfer of political
          rights in some African tribes." *Journal of the
          Royal Anthropological Institute*, 90, 2, 175-90.

1956   *Chisungu : A Girls' Initiation Ceremony Among the
          Bemba of Northern Rhodesia*. London: Faber.

Richards, Audrey I.
1951   "The Bemba of north-eastern Rhodesia." In *Seven
          Tribes of British Central Africa*, ed. E. Colson and
          M. Gluckman, 164-93.

1940   "The political system of the Bemba tribe--north-eastern Rhodesia." In African Political Systems, ed. M. Fortes and E.E. Evans-Pritchard, 83-120.

1939   Land, Labour and Diet in Northern Rhodesia: An Economic Study of the Bemba Tribe. London: Oxford University Press.

1936   "The life of Bwembya." In Ten Africans, ed. M.F. Petham, 17-40.

1935   "A modern movement of witch-finders." Africa, 8, 4, Oct. 448-61.

1932   "Anthropological problems in northeastern Rhodesia." Africa, 5, 2, 121-44.

Ricoeur, Paul
1967   The Symbolism of Evil. New York: Harper and Row.

Roberts, Andrew D.
1976   A History of Zambia. New York: African Publishing Co.

1973   A History of the Bemba: Political Growth and Change in North-Eastern Zambia before 1900. Madison: University of Wisconsin Press.

1970   "The Lumpa Church of Alice Lenshina." In Robert Rotberg and Ali A. Mazrui (eds.) Protests and Power in Black Africa. New York: Oxford University Press.

1968a   "The nineteenth century in Zambia." In T.O. Ranger (ed.) Aspects of Central African History, 71-96. Evanston: Northwestern University Press.

1968b   "The political history of twentieth century Zambia." In T.O. Ranger (ed.) Aspects of Central African History, 154-89. Evanston: Northwestern University Press.

Robertson, W.G.
1904   An Introductory Handbook to the Language of the Bemba People (Awemba). London: London Missionary society.

Rothberg, Robert I.
1965   Christian Missionaries and the Creation of Northern Rhodesia, 1880-1924. Princeton: University Press.

Russell, Jeffrey B.
1972   Witchcraft in the Middle Ages. Ithaca: Cornell University Press.

Sarpong, P.K.
   1972   "The search for meaning: the religious impact of
            technology in   Africa."   Ecumenical Review,   24,
            July, 300-09.

Scheub, Harold
   1971   "Translation   of   African   oral   narrative.
            Performances to the written word.   Yearbook of
            Comparative and General Literature, 20, 28-36.

   1975   "Oral narrative process and the use of models."
            New Literary History, 6, 11, Winter, 353-77.

Schneidau, Herbert N.
   1976   Sacred   Discontent: The   Bible   and   Western
            Tradition.   Baton   Rouge: Louisiana   State
            University Press.

Schoeffer, Pere
   1910   Katechishimu: Chitika cha Bakatekumeni . Algers:
            (Mission Press).

Schuster, Ilsa M.G.
   1979   New Women of Lusaka. Palo Alto: Mayfield.

Scollon, Ron and Suzanne, B.K.
   1980   "Literacy as   focused interaction."   Quarterly
            Newsletter of the Laboratory of Comparative Human
            Cognition.   University of California, San Diego.
            April, 2, 2, 26-9.

Scribner, Sylvia and Cole, Michael
   1978   "Literacy   without   schooling: Testing   for
            intellectual   effects."   Vai Literacy   Project,
            Rockefeller University, Laboratory of Comparative
            Human Cognition. April, 2.

Sendwe, Edouard
   1963   "L'homme dans la genese et l'homme chez les Bantu."
            Thesis, Montpelier: Faculte Libre de Theologue
            Protestante.

Serpell, Robert
   1977   "Strategies for investigating intelligence in its
            cultural context." Quarterly Newsletter of the
            Institute   for   Comparative Human Development,
            Rockefeller University, 1, 3, 11-15.

   1976   Culture's   Influence   on   Behaviour.   London:
            Methuen.

   1974   "Estimates of intelligence in a rural community of
            Eastern Zambia." Human Development Research Unit
            Reports, University of Zambia, 25.

Sharman, John C. and Meussen, A.E.
1955   "The representation of structural tones with
          special reference to the tonal behaviour of the
          verb in Bemba, Northern Rhodesia." _Africa_ 25, 4:
          393-404.

Sheane, J.H. West
1906   "Some aspects of the _Awemba_ religion and
          superstitous observances." _Journal of the
          Anthropology Institute_ 36, 150-8.

Shorter, Aylward
1977   _African Christian Theology--Adaptation or
          Incarnation?_ New York: Orbis Books.

Simmance, Alan J.
1972   _Urbanization in Zambia_. New York: Ford
          Foundation.

Simukoko, Youngson T.
1978   "The orate illiterate and the inorate literate:
          expressiveness in authentic Zambian oral
          literature." _Bulletin of the Zambia Language
          Group_, 3/2, 7-16.

1977   "Towards a search for an authentic drama and
          theatre idiom: the linguistic dimension." _Bulletin
          of the Zambia Language Group_, 3, 1.

Skorupski, John
1976   _Symbol and Theory: A Philosophical Study of
          Theories of Religion in Social Anthropology_. New
          York: Cambridge University Press.

Smith, Michael
1978   "An ethnography of literacy in a Vai town." _Vai
          Literacy Project, Rockefeller University,
          Laboratory of Comparative Human Cognition_. March,
          1.

Snelson, Peter D.
1974   _Educational Development in Northern Rhodesia, 1883-
          1945_. Ndola: NECZAM.

Sperber, Dan
1975   _Rethinking Symbolism_. Cambridge: Cambridge
          University Press.

Stefaniszyn, Bronislaw
1964   _Social and Ritual Life of the _Ambo_ of Northern
          Rhodesia_. London: Oxford University Press.

Stuart, Richard G.
1972   " *Mchape* and the UMCA 1933." Paper presented at
          the Lusaka Conference in the History of Central
          African Religious Systems.

Tanguy, Father
1949   *Imilandu ya Babemba* . London: Oxford University
          Press.

Tannen, Deborah (ed.)
1982   Spoken and Written Language: Exploring Orality and
          Literacy. Norwood, N.J.: Ablex.

Tanner, Ralph E.S.
1967   Transition in African Beliefs: Traditional
          Religion and Christian Change: A Study in
          Sukumaland, Tanzania, East Africa. New York:
          Maryknoll.

Taylor, John V. and Lehmann, Dorothea
1961   Christians of the Copperbelt: The Growth of the
          Church in Northern Rhodesia. London: S.C.M.
          Press.

Tempels, Placide
1945   La Philosophie Bantoue. Elizabethville: Lovania.

Theuws, Theodore
1964   "Outline of Luba culture." Cashiers of economiques
          et sociaux 11, 1, Leopoldville (Kinshasa) 15.

Tillich, Paul
1951   Systematic Theology. Chicago: University of
          Chicago Press.

Torrey, E. Fuller
1972   The Mind Game: Witchdoctor and Psychiatrists. New
          York: Emerson Hall.

Tracy, David
1981   The Analogical Imagination: Christian Theology and
          the Culture of Pluralism. New York: Crossroad.

1979   "Metaphor and religion: the test case of Christian
          texts." In On Metaphor, edited by Sheldon Sacks.
          Chicago: The University of Chicago Press, 89-104.

1975   Blessed Rage for Order: The New Pluralism in
          Theology. New York: Seabury Press.

1970   The Achievement of Bernard Lonergan. New York:
          Herder and Herder.

Turner, Arthur
    1972   "The effect of urban conditions on indigenous Zambian religious institutions in Kabwe." Paper presented at the Lusaka Conference on the History of Central African Religious Systems.

Turner, Victor W.
    1975   Revelation and Divination in *Ndembu* Ritual. Ithaca: Cornell University Press.

    1969   The Ritual Process: Structure and Anti-Structure. Chicago: Aldine.

    1968   The Drums of Affliction: A Study of Religious Processes Among the *Ndembu* of Zambia. Oxford: Oxford University Press.

    1967   The Forest of Symbols: Aspects of *Ndembu* Ritual. Ithaca: Cornell University Press.

    1957   Schism and Continuity in an African Society. Manchester: Manchester University Press.

Tweedie, Ann
    1966   "Towards a history of the Bemba from oral tradition." In Eric Stokes and Richard Brown (eds.) The Zambesian Past. Manchester: University Press.

Tyler, Stephen A.
    1981   "Words for deeds and the doctrine of the secret world: testimony to a chance encounter somewhere in the Indian jungle." Paper presented at the meeting of the Chicago Linguistic Society (Spring).

    1978   The Said and the Unsaid: Mind, Meaning, and Culture. New York: Academic Press.

    1975   "A point of order." Rice University Studies, 61, 2 (Spring), 111-161.

Van der Leeuw, Gerhardus
    1963   Religion in Essence and Manifestration. New York: Harper & Row.

Vansina, Jan
    1971   "Les mouvements religieux *Kuba* (*Kasai*) a l'epoque coloniale." Etudes d'Histoire Africaine 11.

    1965   Oral Tradition. London: Routledge & Kegan Paul.

Wallace, Anthony F.C.
  1966   _Religion: An Anthropological View_. New York: Random House.

  1961   _Culture and Personality_. New York: Random House.

  1956   "Revitalization movements." _American Anthropologist_, 58, 2, 264-81.

Weber, Max
  1947   _The Theory of Social and Economic Organization_. London: n.p.

Welfele, Pere
  1920   _Milandu ya kwa Mulungu: Bwana Jesu ali talaisa._ Bangewolo: (Mission Press).

Werbner, Richard P.
  1967   "Federal administration, rank, and civil strife among Bemba royals and nobles." _Africa_, 37, 1, 22-48.

Werner, Douglas
  1972   "Aspects of history in the Miao spirit-system of the southern Lake Tanganyika region: the case of Kapembwa." Paper presented at the Lusaka Conference in the History of Central African Religious Systems.

  1971   "Some developments in Bemba religious history." _Journal of Religion in Africa_, 4, 1, 1-24.

White Fathers
  N.D.   _Ifyabukaya_ . Chilubula: White Fathers Mission Press.

  1954   _Bemba-English Dictionary_. London: Longmans Green.

Wilson, Monica
  1971   _Religion and the Transformation of Society: A Study of Social Change in Africa_. Cambridge: University Press.

  1959   _Communal Rituals of the Nyakusa_ . Oxford: University Press.

Winter, Gibson
  1966   _Elements for a Social Ethic: Scientific Perspectives on Social Process_. New York: Macmillan.

Wober, M.
    1966   "Sensotypes." _Journal of Social Psychology._   70:
            181-89.

Yamba, Dauti L.
    1947   _Ficoleko ne Nyimbo._   _Ndola_: African   Literature
            Committee.

Zahan, Dominique
    1970   _Religion, Spiritualite, et Pensee Africaines._
            Paris: Payot.

    1963   _La Dialectique du Verbe Chez Les Bambara._   Paris:
            Mouton.